"*Social Equity & LGBTQ Rights* is an important and well-written book for public administration and public policy students and practitioners. It is a welcome addition to the literature on social equity and social justice and should be assigned as a supplemental textbook in public affairs programs."

Mohamad Alkadry, University of Connecticut, USA

"Dr. Naylor's book is a major contribution to the field. It is well-written, and it comprehensively covers LGBTQ issues in the context of social equity. These issues tend to receive marginal coverage in our courses, yet they are so critical today. I recommend this book with great enthusiasm; it should be required reading in all public administration, affairs and policy courses."

Norma M. Riccucci, Rutgers University, Newark, USA

"Dr. Naylor presents the reader with important cases and a deep understanding of LGBTQ matters framed within social equity. Her contribution is especially important as many parts of the US experience a rollback of LGBTQ rights and protections. Dr. Naylor's book is an essential read for any college/university course on social equity and uplift."

Richard Greggory Johnson, University of San Francisco, USA

"In this important addition to the social equity literature, Dr. Lorenda A. Naylor connects the dots between theory and practice while providing a historical perspective and incorporating milestone events and landmark U.S. Supreme Court rulings. I recommend this book to public administration scholars and students, policymakers, government employees, and those who strive to 'walk the talk' when it comes to social equity."

Erik Bergrud, Park University, USA

Social Equity and LGBTQ Rights

Can a baker refuse to make a wedding cake for a gay couple? Despite the U.S. Supreme Court decision guaranteeing marriage equality in 2015, lesbian, gay, bisexual, transgender, and queer (LGBTQ) citizens in the United States continue to be discriminated against in fundamental areas that others take for granted as a legal right. Using social equity theory and intersectionality but written in an accessible style, this book demonstrates some of the ways in which LGBTQ citizens have been marginalized for their identity and argues that the field of public administration has a unique responsibility to prioritize social equity. Categories utilized by the U.S. Census Bureau (male or female, heterosexual or homosexual), for example, must shift to a continuum to accurately capture demographic characteristics and citizen behavior. Evidence-based outcomes and disparities between cisgender and heterosexual and LGBTQ populations are carefully delineated to provide a legal rationale for a compelling governmental interest, and policy recommendations are provided – including overdue federal legislation to prohibit discrimination based on sexual orientation and gender identity.

Lorenda A. Naylor is an associate professor at the University of Baltimore, College of Public Affairs, School of Public & International Affairs. She is the program director for the undergraduate degree program Policy, Politics and International Affairs, and is a Faculty Fellow with the Schaefer Center for Public Policy. Dr. Naylor has recently been approved as a U.S. Fulbright Specialist. She is a social equity researcher. Her research focuses on the intersection of marginalized populations, government access, and constitutional rights. Prior to joining the academy, she worked in state and local government in maternal child health, foster care, and adoption.

PUBLIC ADMINISTRATION AND PUBLIC POLICY
A Comprehensive Publication Program

EDITOR-IN-CHIEF

DAVID H. ROSENBLOOM
Distinguished Professor of Public Administration
American University, Washington, DC

RECENTLY PUBLISHED BOOKS

The Economic Survival of America's Isolated Small Towns
Gerald L. Gordon

Development and the Politics of Human Rights
Scott Nicholas Romaniuk and Marguerite Marlin

Democracy and Civil Society in a Global Era
Scott Nicholas Romaniuk and Marguerite Marlin

Contracting for Services in State and Local Government Agencies, Second Edition
William Sims Curry

The Constitutional School of American Public Administration
Edited by Stephanie P. Newbold and David H. Rosenbloom

Cost and Optimization in Government: *An Introduction to Cost Accounting, Operations Management, and Quality Control, Second Edition*
Aman Khan

The Nonprofit Human Resource Management Handbook: *From Theory to Practice*
Edited by Jessica E. Sowa and Jessica K. A. Word

The Practice of International Development
Edited by Jerrold Keilson and Michael Gubser

Performance Measurement in Local Sustainability Policy
Susan M. Opp, Samantha L. Mosier, and Jeffrey L. Osgood, Jr., with Mark W. Davis

Governance Networks in Public Administration and Public Policy
Christopher J. Koliba, Jack W. Meek, Asim Zia, and Russell W. Mills

Building the Compensatory State: *An Intellectual History and Theory of American Administrative Reform*
Robert F. Durant

Social Equity and LGBTQ Rights: *Dismantling Discrimination and Expanding Civil Rights*
Lorenda A. Naylor

For more information about this series please visit: www.routledge.com/Public-Administration-and-Public-Policy/book-series/AUEPUBADMPUP

Social Equity and LGBTQ Rights

Dismantling Discrimination and Expanding Civil Rights

Lorenda A. Naylor

NEW YORK AND LONDON

First published 2021
by Routledge
52 Vanderbilt Avenue, New York, NY 10017

and by Routledge
2 Park Square, Milton Park, Abingdon, Oxon, OX14 4RN

Routledge is an imprint of the Taylor & Francis Group, an informa business

© 2021 Taylor & Francis

The right of Lorenda A. Naylor to be identified as author of this work has been asserted by her in accordance with sections 77 and 78 of the Copyright, Designs and Patents Act 1988.

All rights reserved. No part of this book may be reprinted or reproduced or utilised in any form or by any electronic, mechanical, or other means, now known or hereafter invented, including photocopying and recording, or in any information storage or retrieval system, without permission in writing from the publishers.

Trademark notice: Product or corporate names may be trademarks or registered trademarks, and are used only for identification and explanation without intent to infringe.

Library of Congress Cataloging-in-Publication Data
A catalog record for this book has been requested

ISBN: 978-0-8153-8030-6 (hbk)
ISBN: 978-0-3676-4986-9 (pbk)
ISBN: 978-1-351-21350-9 (ebk)

Typeset in Adobe Garamond Pro
by Apex CoVantage, LLC

This book is dedicated to my late uncle Darrel.

Contents

List of Figures xi
List of Tables xiii
Acknowledgments xv
Preface xvii

1 Social Equity and Public Administration 1

2 Marriage Equality: A Fundamental Right 21

3 Foster Care, Adoption, and Assisted Reproductive Technology 45

4 LGBTQ Employment Protections 67

5 LGBT Rights and the U.S. Military Service 95

6 Public Accommodations, Title IX, and Government ID 111

7 Next Steps 133

Glossary 139

Appendix: List of Federal Statutes Protecting Sex Discrimination 141

Index 147

Figures

2.1 Gay Marriage Around the World 22
2.2 Number of Same-Sex Married Couples in the U.S. 36
4.1 U.S. LGBTQ Employment Protections by State 74

Tables

2.1 Summary of U.S. Supreme Court Cases 39
3.1 Foster Care and Adoption Legal Cases 62
4.1 Levels of Judicial Scrutiny by Classification 76
6.1 Federal Policy by Protected Class 120
6.2 Identity Record by Government Level, Demographics, and Cost 127

Acknowledgments

I would like to thank the series editor, David Rosenbloom, for his guidance and continual support in writing this book. I have had the distinct opportunity to work with David over the years and am in awe of his intellect and deep understanding of administrative law and legal analysis. I once drove five and a half hours to hear David speak and it was worth every mile. He is a gifted scholar and exceptional individual. I also want to thank the Taylor & Francis team, editor Laura Stearns Varley, and editorial assistant Katie Horsefall. Your many contributions and patience made this book a reality. I am grateful. I am also indebted to the reviewers who read the draft manuscript and provided insightful suggestions. As a result, the book is a better product.

I am grateful to my colleagues who I have worked with over the years on research projects, symposiums, and conference panels on social equity: Heather Wyatt-Nichol, Blue Wooldridge, Richard Gregory Johnson III, Kris Norman-Major, Sam Brown, Stephanie Dolamore, Sean McCandless, Brandi Blessett, Tia Gaynor, Renita Seabrook, Mohamad Alkadry, Suzanne Piotrowski, Carole Jurkiwiecz, Susan Gooden, RaJade Berry, GiGi Harris, Patria de Lancer Julnes, Mary Hamilton, Jennifer Brinkerhoff, James Svara, Erik Bergrud, Claire Mostel, Ines Beecher, Craig Donovan, Bill Solomon, Steve Bobes, Wally Swan, Ann Braga, Staci Zavattaro, Kendra Stewart, Maria D'Agnostio, Hillary Knepper, Patrice Mareschal, Margaret Stout, and Victoria Gordon.

I want to thank my colleagues at the University of Baltimore who have mentored, guided, and supported me over the years: Dr. Alan Lyles, professor and senior fellow Hoffberger Center for Professional Ethics; Dr. Lenneal Henderson, professor emeritus; and Dr. John Callahan, executive in residence and former assistant secretary of management and budget, U.S. Department of Health and Human Services (1999–2001), all three of whom are National Academy of Public Administration fellows. The trio consistently mentored me, supported me, and encouraged me to strive for excellence. I am thankful to Dr. Larry Thomas who first hired me as a visiting professor and later as an assistant professor. In addition, I want to thank the following University of Baltimore colleagues in the School of Public and International Affairs: George Julnes, Tom Darling, John Willis, Heather Wyatt-Nichol, Carol Molinari, Bridal Pearson, Tiffany Packman, Ed Gibson, Don Haynes, Joe Adler, Al Gourrier, Jennica Larrison, Mariglynn Edlins, Kelechi Uzochuku, Yunzi Rae Tan, Aaron Wachhaus Sarah Federman, Nusta Carranzo Ko, and Jiwon Nam Spears. I am also thankful to the College of Public Affairs: Dean Roger Hartley for his leadership and ongoing support for social equity over the years, to Associate Dean Laura Wilson Gentry, who has mentored me and I have co-authored with, and Dr. Sascha Sheehan, Executive Director, School of Public and International Affairs, for his support and ongoing encouragement. I gratefully acknowledge the University of Baltimore, College of Public Affairs, School of Public & International Affairs for research funding to complete this book. I am thankful. I also want to thank Dr. Ann Cotten, Executive Director, Schaefer Center for Public Policy for her ongoing leadership in applied research.

I am also thankful to Stephanie Pinkney Lee for her highly valuable service. I am indebted to the late Lou Gawthrop, whose vast theoretical knowledge spanning public administration, political science, and theology kept me engaged and on task. When we finished meetings in my office Lou would always conclude by knocking on my desk and encouraging me to "keep the faith." I have done my best to keep the faith.

I also want to thank Krishna Tummala, professor emeritus Kansas State University, for mentoring me, flying to South Africa to ensure my travel abroad success as a graduate student and encouraging me to get my PhD. I am forever grateful. I also want to thank Dr. Norge Jerome, professor emerita, The University of Kansas Medical Center, School of Medicine, for her encouragement to pursue my PhD. Your support propelled me to apply for my PhD. I would like to thank the team at Apex for the attention to detail in formatting and editing the book.

Last but not least, I thank my children and family, for their patience and understanding. For all the times, I worked late nights and on weekends I thank you for supporting my writing.

Preface

The Stonewall riots of 1969 marked the beginning of the lesbian, gay, bisexual, transgender, and queer (LGBTQ) rights movement in America. The riots began at the Stonewall Inn, a gay bar in New York City, which now serves as a national historic landmark (National Park Service, n.d.).

Over the past 50 years, significant social, legal, and political advances have been made in securing LGBTQ rights.

Public Opinion Polls

Socially, there is more acceptance and support for LGBTQ people. Numerous polls illustrate that the majority of Americans support LGBTQ rights. A Gallup poll conducted in 2019 found that 55 percent think gay or lesbian relations are acceptable by Americans compared to 21 percent in 2001, and 49 percent believe that people are born gay compared to 13 percent in 1977. Equally remarkable is the increase in support for LGBTQ legal rights. In 2019, 63 percent support same-sex marriage, 93 percent support equal rights in terms of job opportunities for gays and lesbians, 75 percent support gays and lesbians adopting children, and 71 percent favor transgender men and women serving in the military (Gallup, 2019). These polls reflect remarkable changes in attitudes and beliefs about LGBTQ people in American society. These significant social and cultural changes are reflected in major political and legal advancements.

Political Representation

The LGBTQ community has made tremendous strides in political representation. More LGBTQ members are running for office and getting elected to office. The 2020 presidential race marks the first time in U.S. history an openly gay candidate ran for president of the United States: Pete Buttigieg, former mayor of South Bend, Indiana, and a U.S. veteran. This is historic and momentous. According to the Victory Institute, which promotes and trains LGBTQ candidates for public office, there are currently nine U.S. members of Congress who are openly LGBTQ. In 2012, Tammy Baldwin, a Wisconsin Democrat, became the first openly gay person to win a seat in the U.S. Senate. In 2016, Kyrsten Sinema, a Arizona Democrat, became the first openly bisexual person elected to the U.S. Senate. At the state level, as of 2019, there are two openly LGBTQ governors: Jared Polis (Colorado, Republican), the first openly gay elected governor in the country, and Kate Brown (Oregon, Democrat). In addition, there are 22 openly LGTBQ officials serving in state legislatures across the country. In 2017, the first openly transgender person to win a public office in the country,

Danica Roem, was elected as a Virginia delegate. In 2019, she was reelected to office, creating a path for more transgender candidates to run for public office. In June 2020, West Virginia elected its first openly transgender person, Rosemary Ketchum, to a Wheeling city council seat. As of 2020, there are at least 27 openly transgender elected officials (Asmelash, 2020). In 2019, the highest ranking openly LGBTQ mayor was elected in U.S. history: Lori Lightfoot, mayor of Chicago. The LGBTQ community has come a long way since electing its first openly LGBTQ member to a state legislature in 1974, Elain Noble, Massachusetts House of Representatives, and in 1977 the first openly LGBTQ member to win a city seat: Harvey Milk, San Francisco, California, Board of Supervisors. Milk was assassinated in 1978 and was posthumously awarded the Medal of Freedom by President Obama in 2009. In 1990, there were an estimated 50 openly LGBTQ elected officials, and by 2019, the number increased to approximately 700 officials.

The dramatic increase in political representation is historic. It increases the direct participation of LGBTQ citizens in the political process. It elevates LGBTQ visibility, strengthens the voice of the LGBTQ community, and provides the much-needed diversity in public office. The LGBTQ community now has a seat at the table of power and can influence public policy. However, political representation remains disproportionate compared to straight people. As of 2020, there are 698 openly LGBTQ elected officials in the United States out of approximately 520,000 elected positions (Lawless, 2012). LGBTQ people compose 4.9 percent of the population and only 0.13 percent (less than half of 1 percent) of elected public officials. This means that to achieve equal representation an additional 22,638 LGBTQ public officials need to be elected in municipal governments, townships, county governments, school districts, special districts, and state and federal offices.

Legal Rights

Recent landmark rulings by the U.S. Supreme Court have created new LGBTQ rights, benefits, and protections in marriage equality, federal spousal benefits, sexual privacy, adoption, and employment protections. These court decisions are historic and momentous. They expand civil rights in America, and they represent a sea change of rights and protections for LGBTQ citizens, which is the subject of this book. This book describes the marginalization and discrimination of LGBTQ people as a legal class and analyzes the creation of LGBTQ legal rights utilizing a public administration framework. Relying on social equity theory and intersectionality as the foundation, the argument is made that LGBTQ people should be treated fairly, equally, and equitably by its government. This includes procedural fairness, equal access to services, distribution of resources, and targeted interventions to reduce LGBTQ disparities and inequalities. This book addresses salient issues facing LGBTQ people and captures the ideological division in our country: a political debate between equal treatment and religious rights.

Book Organization

Chapter 1 defines social equity theory as a pillar in public administration, delineates the difference between equity and equality, defines LGTBQ terms, and lays the legal foundation for LGBTQ rights. It links social equity to the rule of law, which is critical for enforcing and upholding LGBTQ legal protections, rights, and benefits. Social equity and equality must be based on law to have sustainability and enforceability. Chapter 2 describes the ideological debate on same-sex marriage and the historical role of states in regulating and administering marriage licenses. It identifies the legal advances in marriage equality focusing on landmark U.S. Supreme Court rulings, *Obergefell v. Hodges* (2015) and *U.S. v. Windsor* (2013). Chapter 3 explores foster care, adoption, and assisted reproductive technology identifying obstacles faced by LGBTQ people in creating families. International adoption is also addressed along with the utilization of international surrogacy and the challenges faced by LGBTQ individuals and couples: immigration laws. Equally important, it summarizes the political and legal debate: religious rights of service providers versus equal protection rights of LGBTQ people in creating families, granted in *Obergefell v. Hodges* (2015). Chapter 4 discusses employment discrimination based on sexual orientation and gender identity. It analyzes the recent landmark decision by the U.S. Supreme Court, which ruled that 'sex' under Title VII of the Civil Rights Act of 1964 protects gays and transgender people (*Bostock v. Clayton County*, 2020). It is now a violation of Title VII to fire an individual based on sexual orientation or gender identity. This chapter traces the legal development that led up to the *Bostock* (2020) decision and its implications on the Affordable Care Act, the Fair Housing Act, and over 100 federal statutes that prohibit discrimination based on sex. Chapter 5 reviews the history of LGBTQ rights in the U.S. military with an emphasis on lesbian and gay rights. It addresses Don't Ask Don't Tell and the repeal of Don't Ask Don't Tell. Chapter 6 covers public accommodations and government identity. It describes the passage of state bathroom bills and public accommodations under Title IX. It also identifies obstacles for LGBTQ people in complying with the federal REAL ID law and obtaining government-issued identification documents such as marriage licenses, birth certificates, and U.S. passports. Last is Chapter 7, which summarizes key judicial rulings, legislation, and policy outcomes as they relate to LGBTQ rights, public administration, and social equity. The next steps to securing full LGBTQ legal rights are identified.

Chapter 1

Social Equity and Public Administration

Introduction

Can a baker refuse to make a wedding cake for a gay couple? According to the U.S. Supreme Court, the answer is yes, as long as the cake is custom-made. In 2012, a same-sex couple named Charlie Craig and David Mullins decided to order a customized cake for their wedding. They wanted to place an order at Masterpiece Cake located in Lakewood, Colorado. The baker, Jack Phillips, a devout Christian, refused to create a cake for the couple citing religious beliefs. He did not want to use his artistic skills to create a cake that went against his religious beliefs. Phillips did offer to sell the couple other bakery items in his store. The couple filed a charge with the Colorado Civil Rights Commission under the state law, the Colorado Anti-Discrimination Act, which prohibits discrimination based on sexual orientation in a place of business. After the commission issued a finding of probable cause, the couple filed a complaint with the Office of Administrative Courts. The administrative law judge ruled in favor of the couple. Masterpiece Cake appealed the case and the Colorado Court of Appeals affirmed the commission's ruling. The legal question before the U.S. Supreme Court was, Does the application of a state law forcing a cake maker to design a cake that contradicts his religious beliefs on same-sex marriage violate the Free Speech or Free Exercise Clauses of the First Amendment? In a 7–2 decision, the U.S. Supreme Court ruled the baker's artistic skills were an expression of free speech and to create the cake violated the baker's religious beliefs under the First Amendment (*Masterpiece Cakeshop, Ltd. v. Colorado Civil Rights Commission*, 2018). Under the Constitution's free exercise clause, Phillips had a right to neutral treatment and consideration by the state commission. The court made the ruling based on religious animus. Justice Kennedy wrote the majority opinion, stating that the commission showed elements of a

> clear and impermissible hostility toward the sincere religious beliefs motivating his objection . . . [they] disparaged Phillips' faith as despicable and characterized it as merely

rhetorical, and compared his invocation of his sincerely held religious beliefs to defenses of slavery and the Holocaust.
(*Masterpiece Cakeshop, Ltd. v. Colorado Civil Rights Commission*, 2018, p. 2)

The Court found in favor of Masterpiece Cake. The Court's decision was criticized for focusing on religious animus and avoiding the core principle between gay rights and religious liberty (Kendrick & Schwartzman, 2018). Would the court had ruled differently if the state commission was respectful of Phillips's religious beliefs and provided neutral treatment? In the dissenting opinion, Justice Ginsburg and Justice Sotomayor agree with the court's majority opinion that "[P]urveyors of goods and services who object to gay marriages for moral and religious reasons [may not] put up signs saying 'no goods or services will be sold if they will be used for gay marriages'" (*Masterpiece Cakeshop, Ltd. v. Colorado Civil Rights Commission*, 2018, p. 1), but argued that the Commissioner's negative comments on Phillip's religious beliefs and the treatment of bakers did not justify a favorable ruling for Masterpiece Cakeshop, Ltd. Justice Ginsburg opined that "what matters is that Phillips would not provide a good or service to a same-sex couple that he would provide to a heterosexual couple" (Justice Ginsburg, Dissenting Opinion, *Masterpiece Cakeshop, Ltd. v. Colorado Civil Rights Commission*, 2018, p. 5). Gay people should be able to buy products on the same terms and conditions as other people: Gay couples have a right to store-bought wedding cakes but not customized wedding cakes. When it comes to artistic expression, religious freedom trumps discrimination in private businesses.

As noted earlier, lesbian, gay, bisexual, transgender, and queer (LGBTQ) rights in the United States are still in the process of being determined by the courts. LGBTQ rights vary widely around the world. Western democracies provide the greatest legal protections while the Middle East and Africa have the most severe punishments. As of 2019, 30 countries have legalized same-sex marriage, 30 countries permit same-sex second-parent adoption, and 9 countries have constitutional provisions protecting sexual orientation from discrimination. On the other end of the legal continuum, men who have sex with men are executed in 6 countries (Iran, Nigeria, Saudi Arabia, Somalia, Sudan, and Yemen), 5 countries can technically execute (Afghanistan, Mauritania, Pakistan, Qatar, and United Emirates), and 70 countries criminalize same-sex activity (International Lesbian, Gay Association, 2019).

In the U.S., LGBTQ rights and protections are based on U.S. Supreme Court rulings, federal case law, statutory laws, and executive orders, as well as state, county, and city laws; rules; and regulations. In the end, rights and justice are determined by the U.S. Supreme Court. Although court rulings specifically address lesbians, gays, and transgender people the book includes the term *queer* and refers to the group collectively as LGBTQ. In the field of public administration, which trains public servants, LGBTQ rights fall under the theory of social equity and the umbrella of civil rights laws. Social equity theory postulates that everyone should be treated fairly and justly. In the preceding case, it would argue that all couples, including gay couples, are entitled to a custom wedding cake regardless of the baker's religious beliefs. This position is in direct opposition to the Court's ruling in *Masterpiece Cakeshop, Ltd. v. Colorado Civil Rights Commission*, 2018). As such, for social equity theory to have power, it must be based on the rule of law (Rosenbloom, 2018), regardless if one agrees with the ruling. This chapter provides an overview of the development of social equity. Specifically, it defines and operationalizes social equity, describes the institutionalization of social equity in the field of public administration, describes relevant research, and discusses key legal components as it relates to the LGBTQ population.

Social Equity Defined

The terms *equality* and *equity* are used interchangeably. However, from a legal perspective, there are core differences. *Equality* refers to equal parts and has a constitutional basis. The U.S. Constitution's Fourteenth Amendment provides for equal protection under the law. In application,

> the courts use it to judge whether a challenged law creates suspect categories whose members are subject to discrimination. The criterion considers whether group members have been historically discriminated against, have a highly visible trait, or have little to no power to protect themselves.
>
> (Guy & McCandless, 2012, p. S6)

In comparison, *equity* is concerned with fairness and is rooted in philosophy, specifically social contract theory (Guy & McCandless, 2012), Locke (1689), and Hobbes (1660) laid the foundation that government must provide alienable rights and equalities in order to secure validity and legitimacy. People will abide by its government in exchange for protection. In *A Theory of Justice*, Rawls (1971) advocates for equity and insists that justice should be delivered "behind a veil of ignorance" to ensure fairness. The term *equity* is related to affirmative action, disparities, diversity, justice, and representative bureaucracy. Guy and McCandless (2020, 2012) point out that the concept of social equity evolved from a social contract, as described earlier, to a constitutional issue to an administration concern.

Social equity is a pillar of public administration. It is not as well known as the traditional pillars, which include economy, efficiency, and effectiveness, often referred to as the 3Es (Frederickson, 2010, 1990, 1980; Gooden, 2015, 2014; Gooden & Portillo, 2011; Johnson III, 2012a; Rutledge, 2002), but is equally important and recognized. As stated by the U.S. Supreme Court, "although efficacious administration of governmental programs is not without some importance, 'the Constitution recognizes higher values than speed and efficiency'" (*Frontiero v. Richardson*, 1973, p. 1764; as quoted in *Ely v. Saul*, 2020, p. 16). However, the concept of social equity wasn't introduced until much later in the field of public administration's development. Specifically, it was introduced in 1968 at the first Minnowbrook Conference led by Dwight Waldo. At the conference, scholars assessed the state of the field and discussed the future of public administration within the context of great political turmoil including the Vietnam War, the civil rights movement, and multiple political assassinations. Out of the debate emerged the New Public Administration and the concept of social equity. Since Minnowbrook I, social equity has been recognized as one of the pillars of public administration (Blessett et al., 2019; Blessett et al., 2017; Frederickson, 2010, 1990, 1980; Gooden, 2015, 2014; Gooden & Portillo, 2011; Guy & McCandless, 2012; Rutledge, 2002; Wooldridge & Bilharz, 2017; Wooldridge & Gooden, 2009). However, because it joined the public administration lexicon much later than the three traditional pillars, social equity has been more difficult to define, operationalize, and measure, and as such, it has been less utilized (Norman-Major, 2011).

Several definitions of social equity exist in the academic literature. Shafritz and Russell define social equity as "[f]airness in the delivery of public services; it is egalitarianism in action – the principle that each citizen, regardless of economic resources or personal traits, deserves and has the right to be given equal treatment by the political system" (2000, p. 436). According to Gooden, "social equity is directly related to the democratic principle of justice. It is the concept of fairness applied to all, not just select groups" (Gooden, 2014, p. 13). An earlier definition by Gooden and Myers states that it is "fairness or social justice" (2004). In the book *Justice for All: Promoting Social Equity in Public Administration*, authors Johnson and Svara (2011) state the goal of social equity is "members of all social groups will have the same prospects for success and the same opportunity to be protected from the adversities of life" (p. 4). These definitions implicitly include LGBT people. Johnson and Svara (2011) go on to provide a comprehensive definition that operationalizes the concept:

> Social Equity is the active commitment to fairness, justice, and equality in the formulation of public policy, distribution of public services, implementation of public policy, and management of all institutions serving the public directly or by contract. Public administrators, including all persons involved in public governance should seek to prevent and reduce inequality and injustice based on significant social characteristics and to promote greater equality in access to services, procedural fairness, quality of services and social outcomes. Public administrators should empower the participation of all persons in the political process and support the exercise of constructive personal choice.
> (Johnson & Svara, 2011, p. 282)

As illustrated above there are numerous definitions of social equity, but there is no consensus on a single definition, which makes it difficult to operationalize (Rosenbloom, 2018). Rutledge (2002) summarized it as "our failure as a profession to develop the quantitative tools, indicators, and benchmarks to define objectives and measure progress in the pursuit of social equity" (p. 391).

Institutionalizing Social Equity

Despite a lack of consensus on a definition, great strides have been made in the field of American public administration. The concept of social equity has been institutionalized in U.S. public administration by the field's three professional organizations. These include (1) the National Academy of Public Administration (NAPA), (2) the American Society for Public Administration (ASPA), and (3) the Network of Schools of Public Policy, Affairs, and Administration (NASPAA). Each of their contributions is discussed in the following sections.

NAPA

The NAPA, which was chartered by Congress, created a standing panel on social equity in 1997. The panel meets regularly in Washington, D.C., and provides a speaker series on cutting edge issues related to social equity. Dr. Phil Rutledge created the standing panel on social equity (Frederickson, 2010). In 2005, the NAPA recognized social equity as the fourth pillar of public administration. In its strategic plan, it states, "The Academy's Board of Directors adopted social equity as the fourth pillar of public administration, along with economy, efficiency and effectiveness" (NAPA, 2005; as stated in Wooldridge & Bilharz, 2017). In addition, the NAPA provides a definition for social equity and created an annual conference on social equity. Since 2001 the annual Social Equity and Leadership Conference has been held to advance the subject through panels and workshops. The NAPA president and chief executive officer, Teresa Gerton, consistently promotes and fosters social equity in meetings such as Grand Challenges in Public Administration and the daily NAPA newsletter *Management Matters*. These contributions are significant because NAPA continues to elevate the role of social equity in the academy and field of public administration (Frederickson, 2010; Wooldridge & Bilharz, 2017). It was the first professional organization to provide a definition of social equity giving the concept organizational validity. NAPA defines social equity as

> the fair, just, equitable management of all institutions serving the public directly or by contract: the fair, just and equitable distribution of public services and implementation of public policy. The commitment to promote fairness, justice, and equity in the formation of public policy.
> (National Academy of Public Administration, 2000a, 200b)

This definition implicitly includes LGBT people as a result of ongoing discrimination and disparities.

Measuring Social Equity

To operationalize the term a set of criteria was created. Svara and Brunet (2018) collaborated with NAPA members and identified a set of measurement criteria for social equity. The four criteria are outlined as follows:

1. Procedural fairness – process under which due process, equal protection, hiring, promotion, awarding of contracts are all guaranteed.
2. Distributional equity – process assures equal access, targeted intervention, and commitment of resources to achieve fair results.
3. Process equity – guarantees consistency in the level of service delivery regardless of distributional criterion used, and
4. Outcome disparities – probes for reasons why disparities may still exist as a result of policies and programs that may in fact meet all input criteria (National Academy of Public Administration, n.d.).

In an article titled "Counting an Invisible Class of Citizens: The LGBT Population and the U.S. Census," Naylor (2018) utilizes the four criteria outlined earlier to illustrate the negative economic and political impact of the U.S. Census Bureau's 2017 decision to omit two demographic variables, sexual orientation and gender identity, from the 2020 decennial census. The census, which provides population and housing estimates by counting the location and number of people, is used to allocate over $650 billion in funding to state and local governments and determine political apportionment in the U.S. House of Representatives. The author argues that by excluding these two demographic variables, the LGBTQ population is shortchanged in the allocation of federal funding (distributional equity) and may not receive equal opportunities in education, employment, health care, homeownership, and public accommodations, which can lead to disparities and negative outcomes for LGBTQ people.

There are two reports in the field of public administration providing examples on how to assess and measure social equity. In *Linking Social Equity and Performance Management: A Practitioner's Roadmap*, the authors, from the University of Colorado Denver, School of Public Affairs, Larson et al. (2017), provide concrete examples for administrators in local government to measure social equity. The authors apply social equity and performance measurement to three case studies: Seattle, Washington; Louisville, Kentucky; and Fort Collins, Colorado. In *Moving From Theory to Practice: An Evaluative Assessment of Social Equity Approaches*, Blessett et al. (2017) provide definitions, measurements, and resources on social equity. In addition, they describe successful social equity tools and frameworks, including Virginia Performs, which utilizes a scorecard to assess social indicators in the state; National Equity Atlas, which assesses a list of comprehensive indicators on economic inclusive growth; Sustainability Tools for Assessing and Rating Communities, which assesses local government sustainability; and the Seattle Race and Social Justice Initiative, which assesses institutionalized racism and racial disparity. All four assessment tools measure social equity.

ASPA

The second professional organization to institutionalize social equity is the ASPA. It is a membership organization for public administration and includes both government practitioners and academics. It has anchored social equity to the profession by giving annual awards, hosting luncheons, creating sections, and developing codes of ethics. These activities and events are important in institutionalizing values into an organization's culture (Khademian, 2002). Regarding awards, since 2003, the ASPA has hosted the Gloria Hobson Nordin Social Equity luncheon at the annual conference. Practitioner James Nordin endowed the luncheon, naming it after his late wife, Gloria Hobson, who was a public servant. The award recognizes lifetime achievement in social equity (ASPA, n.d.). Most recently, the Conference of Minority Public Administrators (COMPA) awarded the 2020 Public Service Award to Dr. Blue Woodridge for his 50 years of service and unwavering support of social equity. The Section on Women in Public Administration (SWPA) also issues annual awards recognizing important research and professional contributions for women and vulnerable populations. With regard to sections, the ASPA offers at least eight sections that address social equity issues: (1) COMPA, (2) democracy and social justice, (3) LGBT Advocacy Alliance, (4) ethics and integrity in governance, (5) public law and administration, (6) personnel administration and labor relations, (7) public administration education, and (8) women in public administration. These sections are instrumental in supporting social equity research and recognizing exemplary contributions in the field. The LGBT Advocacy Alliance section was created in December 2011 by ASPA member Claire Mostel in conjunction with Erik Bergrud, a past president of ASPA (Mostel, n.d.). Its mission is to "provide a safe and supportive environment within ASPA and its partners by:

- Focusing on equal rights, diversity and workplace issues
- Providing policy assistance through research and education on critical/relevant issues
- Being a clearinghouse for information – resources and materials
- Facilitating and supporting community engagement/development and coalition building
- Increasing awareness of cultural competency" (Mostel, n.d.).

In addition to holding annual meetings, the section provides annual awards for outstanding contributions to LGBT issues. Past Visionary award winners include Erik Bergrud and Claire Mostel; Visionary Award – Chet Newland (2016), Public Service Award – Richard Gregory Johnson III (2018), and Seth Meyer (2019); and Best Article Award – Peter Stanley Federman and Nicole Elias; Meghna Sabharwal, Helisse Levine, Maria D"Agostino, Tiffany Ngyuyen, Mitchell Dylan Sellars (2018) and Nicole Elias and Roddrick Colvin (2019). The creation of the LGBT section is significant because it promotes LGBT research, provides scholars who identify as LGBT a safe place to speak about issues in a professional setting, provides mentoring, and challenges bias and intolerance in public administration.

One vehicle utilized to incorporate values of fairness, tolerance, and justice is through the adoption of a professional code of ethics. The ASPA adopted social equity as a core principle in its code of ethics. Principle four of the code states: "Strengthen social equity: treat all persons with fairness, justice and equality and respect individual differences, rights, and freedoms. Promote affirmative action and other initiatives to reduce unfairness, injustice, and inequality in society" (ASPA, Code of

Ethics, 2014). This principle is important because LGBT citizens are more likely to face inequality and injustice through discrimination, harassment, and physical attacks than their heterosexual peers (Dolamore & Naylor, 2017; Naylor, 2018; Swan, 2015).

NASPPA

The third professional organization to address social equity is the NASPAA. The NASPAA is the accrediting body for U.S. and international graduate schools in public affairs which include the Master of Public Administration (MPA) and Master of Public Policy. Currently, there are over 300 NASPAA-accredited schools. Accreditation is important because it sets standards that outline expectations, competencies, and values in teaching public administration. Programs seeking reaccreditation or new accreditation are reviewed by the Commission on Peer Review and Accreditation on seven standards. Three of these standards relate to social equity: (1) standard 3.2 faculty diversity, (2) standard 4.4 student diversity, and (3) standard 5.1 universal required competencies. Specifically, standard 5.1 identifies the competency "to communicate and interact productively with a diverse and changing workforce and citizenry" (NASPAA, 2019). This means that accredited graduate programs must measure both student diversity and faculty diversity. Does faculty diversity reflect or represent student diversity? In addition, accredited schools should teach diversity in their programs. The expectation is that concepts such as diversity, social equity, social justice, and representative bureaucracy are taught in courses such as human resources, public personnel management, public policy, ethics, and administrative law. The goal is for graduate students to enter public service and incorporate diversity and social equity as a core value in the workplace. In other words, graduates should practice social equity. Public servants have a lot of discretion in their interactions with citizens (Lipsky, 2010), and through education and training, it is more likely they will treat all people seeking government services equally and fairly, including LGBT citizens.

According to Blessett et al. (2019), which conducted research on barriers to teaching social equity, NASPAA has recognized several MPA programs for emphasizing social equity in the curriculum and program. These include John Jay College of Criminal Justice, Long Island University, Rutgers University, State University of New York – Albany, the University of Baltimore, the University of Cincinnati, the University of Massachusetts Amherst, and Virginia Commonwealth University. Faculty at these institutions conduct research on social equity and advocate for the incorporation of social equity in the MPA curriculum. However, across all MPA programs in the U.S., social equity courses remain underrepresented in graduate programs that train government employees. McCandless and Larson (2018) found that only 10 percent of MPA programs emphasize social equity in their programs, and roughly 74 percent do not require courses on social equity. Despite its importance in training public servants, social equity remains underrepresented in public affairs education (Gooden, 2015; Norman Major, 2011; Wyatt-Nichol et al., 2011).

More work needs to be done to ensure social equity is embedded in MPA curriculum and other graduate public affairs programs. In the professional membership organizations (the ASPA and the NAPA), social equity has been institutionalized through conferences, awards, sections, and codes of ethics. Next, social equity research is discussed.

Research

With regard to academic literature in public administration, in the past social equity research has not received the attention or recognition other subjects in the field have received. *Social equity* is a broad term and includes concepts such as affirmative action, civil rights, diversity, equal opportunity, social justice, and representative bureaucracy. It is applied to demographic categories, including race, ethnicity, national origin, gender, gender identity, sexual orientation, disability, and veteran status. It focuses on disparities and inequalities and intersects with education, employment, health, housing, and income. There are hundreds of articles and books on these subjects. In public administration, these concepts are covered in the area of administrative law, diversity, ethics, public personnel management, and representative bureaucracy. The seminal book on social equity was written by H. George Frederickson (2010), titled *Social Equity and Public Administration: Origins, Developments, and Applications*. More recent titles include *Achieving Social Equity: From Problems to Solutions* (Guy & McCandless, 2020), *Social Equity in a Time of Change: A Critical 21st Century Social Movement* (Johnson, 2017), *Race and Social Equity: A Nervous Area of Government* (Gooden, 2014), *Justice for All: Promoting Social Equity in Public Administration* (Johnson & Svara, 2011), *Cultural Competency for Public Administrators* (Norman-Major & Gooden, 2015), and *Cultural Competence for Public Managers: Managing Diversity in Today's World* (Borrego & Johnson, 2011). Also see *Teaching College Students Communication Strategies for Effective Social Justice Advocacy* (Johnson III, 2011).

Regarding diversity, there is a rich depository on the subject including *Personnel Management in Government* (Naff et al., 2017), *Public Personnel Management: Contexts and Strategies* (Llorens et al., 2015), *Public Personnel Management: Current Concerns, Future Challenges* (Riccucci, 2017), *Managing Diversity in Public Service Workforces* (Riccucci, 2002), *Promoting and Valuing Diversity in Municipal Government Workforces* (Riccucci, 1992), and *Federal Equal Employment Opportunity* (Rosenbloom, 1977).

The majority of books and peer-reviewed articles have been written on representative bureaucracy. See Krislov and Rosenbloom's (2012) seminal book on the subject titled *Representative Bureaucracy and the American Political System*. Additional titles include *Representative Bureaucracy: Classic Readings and Continuing Controversies* (Dolan & Rosenbloom, 2003); *The Promise of Representative Bureaucracy: Diversity & Responsiveness in a Government Agency* (Coleman Selden, 2015); *To Look like America: Dismantling Barriers for Women and Minorities in Government* (Naff, 2001); *Politics of Representative Bureaucracy: Power, Legitimacy & Performance* (Peters et al., 2015); and *Bureaucracy and Representative Government* (Niskanen, 1971), to name a few.

For books on the legal aspect of social equity, the most prolific writer has been David Rosenbloom. See *Administrative Law for Public Managers* (Rosenbloom, 2015); *Public Administration and Law* (Rosenbloom et al., 2019); *Public Administration: Understanding Management, Politics, and Law in the Public Sector* (Rosenbloom et al., 2008); and *Constitutional Competence for Public Managers: Cases and Commentary* (Rosenbloom et al., 2000).

In the area of sexual orientation and gender, several books and an encyclopedia have been written in the field of public administration. Swan has edited three books, two handbooks, one encyclopedia article as well as two chapters on the subject. Swan's (2019) *The Routledge Handbook of LGBTQIA Administration Policy* serves as a repository for LGBT issues and policies. Swan also edited *The Handbook of Gay, Lesbian Bisexual and Transgender Administration and Policy* (2004). Edited books by Swan include *Gay, Lesbian, Bisexual, and Transgender Civil Rights: A Public Policy Agenda for Uniting a Divided America* (Swan, 2015), which focuses on conservative and liberal states and implications for marriage equality; *Gay, Lesbian, Bisexual, Transgender Public Policy Issues: A Citizen's and Administrators Guide to the New Struggle* (1997); and *Breaking the Silence: Gay, Lesbian, and Bisexual Issues in Public Administration* (1995, ASPA).

These are just a few of the books on social equity; the list is not exhaustive. It illustrates that social equity, diversity, and representative bureaucracy have been well researched in public administration. What remains an issue is that social equity has not been given the emphasis deserved in top published journals compared to other subjects. For example, Gooden found that only 4.2 percent of articles published in *Publication Administration Review*, the leading journal in public administration, focused on social equity (Blessett et al., 2019, p. 287; Gooden, 2015). For examples of articles on social equity in *Publication Administration Review*, see Glaser et al. (2011, 2014), Johnson III (2012a), Glaser (2012), and Maynard-Moody and Musheno (2012). Part of the bias may stem from the fact that research on social equity is normative, not quantitative, making it less attractive to journal editors.

To address this concern and ongoing documented inequalities, scholars decided to elevate the subject by creating a manifesto.

Social Equity Manifesto

In 2018, the "Minnowbrook 50" conference was held to celebrate the 50th anniversary of Minnowbrook I and to reflect on progress in the field. Scholars noted the progress made and the work that still needed to be done. Inequalities still exist by race, ethnicity, gender, sexual orientation, and, especially, gender identity and orientation. Attendees declared that social equity must be a core value and foundational anchor for the field of public administration. This resulted in a manifesto of seven principles to "integrate social equity in the research, teaching, and practice of public administration" (Blessett et al., 2018; also see Gooden & Portillo, 2011). The manifesto states:

> Below are a set of principles that seek to move public administration toward making social equity an embedded value and practice in the field:
>
> I. Social equity is a foundational anchor, not just a pillar, of public administration. There is a responsibility to promote social equity in our roles as researchers, teachers, and practitioners.
> II. Our commitment to the field of public administration requires us to stand up for good governance, social equity, and strong communities. As scholars and practitioners, we must be open to professional development opportunities that challenge conscious and unconscious bias, be willing to engage in difficult conversations with colleagues and constituents, and commit ourselves to be life-long learners as a way to incorporate the values of social equity and cultural understanding as part of our daily process.
> III. A goal of social equity is to eliminate inequalities of all kinds. This requires a commitment to structural, institutional changes and deep personal work on behalf of public administration scholars and practitioners. As academics, we support social equity in our instruction, in the hiring and promotion of our colleagues, in our research, and in our service to the field. As practitioners, we support social equity in the development, implementation, and evaluation of managerial practices and public policies.
> IV. Research needs to be utilized as a tool for examining whether social equity goals are being realized. As researchers, we can use equity frameworks, such as Representative Bureaucracy and Intersectionality, to inform the questions we ask as well as broaden our methodological choices to incorporate more qualitative work. Representative bureaucracy can demonstrate the effectiveness of equity-based approaches to hiring and promotion.
> V. Violations of equity are contrary to democracy. As researchers, we should be more conscious of the questions we ask, the paradigms/frameworks/theories we use and

propose, and the implications of our research as it pertains to equity. As practitioners, a democratically responsible administration includes passionate action that is equitable, inclusive, intentional, person-centered and encapsulated by an ethos of care.

VI. As a whole, academic programs of public administration are not currently equipping or preparing the future of public administrators for the practical work of equity in public service. Public administration programs need core courses focused centrally on equity that are not relegated to "special topics" courses or electives. In addition, equity concepts, processes, issues, and outcomes should be incorporated within every core class in public administration curricula.

VII. Practitioners are fundamental actors in extending democracy and promoting equity. Administrators must be committed to and manifest the ideals of democracy, justice, and equity for all citizens through their actions, professional development, and engagement with all individuals and communities. As practitioners, the upper levels of management with promotion authority need to create pipelines to promote social equity at the higher levels of government.

(Blessett et al., 2018)

The manifesto is a call to action to ensure social justice in our democracy. The challenge is to operationalize and measure social equity to ensure progress. This is important because significant disparities exist between LGBTQ people and heterosexual citizens. For example, LGBTQ people are more likely than their heterosexual peers to suffer from homelessness (McCandless, 2018; Shelton, 2018; Johnson III et al., 2018; Johnson III, 2018), depression, substance abuse, mental illness, violence, and poverty (Dolamore & Naylor, 2017; Fraser et al., 2019; Kates et al., 2018). LGBTQ youth are proportionally three times more likely to report being raped than their straight peers (16 percent versus 5 percent; U.S. Centers for Disease Control and Prevention, 2010), and transgender people are more likely to be killed than straight peers. According to the Federal Bureau of Investigation, in 2017, approximately 17 percent of hate crime incidents in the U.S. were due to perceived sexual orientation (U.S. Federal Bureau of Investigation, 2017). LGBT citizens are more likely to experience discrimination, harassment, and physical attacks than their heterosexual counterparts. LGBT citizens have been murdered based on sexual orientation (U.S. Federal Bureau of Investigation, 2018). Approximately 25 transgender people are murdered each year based on gender identity and orientation.

Rule of Law

The fourth component is the rule of law. Social equity theory must be based on the rule of law to have power and sustainability. This includes the U.S. Constitution, U.S. Supreme Court decisions, case law, and statutes. The connection between social equity and law is evident and begins with the U.S. Constitution. The Fifth Amendment's due process clause states that "no person . . . shall be deprived of life, liberty or property without due process of law" (U.S. Constitution, 1789). It applies directly to social equity and classifications (see *Adarand v. Pena*, 1995). The Fourteenth Amendment gives citizens' rights in the form of due process and equal protection. It states, "[N]or shall any State deprive any person of life, liberty, or property; without due process of law, nor deny to any person within its jurisdiction the equal protection of the laws" (U.S. Constitution, Fourteenth Amendment, ratified 1868). This is known as the due process clause, and numerous U.S. Supreme Court rulings are based on it. This is not to state that the language in the Constitution is perfect. It is not.

There are imperfections and clear flaws, including outright discrimination (see Article I, Section II reference to treating slaves as three-fifths of a person and exclusion of Indians and women).

Constitutional interpretation, which is often contradictory, evolves over time as a reflection of social norms and public opinion. Over time, the courts have ruled to protect marginalized groups and minorities from legislation that promotes hate, discrimination, and bias. The U.S. Supreme court has a special role in protecting unpopular groups by ensuring civil rights and equality. For example, in *Plessy v. Ferguson* (1896), the court ruled separate but equal was constitutional; 50 years later in *Brown v Board of Education Topeka I* (1954) the court reversed and ruled the equal rights clause made it unconstitutional to operate racially segregated educational systems. In *Brown v. Board of Education Topeka* II (1955), the court required racial integration with deliberate speed. Prior to 1967, it was illegal in numerous states for whites and blacks to marry. In 1967, the court ruled that it was unconstitutional to prohibit interracial marriage (*Loving v. Virginia*, 1967), which cleared the legal path for interracial marriages across the country. At the core of inequality is animus. In 1973, the U.S. Supreme Court ruled that "if the constitutional conception of 'equal protection of the laws' means anything, it must at the very least mean that a bare congressional desire to harm a politically unpopular group cannot constitute a legitimate governmental interest" (*U.S. Department of Agriculture v. Moreno*, 1973; also see *City of Cleburne v. Living Center, Inc.*, 1985; *Romer v. Evans*, 1996; *U.S. v. Windsor*, 2013).

The following is a timeline of landmark U.S. Supreme Court decisions that guarantee civil rights and equal treatment and promote social equity.

Timeline of U.S. Supreme Court Decisions

In 1932, the U.S. Supreme Court ruled in *Powell v. Alabama* (287 U.S. 45) that defendants have a right to legal counsel before being tried in court. This case involved nine black males (the Scottsboro Boys) who were tried, convicted, and sentenced to death for raping two white women without evidence and without an attorney. The court ruled the trials violated the due process clause of the Fourteenth Amendment.

In 1942, the U.S. Supreme Court ruled in *Glasser v. U.S.* (315 U.S. 60) that it was unconstitutional to exclude women from the jury pool. The court ruled it violated the Sixth Amendment (impartial jury clause).

In 1944, the U.S. Supreme Court ruled in *Smith v. Allright* (321 U.S. 649) that all individuals of all races are guaranteed to vote in primary elections. The court ruled it violated the equal protection clause of the Fourteenth Amendment.

In 1948, the U.S. Supreme Court ruled in *Shelley v. Kraemer* (334 U.S. 1) that it was unconstitutional to enforce racial covenants on real estate, creating segregated neighborhoods.

In 1954, the U.S. Supreme Court ruled in *Brown v. Board of Education Topeka I* (347 U.S. 483) that educational segregation was unconstitutional.

In 1955, the U.S. Supreme Court ruled in *Brown v. Board of Education Topeka II* (349 U.S. 294) that local jurisdictions were responsible for integrating schools with "deliberate speed."

In 1960, the U.S. Supreme Court ruled in *Boynton v. Virginia* (364 U.S. 454) that racial segregation in public transportation is unconstitutional under the Interstate Commerce Act of 1887.

In 1964, the U.S. Supreme Court ruled in *Heart of Atlanta Motel v. United States* (379 U.S. 241) that it was a violation for the hotel owner to refuse service to black travelers under the Constitution's commerce clause.

In 1967, the U. S. Supreme Court ruled in *Loving v. Virginia* (388 U.S. 1) that state laws banning interracial marriage violated the U.S. Constitution. The decision made it legal for interracial couples to marry.

In 1973, the U.S. Supreme Court ruled in *U.S. Department of Agriculture v. Moreno* (413 U.S. 528) that the Food Stamp Act of 1964 (as amended) cannot prohibit households from receiving food stamps if there is an unrelated individual living in the household. It does not advance a legitimate government interest. "A congressional desire to harm a politically unpopular group cannot constitute a legitimate governmental interest" (*U.S. Department of Agriculture v. Moreno*, 1973, p. 534).

In 1973, the U.S. Supreme Court ruled in *Frontiero v. Richardson* (411 U.S. 677) that it was a violation of the Fifth Amendment's due process clause for a federal law to treat similarly situated female military members different than males regarding spousal dependency and benefits.

In 1974, the U.S. Supreme Court ruled in *Cleveland Board of Education v. LaFleur* (414 U.S. 632) that it is unconstitutional to force mandatory maternity leave on public employees.

In 1976, the U.S. Supreme Court ruled in *Craig v. Boren* (429 U.S. 190) it is unconstitutional to have different age minimums, females (age 21) and males (age 18) to purchase beer.

In 1985, the U.S. Supreme Court ruled 9–0 in *City of Cleburne v. Cleburne Living Center, Inc.* (473 U.S. 432) that denying a special permit to operate a home for the mentally challenged violates the equal protection clause of the Fourteenth Amendment.

In 1995, the U.S. Supreme Court ruled in *Adarand Constructors v. Pena* (515 U.S. 200) that all racial classifications, including federal, state, and local governments, must pass a strict scrutiny standard and must "serve a compelling government interest and must be narrowly tailored to further that interest" (*Romer v. Evans*, 1996, pp. 93–1841).

In 1996, the U.S. Supreme Court ruled in *Romer v. Evans* (517 U.S. 620) that Amendment 2 of the Colorado State Constitution was unconstitutional. It violated the equal protection clause by denying homosexual and bisexual people legal protections against discrimination. The court held that "a bare desire to harm a politically unpopular group cannot constitute a legitimate governmental interest" (*U.S. Department of Agriculture v. Moreno*, 1973).

In 2003, the U.S. Supreme Court ruled in *Lawrence v. Texas* (539 U.S. 558, 2003) that a Texas sodomy law was unconstitutional. The ruling made sodomy legal in every state.

In 2013, the U.S. Supreme Court ruled in *United States v. Windsor* (570 U.S. 744) that Section 3 of the Defense of Marriage Act (DOMA), which defined marriage as a union between a man and a woman, was unconstitutional. The court held that harming a politically unpopular group is not a legitimate governmental interest (*U.S. Department of Agriculture v. Moreno*, 1973).

In 2014, a U.S. Court of Appeals, Ninth Circuit ruled in *SmithKline Beecham Corporation v. Abbott Laboratories* (740 F.3d 471) that it is a violation of the equal protection clause to deny a citizen jury duty based on sexual orientation.

In 2015, the U.S. Supreme Court ruled in *Obergefell v. Hodges* (576 U.S. 644) that marriage was a fundamental right regardless of sexual orientation. The decision secured marriage equality for same-sex couples across the country.

In 2020, the U.S. Supreme Court ruled in Bostock v Clayton County (590 U.S._) that sex under Title VII of the Civil Rights Act includes sexual orientation and gender identity. It is a violation to fire an individual for being gay or transgender. The preceding list is not exhaustive but rather documents the connection between the rule of law, civil rights, and social equity. These court decisions address the fair and equal treatment of individuals within the pillar of social equity and the umbrella of civil rights laws. Because social equity is based on the rule of law it is legally enforceable. The next section focuses on federal statutes.

Federal Laws

In addition to U.S. Supreme Court decisions, there is federal legislation that promotes fair and equal treatment of citizens. For example, the U.S. Congress has passed numerous laws to enforce civil rights in America. The most well known of these is the landmark Civil Rights Act of 1964 (Pub. L. 88–352), which made segregation illegal. Specifically, it made discrimination based on race, color, sex, national origin, or religion illegal. It provides the basis for equal employment opportunity. Its purpose is to

> enforce the constitutional right to vote, to confer jurisdiction upon the district courts of the United States to provide injunctive relief against discrimination in public accommodations, to authorize the Attorney General to institute suits to protect constitutional rights in public facilities and public education, to extend the Commission on Civil Rights, to prevent discrimination in federally assisted programs, to establish a Commission on Equal Employment Opportunity.
> (Civil Rights Act of 1964, Pub. L. 88–352)

The law was broad sweeping in nature and sought to change deeply embedded racism. As such, it was met with great resistance ranging from peaceful demonstrations to rioting and murder.

The Civil Rights Act of 1964 has made great strides in advancing equality and fairness, but work still remains to be done. Segregation in schools and neighborhoods continues to exist today but not at the level witnessed during the 1960s. Voting rights have achieved moderate success, but voter suppression still exists. There is less employment discrimination but minorities and women continue to be underrepresented in high-level positions, which earn much higher salaries, whereas eliminating segregation in public accommodations (restaurants, hotels, movie theaters, etc.) has achieved the greatest success.

Another landmark piece of legislation is the Matthew Shepard Jr. and James Byrd Hate Crimes Prevention Act of 2009 (Pub. L. 111–84). It involves the highly publicized 1998 murder of Matthew Shepard, an openly gay man. He was robbed, beaten, and tortured to death near Laramie, Wyoming. His two attackers hit him in the head with a .357-caliber pistol 19 to 21 times. He was treated at a hospital where he later died (Marsden, 2014). His death combined with James Byrd's murder resulted in federal legislation to prevent hate crimes known as the Matthew Shepard Jr. and James Byrd Hate Crimes Prevention Act of 2009 (Pub. L. 111–84), which allows for federal prosecution of a hate crime. James Byrd was a black man who was dragged behind a pickup truck by white supremacists in Texas and decapitated. The 2009 law expands the term *hate crimes* to include "offenses involving actual or perceived national origin, gender, sexual orientation, gender identity, or disability" (18 U.S.C., Section 249). Prior to 2009, crimes against LGBTQ people could not be charged as hate crimes. The intent of the 2009 law is to recognize that criminals target individuals based on bias (real or perceived) including sexual orientation and gender (as well as race, national origin, and disability). As a result of the law, the U.S. Federal Bureau of Investigations tracks data on hate crimes against people (murder, rape, assault, intimidation), property (robbery, burglary, vandalism), and society (prostitution, drugs, narcotics) (U.S. Federal Bureau of Investigation, 2017). Before the law was passed, perpetrators would not be prosecuted for a hate crime, which carries a more severe penalty.

The two pieces of federal legislation described earlier represent a large body of public laws that promote civil rights and advance social equity and justice. A timeline of federal legislation is provided below to give the reader an overview of key legislation that supports social equity theory.

Timeline of Laws

In 1789, the first Congress under the U.S. Constitution convenes. It was passed ensuring citizens have a right to due process and equal protection under the law.

In 1963, Congress passed the Equal Pay Act (Pub. L. 88–38), which requires employers to pay equal pay for equal work regardless of sex.

In 1964, the Civil Rights Act was passed (Pub. L. 88–352, 78 Stat. 241). Title VII of the law guarantees employment without regard for race, color, religion, sex, and national origin.

In 1965, Congress passed the Voting Rights Act (Pub. L. 89–110) which prohibits restrictions on the right to vote. In 1967, Congress passed the Age Discrimination in Employment Act (Pub. L. 90-202).

In 1968, Congress passed the Fair Housing Act (Title VIII of the Civil Rights Act of 1968), which prohibits discrimination basis on race, sex, religion, disability, and familial status.

In 1972, Congress passed Title IX of the Educational Amendments (Pub. L. 92-318), which prevents sex discrimination in programs that receive federal funding and encourages female participation in athletics.

In 1972, Congress passed the Equal Employment Opportunity Act which amends section 706 Title VII of the Civil Rights Act of 1964 (78 Stat. 253; 42 U.S.C. 2000e).

In 1975, Congress passed the Age Discrimination Act (42 U.S.C. Sections 6101–6107), which prohibits discrimination by programs that receive federal funding.

In 1978, Congress passed the Pregnancy Discrimination Act (Pub. L. 95–555) to prevent women from being discriminated against in the workplace.

In 1991, Congress passed the Civil Rights and Women's Equity in Employment Act (Pub. L. 102–166).

In 2009, Congress passed the Matthew Shepard Jr. and James Byrd Hate Crimes Prevention Act of 2009 (Pub. L. 111–84). Provides for federal prosecution of hate crimes including national origin, gender, sexual orientation, gender identity, and disability.

The federal laws identified above represent a commitment to equality and fairness by Congress, thus advancing civil rights and social equity. These laws are directly applicable to the goals of social equity and LGBTQ people. LGBTQ and related gender identity terms are defined in the next section, which is followed by a discussion on intersectionality as it relates to LGBTQ people and social justice.

Gender Identity Definitions

Historically, gender has been viewed as binary; either male or female. Today, it is conceived on a spectrum; rejecting the binary model. It is important to define gender identities because each identity has different needs and legal rights. The American Psychological Association (2015), defines sexual orientation and gender identity on key distinctions. Transgender and gender nonbinary people are individuals whose gender identity does not conform to their sex assigned at birth (often referred to as biological sex or birth sex) (Nolan et al., 2019). These individuals may seek hormonal and psychological treatment, be diagnosed with gender dysphoria, and seek sex reassignment surgery. Gender identity is different than gender expression. In contrast, "cisgender" refers to individuals whose biological sex matches their gender identity, which is the vast majority of the U.S. population. Nonbinary individuals do not associate with either sex (male or female). Lesbian refers to women who are attracted to other women. Gay men are attracted to other men. Bisexual refers to people who are attracted to both men and women. In contrast, sexual orientation refers to whom a person finds sexually attractive. Individuals attracted to the opposite sex are known as heterosexual. Individuals attracted to the same-sex are referred to as either lesbian, gay, or homosexual. As described earlier, gender is no longer viewed as a dichotomous variable, a simple checkbox of either male or female. It exists on a continuum. This significant change in society from a binary model to a gender continuum model is important to note because public policies in federal, state, and local governments have not been amended to incorporate these changes. For example, the 2020 U.S. Census does not count the number of gay, lesbian, transgender, bisexual, or queer singles. It counts the number of LG people living in the same household and their relationship to each other (spouse or partner). The difference is significant because the majority of LGBTQ people are single, 80 percent; the remaining 20 percent are married or have partners. This means the majority of LGBTQ people are not counted in the census or factored into funding formulas based on the census, which is utilized to allocate federal funding for education, health, housing, policing, and social policies (Naylor, 2018). This is important because LGBTQ people are discriminated against in employment, health care, and housing.

Intersectionality

The changes described earlier from a binary gender model to a gender continuum model take place against the backdrop of intersectionality. The term *intersectionality* was coined by Crenshaw (2001, 1991, 1989) to describe how African American women are discriminated against based on race, gender, and income. These three variables form a layered identity in an individual. The intersectionality framework posits that when race, gender, and income are combined or intersect, it can lead to multiple levels of discrimination, injustice, and oppression. Harris refers to this as multiple marginality (2012). The impact is cumulative. The framework argues that the more negative characteristics or demographic variables that intersect, the greater the potential severity of oppression. Today, the term *intersectionality* has expanded to include gender identity and expression, disability, education, nationality, veteran status, and other demographic variables which, when combined, can lead to greater oppression and injustice than a single, stand-alone demographic variable. For example, a poor, black, transgender, immigrant woman has different life experiences and hardships than a Black man. Intersectionality is a framework to view injustices and is directly applicable to LGBTQ people who are discriminated against, harassed, and often killed due to sexual orientation or gender identity.

Conclusion

This chapter traces the history of social equity in the field of public administration and anchors social equity theory to the rule of law. For social equity to have power and sustainability it must be linked to the rule of law. Federal legislation combined with court rulings and case law provide the legal foundation for social equity theory. Together these policies provide legal rights to protect people who have been marginalized based on race, ethnicity, national origin, gender, disability, age, or other classifications. However, legal rights for LGBTQ people lag behind rights for those groups considered a protected class. (For a full discussion see Rosenbloom, 2003, pp. 39–41). As illustrated in the *Masterpiece Cakeshop, Ltd. v. Colorado Commission Civil Rights Commission* ruling, sexual orientation is treated differently than historically legally protected classes such as race, nationality, or disability. For example, it is unlikely the baker could legally refuse to bake a cake for a black or a Chinese couple. The underlying bias is the belief that sexual orientation is a choice. Kendrick and Schwartzman (2018) argue the U.S. Supreme Court's ruling focuses on the religious animus of state officials while passing on the central question of whether religious liberty authorizes discrimination based on sexual orientation in the purchase of goods and services. Can wedding-related businesses such as florists and photographers invoke religious objections to serving same-sex couples in the absence of animus by state officials? Legal rulings addressing religious rights and LGBTQ rights are evolving and are discussed at greater length in subsequent chapters. The next chapter focuses on marriage equality.

Resources

American Society for Public Administration (ASPA). www.aspanet.org
Code of Federal Regulations. www.govinfo.gov/app/collection/cfr
Library of Congress, Law Library. www.loc.gov/law/help/guide.php
National Academy of Public Administration (NAPA). www.napawash.org/
National Association of Attorney Generals. www.naag.org
Oyez. www.oyez.org/
U.S. Courts. www.uscourts.gov
U.S. Department of Justice. www.doj.gov
U.S. Supreme Court. www.supremecourt.gov/

References

Adarand Constructors v. Pena, 515 U.S. 200 (1995).
Age Discrimination in Employment Act of 1967 (ADEA) (Pub. L. 90–202).
American Psychological Association. (2015). *APA dictionary of psychology*. American Psychological Association.
American Society for Public Administration. (2014). *Code of ethics*. www.aspanet.org/ASPA/About-ASPA/Code-of-Ethics/ASPA/Code-of-Ethics/Code-of-Ethics.aspx?hkey=fefba3e2-a9dc-4fc8-a686-3446513a4533
American Society for Public Administration. (n.d.). *Gloria Hobson social equity award*. www.aspanet.org/ASPA/Make-Connections/Awards/Gloria-Hobson-Nordin-Social-Equity-Award.aspx
Blessett, B., Dodge, J., Edmond, B., Goerdel, H., Gooden, S., Headley, A., Riccucci, N. M., & Williams, B. (2019). Social equity in public administration: A call to action. *Perspectives on Public Management and Governance*, 283–299.
Blessett, B., Dodge, J., Edmond, B., Goerdel, H., Gooden, S., Headley, A., Riccucci, N. M., & Williams, B. (2018, August). *Minnowbrook 50 social equity manifesto*. Syracuse University, Maxwell School of Citizenship and Public Affairs. www.maxwell.syr.edu/minnowbrook/social-equity-manifesto/
Blessett, B., Fudge, M., & Gaynor, T. S. (2017). *Moving from theory to practice: An evaluative assessment of social equity approaches*. Submitted to Center for Accountability and Performance and National Academy for Public Administration's Standing Panel on Social Equity in Governance. https://aspacap.files.wordpress.com/2018/10/cap-theory.pdf
Borrego, E., & Johnson III, R. G. (2011). *Cultural competence for public managers: Managing diversity in today's world*. CRC Press (now Taylor & Francis).
Boynton v. Virginia, 364 U.S. 454 (1960).
Brown v. Board of Education Topeka I, 347 U.S. 483 (1954).
Brown v. Board of Education Topeka II, 349 U.S. 294 (1955).
City of Cleburne v. Living Center, Inc., 473 U.S. 432 (1985).
Civil Rights Act of 1964 (Pub. L. 88–352).
Civil Rights and Women's Equity in Employment Act of 1991. (Pub. L. 102–166).
Cleveland Board of Education v. LaFleur, 414 U.S. 632 (1974).
Coleman, S. S. (2015). *The promise of representative bureaucracy: Diversity & responsiveness in a government agency*. M.E. Sharpe.

Craig v. Boren, 429 U.S. 190 (1976).
Crenshaw, K. W. (2001, September). *The intersectionality of gender and race discrimination*. Paper presented at the World Conference Against Racism. Durban, South Africa.
Crenshaw, K. W. (1991). Mapping the margins: Intersectionality, identity, politics, and violence against women of color. *Stanford Law Review*, *43*(6), 1241–1299.
Crenshaw, K. W. (1989). Demarginalizing the intersection of race and gender: A black feminist critique of anti-discrimination doctrine. *University of Chicago Legal Forum*, *1*, Article 8, 139–167.
Dolamore, S., & Naylor, L. A. (2017). Providing solutions to LGBT homeless youth: Lessons from Baltimore's youth empowered society. *Public Integrity*, *20*(6), 595–610. https://doi.org/10.1080/10999922.2017.1333943
Dolan, J., & Rosenbloom, D. H. (2003). *Representative bureaucracy: Classic readings & continuing controversies*. Routledge.
Ely v. Saul (formerly *Ely v. Berryhill*), CV-18-0557-TUC-BGM (Arizona, May 27, 2020).
Equal Employment Opportunity Act of 1972 (Pub. L. 92–261).
Equal Pay Act of 1963 (Pub. L. 88–38).
Fair Housing Act. Title VIII of the Civil Rights Act of 1968 (Pub. L. 90–284).
Fraser, B., Peirse, N., Chisolm, E., & Cook, H. (2019, July 26). LGBTQ+ homelessness: A review of the literature. *International Journal of Environmental Research & Public Health*. doi:10.3390/ijerph16152677
Frederickson, H. G. (2010). *Social equity and public administration: Origins, developments, and applications* (pp. 125–132). M.E. Sharpe.
Frederickson, H. G. (1990). Public administration and social equity. *Public Administration Review*, *50*(2), 228–237.
Frederickson, H. G. (1980). *New public administration*. University of Alabama Press.
Frontiero v. Richardson, 411 US 677 (1973).
Glaser, M. A. (2012). Social equity and the public interest. *Public Administration Review*, *72*(Supp), S14–S15.
Glaser, M. A., Hildreth, W. B., Mcguire, B. J., & Bannon, C. (2011). Frederickson's social equity agenda applied. *Public Integrity*, *14*(1), 19–38.
Glaser, M. W., Bartley, H. B., McGuire, B. J., & Bannon, C. (2014). Frederickson's social equity agenda applied: Public support and willingness to pay. *Public Integrity*, pp. 19–38. Published online December 8, 2014.
Glasser v. U.S., 315 U.S. 60 (1942).
Gooden, S. T. (2015). PAR's social equity footprint. *Public Administration Review*, *75*(3), 372–381.
Gooden, S. T. (2014). *Race and social equity: A nervous area of government*. Taylor & Francis.
Gooden, S. T., & Myers, S. L. Jr. (2004). "Social equity in public affairs education. *Journal of Public Affairs Education*, *10*(2), 91–97.
Gooden, S. T., & Portillo, S. (2011). Advancing social equity in the Minnowbrook tradition. *Journal of Public Administration Research and Theory*, *21*(Supp 1), 61–76.
Guy, M. E., & McCandless, S. A. (2020). *Achieving social equity: From problems to solutions*. Melvin & Leigh Publishers.
Guy, M. E., & McCandless, S. A. (2012). Social equity: Its legacy, its promise. *Public Administrative Review*, *72*(Supp), S5–S13. https://doi.org/10.1111/j.1540-6210.2012.02635.x
Harris, G. L. A. (2012). Multiple marginality: How the disproportionate assignment of women and minorities to manage diversity programs reinforces and multiplies their marginality. *Administration & Society*, *20*(10), 1–34.
Heart of Atlanta Motel v. United States, 379 U.S. 241 (1964).
Hobbes, Thomas. (1660). *Leviathan*. Penguin Putnam.
International Lesbian, Gay Association. (2019). *State-sponsored homophobia report 2019* (13th ed.). https://ilga.org/ilga-launches-state-sponsored-homophobia-2019
Johnson, N. J., & Svara, J. H. (Eds.). (2011). *Justice for all: Promoting social equity in public administration*. M.E. Sharpe.
Johnson III, R. G. (2018). Public administration's ethical dilemma: Homeless LGBT youth in the twenty-first century. *Public Integrity*, *20*(6), 539–541.

Johnson III, R. G. (2017). *Social equity in a time of change: A critical 21st century social movement*. Birkdale Publishers.

Johnson III, R. G. (2012a). Promoting social equity in public administration: A much needed topic in the 21st century. *Public Administrative Review, 72*(3), 471–473.

Johnson III, R. G. (2012b). The intersection of black men and sexuality in a time of change: Striving for his place in the 21st century. *National Association of Student Affairs Professionals Journal*, (15) 1, 8–16.

Johnson III, R. G. (2011). *Teaching college students communication strategies for effective social justice advocacy*. Peter Lang.

Johnson III, R. G., Rivera, M., & Lopez, N. (2018). A public ethics approach focused on the lives of diverse LGBTQ homeless youth. *Public Integrity, 20*(6), 611–624. https://doi.org/10.1080/10999922.2017.1342217

Kates, J., Ranji, U., Beamsderfer, A., Salganicoff, A., & Dawson, L. (2018, May 3). *Health & access to care and coverage for lesbian, gay, bi-sexual, and transgender (LGBT) individuals in the US*. Kaiser Family Foundation. www.kff.org/report-section/health-and-access-to-care-and-coverage-lgbt-individuals-in-the-us-health-challenges/

Kendrick, L., & Schwartzman, M. (2018, November 9). The etiquette of animus. *Harvard Law Review, 133*, 132. https://harvardlawreview.org/wp-content/uploads/2018/11/133-170_Online.pdf

Khademian, A. M. (2002). *Working with culture: The way the job gets done in public programs*. CQ Press.

Krislov, S., & Rosenbloom, D. H. (2012). *Representative bureaucracy and the American political system* (2nd ed.). Introduction by D. H. Rosenbloom. Quid Pro Books.

Larson, S. J., Jacob, B., & Butz, E. (2017, March). *Linking social equity and performance measurement: A practitioner's roadmap*. University of Colorado, Denver. School of Public Affairs. https://aspacap.files.wordpress.com/2018/10/cap-roadmap-larson.pdf

Lawrence v. Texas, 539 U.S. 558 (2003).

Lipsky, M. (2010). *Street level bureaucrats; Dilemmas of the individual in public services* (2nd ed.). Russell Sage Foundation.

Llorens, J., Klinger, D. E., & Nalbandian, J. L. (2018). *Public personnel management: Contexts and Strategies* (7th ed.). Routledge.

Locke, John. (1689). *Second treatise of civil government*. Prometheus.

Loving v. Virginia, 388 U.S. 1 (1967).

Marsden, J. (2014, November 8). *The murder of Matthew Shepard*. The Wyo-History.Org. www.wyohistory.org/encyclopedia/murder-matthew-shepard

Masterpiece Cakeshop, Ltd. v. Colorado Civil Rights Commission, 16–1584 U.S. (2018).

Matthew Shepard Jr. and James Byrd Hate Crimes Prevention Act of 2009 (Pub. L. 111–84).

Maynard-Moody, S., & Musheno, M. (2012). Social equities and inequities in practice: Street level workers as agents and pragmatists. *Public Administration Review, 72*(Supp), S16–S23.

McCandless, S. (2018). LGBT homeless youth and policing. *Public Integrity, 20*(6), 558–570. Published online December 4, 2017.

McCandless, S., & Larson, J. (2018). Prioritizing social equity in the MPA curricula: A cross program analysis and case study. *Public Affairs Education, 24*(3), 361–379. https://doi.org/10.1080/15236803.2018.1426429

Mostel, C. (n.d.). ASPA creates organization's first LGBT section. *PA Times*. https://patimes.org/aspa-creates-organizationss-first-lgbt-section/

Naff, K. (2001). *To look like America: Dismantling barriers for women and minorities in government*. Taylor & Francis.

Naff, K., Riccucci, N., & Freyss, S. F. (2017). *Personnel management in government: Politics & process* (7th ed.). With the assistance of D. H. Rosenbloom & A. C. Hyde. CRC Press, imprint of Taylor & Francis Group.

National Academy of Public Administration. (2005). *Strategic plan*. Standing Panel on Social Equity in Governance. www.napawash.org/uploads/Social_Equity_Charter_and_Strategic_Goals.pdf

National Academy of Public Administration (NAPA). (2000a, October). *Standing panel on social equity in governance issue paper and work plan*. www.napawash.org/working-groups/standing-panels/social-equity-in-governance

National Academy of Public Administration (NAPA). (2000b, November). www.napawash.org/aa_social_equity/papers_publications.html

National Academy of Public Administration. (n.d.). *Social equity*. www.napa.wash.org/aa_social_equity/index.html

Naylor, L. A. (2018). Counting an invisible class of citizens: The LGBT population and the U.S. census. *Public Integrity*, *22*(1), 54–72. Published online 27 September 2018 doi:10.1080/10999922.2018.1487748

Network of Schools of Public Policy, Affairs, and Administration (NASPAA). (2019). NASPAA Accreditation Standards. Commission on Peer Review and Accreditation.

Niskanen, W. (1971). *Bureaucracy and representative government*. Aldine-Atherton.

Nolan, I., Kuhner, C., & Dy, G. (2019). Demographic and temporal trends in transgender identities and gender confirming surgery. *Translational Andrology and Urology*, *8*(3), 184–190. doi:10.21037/tau.2019.04.09

Norman-Major, K. A. (2011). Balancing the four E's: Or can we achieve social equity in public administration? *Journal of Public Affairs Education*, *17*(2), 233–252.

Norman-Major, K. A., & Gooden, S. (2015). *Cultural competency for public administrators*. Routledge.

Obergefell v. Hodges, 576 U.S. 644 (2015).

Peters, G., von Maravic, P., & Schroter, E. (2015). *Politics of representative bureaucracy: Power, legitimacy & performance*. Edward Elgar Publishing Limited.

Plessy v. Ferguson, 163 U.S. 537 (1896).

Powell v. Alabama, 287 U.S. 45 (1932).

Pregnancy Discrimination Act of 1978 (Pub. L. 95–555).

Rawls, J. (1971). *A theory of justice*. Harvard University Press.

Riccucci, N. M. (2017). *Public personnel management: Current concerns, future challenges* (6th ed.). Routledge.

Riccucci, N. M. (2002). Diversity in sexual orientation. In N. M. Riccucci (Ed.), *Managing diversity in public sector workforces* (pp. 135–151). Westview Press.

Riccucci, N. M. (1992). *Promoting and valuing diversity in municipal government workforces*. International Personnel Management.

Romer v. Evans 517 U.S. 620 (1996).

Rosenbloom, D. H. (2018). Taking social equity seriously in MPA education. *Journal of Public Affairs Education*, *11*(3), 247–252. Published online 11 April. Originally published in 2005. doi:10.1080/15236803.2005.12001397

Rosenbloom, D. H. (2015). *Administrative law for public managers* (2nd ed.). Westview Press.

Rosenbloom, D. H. (2003). *Administrative law for public managers: Essentials of public policy and administration* (pp. 39–41). Westview Press.

Rosenbloom, D. H. (1977). *Federal equal employment opportunity: Politics and public personnel administration*. Praeger.

Rosenbloom, D. H., Carroll, J. D., & Carroll, J. D. (2000). *Constitutional competence for public managers: Cases and commentary*. Peacock Publishers.

Rosenbloom, D. H., & Kravchuk, R. S. (2008). *Public administration: Understanding management, politics, and the law*. McGraw-Hill.

Rosenbloom, D. H., Kravchuk, R., & Clerkin, Richard M. (2008). *Public administration: understanding management, politics and law in the public sector* (7th ed.). McGraw-Hill.

Rosenbloom, D. H., O'Leary, R., & Chanin, J. (2019). *Public administration and law* (3rd ed.). Routledge.

Rutledge, P. (2002). Some unfinished business in public administration. *Public Administration Review*, *62*(4), 390–394.

Shafritz, J. M., & Russell, E. W. (2000). *Introducing public administration* (2nd ed.). Longman, p. 436.

Shelley v. Kraemer, 334 U.S. 1 (1948).

Shelton, J. (2018). LGBT Youth homelessness: What are you going to do about it? *Public Integrity*, *20*(6), 542–545.

Smith v. Allright, 321 U.S. 649 (1944).

SmithKline Beecham Corporation v. Abbott Laboratories, 740 F.3d 471 (2014).

Svara, J. H., & Brunet, James R. (2018). Filling the skeletal pillar: Addressing social equity in introductory courses in public administration. *Journal of Public Affairs Education*, *10*(2), 99–109. Published online April 11, 2018. DOI: 10.10801/15236803.2005.12001398 Originally published in print 2004.

Swan, W. (2019). *Routledge handbook of LGBTQIA of administration policy*. Routledge.

Swan, W. (2015). *Gay, lesbian, bisexual, and transgender civil rights: A public policy agenda for uniting a divided America*. CRC Press.

Swan, W. (2004). *Handbook of gay, lesbian, bisexual, and transgender administration and policy*. Marcel Dekker.

Swan, W. (1997). *Gay, lesbian, bisexual, transgender public policy issues: A citizen's and administrators guide to the new struggle*. Haworth Press.

Swan, W. (1995). The lavender ceiling: How it works in practice. In *Breaking the silence: Gay, lesbian, and bisexual issues in public administration*. American Society for Public Administration.

Title VII of the Educational Amendments of 1972 (Pub. L. 92–318).

United States v. Windsor, 570 U.S. 744 (2013).

U.S. Centers for Disease Control and Prevention. (2010). *NIVS: An overview of 2010 findings on victimization by sexual orientation*. Iwww.cdc.gov/violenceprevention/pdf/cdc_nisvs_victimization_final-a.pdf

U.S. Constitution (1789).

U.S. Department of Agriculture v. Moreno, 413 U.S. 528 (1973).

U.S. Federal Bureau of Investigations. (2019). *Criminal justice information service division: Uniform crime reporting program*. Hate Crime Data, Table 1, 2017. Retrieved March 20, 2019, from https://ucr.fbi.gov/hate-crime/2017/tables/table-1.xls

U.S. Federal Bureau of Investigations. (2018). Hate Crimes Report.

Voting Rights Act of 1965 (Pub. L. 89–110).

Wooldridge, B., & Bilharz, B. (2017). The fourth pillar of public administration. In A. Farazmand (Ed.), *Global encyclopedia of public administration, public policy and governance*. Springer.

Wooldridge, B., & Gooden, S. T. (2009). The epic of social equity. *Administrative Theory & Praxis, 31*(2), 222–234.

Wyatt-Nichol, H., Brown, S., & Haynes, W. (2011). Social class and socio-economic status: Relevance and inclusion in the MPA-MPP programs. *Journal of Public Affairs Education, 17*(2), 187–208.

Chapter 2

Marriage Equality: A Fundamental Right

Introduction

A gay couple in Ohio, James Obergefell and John Arthur, had been partners for over 20 years. John was diagnosed with a debilitating disease with no cure. The couple decided to get married and selected Maryland, where same-sex marriage is legal. Because John's disease had progressed, the couple hired a medical transport plane, flew to Baltimore, got married on the tarmac, and returned to Ohio. John passed away a couple months later. Because Ohio did not recognize same-sex marriages performed in other states, James could not be listed as a spouse on the death certificate. If they were an opposite-sex couple their marriage would have been recognized in every state across the country. The couple filed a lawsuit alleging violation of the equal protection clause and the due process clause of the Fourteenth Amendment (*Obergefell v. Hodges*, 2015).

Who defines marriage? Should same-sex marriage performed in one state be recognized in other states? In the U.S., same-sex marriage is a polarizing issue (Swan, 2015). The demarcation is based on religious and political affiliation; Democrats and unaffiliated religious people tend to support gay marriage, and Republicans and religious people tend to not support gay marriage. Proponents of gay marriage argue they have a constitutional right to marry based on liberty and equal treatment. Opponents argue homosexuality is anti-Christian and goes against the teachings of the Bible (Struening, 2009). While the percentage of those supporting same-sex marriage has consistently increased over the years, there remain clear demarcations. According to the Pew Research Center, based on 2019 data, 71 percent of white Protestant Evangelicals are against same-sex marriage while 79 percent of people who are religiously unaffiliated support same-sex marriage (Masci et al., June 24, 2019). Regarding political affiliation, in 2019, 44 percent of Republicans and those who are Republican-leaning report supporting gay marriage compared to 75 percent of Democrats and those who are Democrat-leaning report supporting gay marriage. The political and religious divide continues to exist, although there is more support for gay marriage.

Marriage Equality

Historically, gays have been marginalized in the U.S. and around the world. Homosexuals were treated like deviates up until the late 20th century. For example, from 1952 to 1973, the American Psychiatric Association considered homosexuality a mental illness (Wyatt-Nichol & Naylor, 2013). Same-sex couples were treated like second-class citizens. In 1996, Congress passed legislation defining marriage as only between a man and woman, denying same-sex couples' federal recognition, benefits, and rights (Defense of Marriage Act of 1996). It wasn't until the 21st century that legal rights for same-sex couples began to emerge. In 2003, same-sex couples were guaranteed the right to sexual privacy (*Lawrence v. Texas*, 2003). In 2013, legally married same-sex couples were recognized by the federal government for the first time, and couples who resided in states that recognized same-sex marriage were granted federal benefits (*U.S. v. Windsor*, 2013). However, same-sex couples who lived in states that did not recognize same-sex marriage did not receive any federal benefits. In other words, federal benefits were based on the state a same-sex married couple lived in. In 2015, same-sex couples were guaranteed the constitutional right to marry in every state and receive all its benefits and rights (*Obergefell v. Hodges*, 2015). The court declares marriage equality is a fundamental right.

This chapter describes the legal history of marriage equality. First, an international overview of same-sex marriage is provided followed by a historical overview of marriage in the U.S., including the constitutional right to marriage and the state regulation of marriage. Next, U.S. Supreme Court cases that led to marriage equality are analyzed.

International Comparison of Marriage

According to the International Lesbian, Gay, Bisexual, Trans and Intersex Association Pew Research Center Analysis (2019), 30 countries have legalized same-sex marriage. As noted in Figure 2.1, most countries with marriage equality are in Western Europe and the Americas. These countries and

Figure 2.1 Gay Marriage Around the World

the corresponding year when same-sex marriage became legal include Argentina (2010), Australia (2017), Austria (2019), Belgium (2003), Brazil (2013), Canada (2005), Columbia (2016), Denmark (2012), Ecuador (2019), England/Wales (2013), Finland (2015), France (2013), Germany (2015), Greenland (2015), Iceland (2010), Ireland (2015), Luxembourg (2014), Malta (2017), The Netherlands (2000), New Zealand (2013), Northern Ireland (2019), Norway (2008), Portugal (2010), Scotland (2014), South Africa (2006), Spain (2005), Sweden (2009), Taiwan (2019), United States (2015), and Uruguay (2013). In Mexico, specific jurisdictions have legalized same-sex marriage: Mexico City and the states of Quintana Roo, Coahuila, and Chihuahua have legalized same-sex marriage. It is important to note the entire country of Mexico has not legalized same-sex marriage, only the specific identified jurisdictions stated earlier.

As noted earlier, the U.S., which legalized same-sex marriage in 2015, lagged behind its European peers. Only five countries legalized same-sex marriage after 2015: Australia, Austria, Northern Ireland, Malta, and Taiwan.

Overview of Marriage

In the U.S. marriage is a constitutional right regulated by state governments. Each state sets its own marriage laws, except in the area of polygamy, which is governed by federal laws. Operating under the system of federalism, marriage laws are a balance between state's rights and constitutional guarantees and protections as defined by the U.S. Supreme Court. First, constitutional rights are discussed.

Constitutional Right

Individuals have a civil right to marry. The U.S. Constitution guarantees this right. It is a liberty protected by the due process clause of the Fifth Amendment and the equal protection clause of the Fourteenth Amendment. The due process clause states "no person shall be denied life, liberty, or property without due process of law" (U.S. Constitution, Fifth Amendment, 1789). In addition, Section 1 of the Fourteenth Amendment states:

> [N]o State shall make or enforce any law which shall abridge the privileges or immunities of citizens of the United States; nor shall any State deprive any person of life, liberty, or property, without due process of law; nor deny to any person within its jurisdiction the equal protection of the laws.
>
> (1789)

State marriage laws are recognized by all states across the nation. The Fourteenth Amendment guarantees the right of marriage. The full faith and credit clause of the Constitution requires a marriage from one state to be legally recognized in every state creating equal recognition and equal protection (U.S. Constitution, 1789; Wyatt-Nichol & Naylor, 2013). Specifically, Article IV, Section 1 states:

> Full faith and Credit shall be given in each State to the public Acts, Records, and judicial Proceedings of every other state; And the Congress may by general Laws prescribe the Manner in which such Acts, Records, and Proceedings shall be approved, and the Effect thereof.
>
> (U.S. Constitution)

This means that public records, such as marriage licenses, must be recognized and honored in every state. For example, a couple married in Delaware who later travels to Louisiana will be recognized by the state government in Louisiana as married. The clause is enforced through the federal statute State and Territorial Statutes and Proceedings; Full Faith and Credit (28 U.S.C. Section 1738). It states:

> The Acts of the legislature of any State, Territory, or Possession of the United States, or copies thereof, shall be authenticated by affixing the seal of such State, Territory or Possession thereto. The records and judicial proceedings of any court of any such State, Territory or Possession, or copies thereof, shall be proved or admitted in other courts within the United States and its Territories and Possessions by the attestation of the clerk and seal of the court annexed, if a seal exists, together with a certificate of a judge of the court that the said attestation is in proper form. Such Acts, records and judicial proceedings or copies thereof, so authenticated, shall have the same full faith and credit in every court within the United States and its Territories and Possessions as they have by law or usage in the courts of such State, Territory or Possession from which they are taken.
> (28 U.S.C. Section 1738)

In summary, each state is legally required to recognize marriage licenses and judicial decisions by other states, in addition to federal laws.

Federal Antipolygamy Laws

During the first 200 years of our country's history, only three federal marriage laws were passed, all of which address polygamy. These laws targeted Mormons and the practice of polygamy. Polygamy or bigamy is when an individual is married to more than one spouse at the same time. In the Mormon faith, it is also called plural marriage or "spiritual wives." In 1862, Congress passed the Morrill Act for the Suppression of Polygamy (Ch. 26, Stat. 501), which made bigamy illegal punishable by a fine up to $500 and imprisonment up to five years. It also revoked the Mormon Church's incorporation and ability to hold property. In 1882, the Anti-Polygamy Act was passed (Ch. 47, section 22 stat. 30). It prohibits marriage and cohabitation with more than one spouse and prohibits polygamists from serving on juries, voting, and holding elected office. In 1887, Congress passed the Edmunds-Tucker Act of 1887 (Ch. 397, 24 Stat. 635), which criminalizes fornication and adultery by polygamists. The law targets Mormon women, often criminalizing them, to obtain testimony against their Mormon husbands (Sigman, 2006). The U.S. Supreme Court ruled that the Morrill Act for the Suppression of Polygamy Act of 1862 is constitutional (*Reynolds v. United States*, 1879). Polygamy is not protected by the First Amendment's free exercise clause. The U.S. Supreme Court also upheld the Edmunds-Tucker Act of 1887 ruling that religious exercise, such as polygamy, is subordinate to criminal laws (*Davis v. Beason*, 1890). In 1890, the Church of the Jesus Christ of Latter-Day Saints formally abandoned the practice of polygamy to gain statehood. As of 2020, federal laws prohibit polygamy; however, enforcement varies by state. In the majority of states, polygamy is a felony. However, Utah, which has the largest polygamy community (estimated between 30,000 to 40,000), is more lenient than other states in enforcing the law. In 2020, it passed a law lowering the penalty from a felony to a misdemeanor for engaging in polygamy (State of Utah, Bigamy Amendments, S.B. 102; Wilkinson, 2020). Excluding antipolygamy laws, which prohibit marriage to more than one spouse, there is "no federal law of domestic relations" (*De Sylva v. Ballentine*, 1956 as quoted in *U.S. v. Windsor*, 2013, p. 17). The regulation of marriage is a right bestowed on the states.

State Regulation

Historically, marriage has been regulated by state laws and considered a 'domestic relation' since America's inception. It is "regarded as a virtually exclusive province of the states" (*Sosna v. Iowa*, 404, 1975; as cited in *U.S. v. Windsor*, 570 U.S. p. 18, 2013). "When the Constitution was adopted the common understanding was that the domestic relations of husband and wife and parent and child were matters reserved for the states" (*Ohio ex re. Popovici v. Angler*, 280 U.S. 379, 383–384, 1930; as cited in *U.S. v. Windsor*, 570 U.S. p. 18, 2013). This means that marriage, divorce, and child custody disputes are managed by individual states, outside the sphere of the federal government. As such, the boundaries of marriage are determined and regulated by state laws. This includes the minimum age to marry, parental consent if under age 18, court approval if under age 16, pregnancy status, degrees of kinship or consanguinity (e.g., marrying a blood relative), the requirement of medical exams, waiting periods, and cost and issuance of marriage licenses. All these requirements and processes are determined by each individual state. As such, marriage laws vary by state. For example, as of 2020, only four states set the minimum age to marry at age 18: Delaware, Minnesota, New Jersey, and Pennsylvania (Kaur, May 11, 2020). The majority of states permit children ages 16 and 17 to marry if parental consent is obtained. The states define marriage requirements and processes, subject to constitutional guarantees. For example, the U.S. Supreme Court expanded the constitutional right to marry to include interracial couples (*Loving v. Virginia*, 1967), men who owe back child support (*Zablocki v. Redhail*, 1978), and prisoners (*Turner v. Safley*, 1987); requiring every state to issue marriage licenses to these three groups. The constitutional right to marry to include same-sex couples was granted to 11 states and the District of Columbia in *U.S. v. Windsor* (2013) and in all 50 states across the nation in 2015 (*Obergefell v. U.S.*). However, most states had bans on same-sex marriage up until 2015. State bans are discussed in the next section.

State Bans on Gay Marriage

The New York City Stonewall riots of 1969 began the lesbian, gay, bisexual, transgender, and queer (LGBTQ) rights movement and specifically the right for gay marriage. The riots served as a rallying cry or triggering mechanism for unified action (Wyatt-Nichol & Naylor, 2013). The Janus Society (formerly the Mattachine Society), the Gay Liberation Front, and the Gay Activists Alliance began working and demanding rights in state and local government, focusing on employment discrimination and domestic partner benefits. Lambda Legal and Gay and Lesbian Advocates and Defenders also joined the movement focusing on marriage equality (Wyatt-Nichol & Naylor, 2013). The movement was a grassroots effort by gay rights activists seeking equal rights and equal status. The 1970s were a period of social change, turmoil, and transformation. The movement met numerous setbacks ranging from assassination to state bans on same-sex marriage. In 1978, Harvey Melk, who was the first openly gay elected official in California, was assassinated. Same-sex couples who attempted to get married were turned away by county clerks and judges. For example, in 1970, a Minnesota gay couple, Richard John Baker and James Michael McConnell, filed a lawsuit when they were turned down by the clerk of the district court in Minneapolis for a marriage license due to being a same-sex couple. The case was denied and appealed to the Minnesota Supreme Court, which also denied their license based on the statute prohibiting marriage between same-sex couples (291 Minn. 310). The couple appealed the decision and lost. The U.S. Supreme Court dismissed the appeal without oral arguments, stating same-sex marriage was not a "substantial federal question" (*Baker v. Nelson*, 1972). The ruling set precedent and was a significant defeat for the LGBTQ movement. It led to nine states issuing statutory bans on gay marriage. State bans on same-sex marriage follow each major court ruling. These are discussed next.

First Wave of State Bans

The first wave of state bans came after the *Baker v. Nelson* (1972) ruling, which led to nine states issuing statutory bans on gay marriage, making it less likely that LGBTQ marriage rights would be secured. In 1973, Maryland passed the first legislative ban on same-sex marriage ban, stating that marriage was between a man and a woman. In 1975, Arizona passed an emergency bill when a same-sex couple attempted to obtain a marriage license. In 1975, a Boulder, Colorado, county clerk began issuing same-sex marriage licenses after obtaining a legal opinion from the district county attorney. The county clerk issued a total of six licenses until the Colorado attorney general intervened and forced her to stop, stating same-sex marriage was not constitutional (Eskridge & Spedale, 2006). In 1977, California followed with a similar legislative ban stating that marriage is a union between a man and a woman. In 1977, Florida enacted legislation banning same-sex marriage as well as banning adoption by same-sex couples. In total, nine states issued same-sex marriage bans in response to the U.S. Supreme Court decision in *Baker v. Nelson* (1972; Maryland, Office of the Attorney General, 2015).

Second Wave of State Bans

The next wave of state bans came in the 1990s after a landmark State Supreme Court ruling in which 30 states issued bans on same-sex marriage. In 1993, a Hawaii Supreme Court ruled that Hawaii's state law limiting marriage to opposite-sex couples used a basis of sex, which is subject to strict scrutiny under the state constitution (*Baehr v. Lewin*, 1993). The ruling was interpreted to mean same-sex marriage could possibly be a state constitutional right. In response to the ruling, more than 30 states enacted legislation banning same-sex marriage and a few states passed constitutional amendments to prevent same-sex marriage (Maryland Office of the Attorney General report, 2015; Wyatt-Nichol & Naylor 2013). This was a major setback for marriage equality and the LGBTQ movement. The state bans were followed by the passage of the federal Defense of Marriage Act of 1996 (DOMA), which is discussed after the third wave of state bans.

Toward the late 1990s two state supreme court rulings found that same-sex marriage bans were unconstitutional. In 1998, the Alaska State Supreme Court ruled that the state must have a compelling state interest for denying same-sex marriage licenses (*Brause v. Bureau of Vital Statistics*, 1998). However, the court ruling was countered by a ballot initiative banning same-sex marriage. In 1999, the Vermont State Supreme Court ruled that same-sex marriage bans violated the state constitution (*Baker v. Vermont*, 1999).

Third Wave of State Bans

The third wave, which includes state legislative bans as well as ballot initiatives, came after 2003 when the Massachusetts State Supreme Court ruled same-sex marriage bans were unconstitutional (*Goodridge v. Department of Public Health*, 2003), requiring the state to recognize and issue same-sex marriage licenses. The court concluded that

> that barring an individual from the protections, benefits, and obligations of civil marriage solely because that person would marry a person of the same sex violated the

Massachusetts Constitution in that such a marriage ban did not meet the rational basis test for either due process or equal protection, where the Commonwealth failed to identify any constitutionally adequate reason for denying civil marriage to same-sex couples.
(*Goodridge v. Department of Public Health*, 2003, p. 1)

The historic ruling made Massachusetts the first state in the country to recognize same-sex marriage. Several states followed this ruling. In 2006, a New Jersey court ordered the legislature to create a legal structure for an equivalent to marriage for same-sex couples (*Lewis v. Harris*, 2006). In 2008, state supreme courts in California, Connecticut, and Iowa all issued rulings stating same-sex marriage bans violate the state constitution (*In re: Marriage cases*, 2008; *Kerrigan v. State Commissioner of Public Health*, 2008; *Varnum v. Brien*, 2009). In 2010, a California court ruled in favor of same-sex marriage (*Perry v. Schwarzenegger*, 2010); then a ballot initiative was passed prohibiting same-sex marriage. The case, *Hollingsworth v. Perry* (2010) was appealed. It is discussed later in the chapter under U.S. Supreme Court cases.) In contrast, several states upheld bans on same-sex marriage, including Arizona (*Standard v. Superior Court*, 2003), New York (*Hernandez v. Robles*, 2006), and Washington, which all upheld DOMA's Section 3 definition of marriage (*Anderson v. King County*, 2006).

In total, state bans and ballot initiatives opposing same-sex marriage spanned a period of over 40 years in American history. LGBTQ activists and allies countered the bans with legal counsel. It was a grassroots effort ignited by the Stonewall riots, which led to substantial legal and social changes in marriage equality and the LGBTQ movement. In 2012, 9 states legally recognized same-sex marriage, and an additional 10 states provided civil unions or domestic partnerships (Human Rights Campaign, 2012). In addition to state laws on same-sex marriage, one federal law was passed during this period, DOMA, which is discussed next.

DOMA of 1996

Although marriage definitions are based on state laws and constitutional guarantees, "Congress, in enacting discreet statutes, can make determinations that bear on marital rights and privileges" (*U.S. v. Windsor*, 2013, p. 14). In 1996, Congress passed DOMA (Pub. L. 104–199). The purpose of the act was to provide a federal definition of marriage that excluded same-sex marriages. The legislation was historic. Before DOMA, there were no federal laws on marriage (except for polygamy; see the Edmunds Anti-Polygamy Act of 1882). The courts had traditionally relied on "reference to the law of the State that created those legal relationships" (*De Dsylva v, Ballentine*, 1956). There were two outcomes of the passage of DOMA. First, the act granted states the right to deny recognition of same-sex marriages performed in other states (DOMA, Section 2; 18 USC Section 1738C), which conflicts with the full faith and credit clause of the Constitution. Second, DOMA's Section 3 amended the Dictionary Act to define the words *marriage* and *spouse*. Specifically, DOMA's Section 3 states that "the word 'marriage' means only a legal union between one man and one woman as husband and wife, and the word 'spouse' refers only to a person of the opposite sex who is a husband or a wife" (1 U.S.C. 7). This was the first time in U.S. history that the federal government defined marriage. Previously, the definition of marriage had been a power granted and exercised by the states. The passage of DOMA meant that same-sex marriages legally performed in a state were not recognized by the federal government.

DOMA divided the states on the issue of same-sex marriage, highlighting the inherent problem of federalism (Kettl, 2020). Without federal recognition of marriage, equal recognition, equal treatment, and equal benefits would depend on the state a same-sex couple lived in. Without federal recognition, benefits would be denied to same-sex couples who were legally married under state law. DOMA's definition of marriage directly applied to over 1,000 federal regulations and statutes, including adoption, bankruptcy, crimes and family violence, employment, food stamps, foster care, government health insurance, housing, immigration and naturalization, Social Security retirement, supplemental security income, taxes, and veterans' benefits (U.S. Government Accountability Office, 2004, 1997). As such, the act was wide in scope and had a quantifiable negative financial impact on same-sex couples (Haulsee & Naylor, 2014). The biggest economic injury was in the form of estate and property taxes, retirement taxes, Social Security benefits, and health care benefits. DOMA placed an economic burden on same-sex married couples, treating them measurably different from opposite-sex married couples. The policy created unequal benefits based on sexual orientation.

Since the passage of DOMA in 1996, Congress has not passed any additional laws pertaining to same-sex marriage. The rights and benefits of same-sex married couples have come from the courts. Specifically, four U.S. Supreme Court decisions have defined the rights of gay marriage, federal benefits, and sexual privacy. These cases are analyzed next.

U.S. Supreme Court Rulings

The federal courts and the U.S. Supreme Court have a unique role in protecting marginalized groups from animus and inequality. Since 2003, the U.S. Supreme Court has intervened to stop state and federal legislation that discriminates against LGBTQ people in the area of sexual privacy and marriage. These key rulings are discussed in the following sections.

Lawrence v. Texas *(2003)*

This case involves a state sodomy law. In the fall of 1998, police near Houston, Texas, responded to a call about a "black man going crazy with a gun" (*Lawrence v. Texas*, 2003). Having probable cause to enter the apartment, the police found two men engaged in anal sex. According to the Texas Penal Code, sexual intercourse with another individual of the same-sex was deviant (Chapter 21, Section 21). It states:

> A person commits an offense if he engages in deviate sexual intercourse with another individual of the same sex. . . . Deviate sexual intercourse is defined as (A) any contact between any part of the genitals of one person and the mouth or anus of the other; or (B) the penetration of the genitals or the anus of another person with an object.
> (Texas Penal Code, Chapter 21, Section 21.6a, 21.01, 2003)

The police charged the two men, Tyrone Garner and John Geddes Lawrence, with an antisodomy law, a Class C misdemeanor. Both men were arrested and jailed. The ex-lover who made the false police report, Robert Eubanks, pled no contest and was sentenced to 30 days in jail. The two men charged with homosexual conduct appealed their case, which eventually made it to the U.S. Supreme Court. The legal questions before the court were (1) should *Bowers v. Hardwick* (1986) be reversed? (2) Is it a violation of the Fourteenth Amendment guarantee of equal protection of laws to criminalize sexual intimacy by same-sex couples but not identical behavior by opposite-sex couples? and (3) Are criminal convictions for adult consensual sex in the privacy of a home a violation of liberty and privacy protected by the due process clause of the Fourteenth Amendment? In a landmark ruling, *Lawrence v. Texas* (2003), the court decided 6–3 that it is unconstitutional to prohibit private homosexual activity between consenting adults. Individuals have a constitutional right to sexual privacy under the due process clause of the Fourteenth Amendment. The majority opinion was written by Justice Kennedy and joined by Justices Stevens, O'Connor, Souter, Ginsburg, and Breyer. Justices Thomas, Scalia, and Rehnquist dissented.

Justice Kennedy, who wrote the majority opinion, states:

> Their right to liberty under the Due Process Clause gives them the full right to engage in their conduct without intervention of the government. The Texas statute furthers no legitimate state interest which can justify intrusion into the personal and private life of the individual.
>
> (*Lawrence v. Texas*, 2003)

As such, individuals are granted a "right to privacy" in their sexual activity because making it a crime "demeans the lives of homosexual persons" (*Lawrence v. Texas*, 539, U.S. 558, 575). Moral disapproval is not a legitimate interest. Justice O'Connor, who wrote a concurring opinion, proclaims,

> A law branding one class of persons as criminal solely based on the State's moral disapproval of that class and the conduct associated with that class runs contrary to the values of the Constitution and Equal Protections Clause, under any standard of review.
>
> (*Lawrence v. Texas*, 2003; also stated in Wyatt-Nichol & Naylor, 2015)

The court found the Texas law unconstitutional because it discriminated against gay couples only; opposite-sex couples could engage in sodomy under the same Texas statute. However, the court did not rule that sodomy was a fundamental right. Justice Kennedy opined:

> Equality of treatment and the due process right to demand respect for conduct protected by the substantive guarantee of liberty are linked in important respects, and a decision on the latter point advances both interests. If protected conduct is made criminal and the law which does so remains unexamined for its substantive validity, its stigma might remain even if it were not enforceable as drawn for equal protection reasons. When homosexual conduct is made criminal by the law of the State, that declaration in and of itself is an invitation to subject homosexual persons to discrimination both in the public and private spheres. The central holding of *Bowers* has been brought into question by this case, and it should be addressed. Its continuance as precedent demeans the lives of homosexual persons.
>
> (*Lawrence v. Texas*, 2003, p. 575)

In her concurring opinion, Justice O'Connor emphasized that "[a] law branding one class of persons as criminal solely based on the state's moral disapproval of that class and the conduct associated with that class runs contrary to the values of the Constitution and Equal Protection Clause, under any standard of review" (*Lawrence v. Texas*, 2003; see also Wyatt-Nichol & Naylor, 2015, p. 123).

The *Lawrence v. Texas* (2003) ruling overturned the U.S. Supreme Court's 1986 decision in *Bowers v. Hardwick*, reflecting changing social norms. In *Bowers v. Hardwick* (1986), Hardwick was charged for violating state law when a police officer found him in his Georgia home engaging in consensual homosexual sodomy. At the time, sodomy was a felony in Georgia, and the state statute prohibited the conduct of sodomy between same-sex couples as well as opposite-sex couples.

In a 5–4 ruling, the U.S. Supreme Court upheld the Georgia statute (*Bowers v. Hardwick*, 1986). There was no sexual right to privacy, upholding a Georgia statute criminalizing oral and anal sex between consenting adults (same sex as well as opposite sex). The 2003 *Lawrence v. Texas* ruling overturned this decision and advanced LGBTQ rights in two significant ways. First, it decriminalized gay sex, also known as sodomy laws, in Texas. The ruling also invalidated sodomy laws across the country (13 states at the time). Before the court ruling, same-sex couples could be charged, jailed, and fined for engaging in sodomy. This had a negative impact on their dignity, relationships, and employment opportunities. Second, it laid the foundation for marriage equality. In his dissenting opinion, Justice Scalia forewarned that the *Lawrence v. Texas* (2003) ruling would create an opening for gay unions. He opined:

> Today's opinion dismantles the structure of constitutional law that has permitted a distinction to be made between heterosexual and homosexual unions, insofar as formal recognition in marriage is concerned. If moral disapprobation of homosexual conduct is "no legitimate state interest" for purposes of proscribing that conduct, *ante*, at 18; and if, as the Court coos (casting aside all pretense of neutrality), "[w]hen sexuality finds overt expression in intimate conduct with another person, the conduct can be but one element in a personal bond that is more enduring," *ante*, at 6; what justification could there possibly be for denying the benefits of marriage to homosexual couples exercising "[t]he liberty protected by the Constitution.
>
> (*Lawrence v. Texas*, 2003, p. 605)

In conclusion, the *Lawrence v. Texas* (2003) decision granting sexual privacy was a major advancement in LGBTQ rights. It moved homosexual behavior from criminal to lawful.

A decade later, legal advancements in the area of marriage equality emerged. In the summer of 2013, the U.S. Supreme Court made twin rulings on LGBTQ rights. In *U.S. v. Windsor* (2013) the court struck down Section 3 of DOMA, the federal definition of marriage. In *Hollingsworth v. Perry* (2013), the court restored same-sex marriage rights in California. These two cases, often referred to as the rainbow rulings, are described next.

U.S. v. Windsor *(2013)*

Edith Windsor and Thea Spyer, a lesbian couple, had been partners for over 40 years. In 1963, Thea asked Edith to marry her and gave her a diamond pendant to symbolize their marriage. In 2007, the couple was legally married in Ontario, Canada, and the marriage was legally recognized in New York where they resided. In 2009, Thea died, leaving her entire estate to Edith. As her spouse and sole beneficiary, Edith attempted to claim the federal tax exemption for surviving spouses. The Internal Revenue Service denied her claim on the grounds that "spouse" refers to marriage between a man and a woman only, citing Section 3 of the federal DOMA (1 U.S.C. Section 7). As a result, Windsor had to pay $363,053 in estate taxes. If Thea had married a man, then she would not have had to pay the $363,053 estate tax. Windsor argued the tax assessment was unconstitutional. She filed a lawsuit against the federal government seeking a tax refund based on differential treatment, alleging DOMA violated the guarantee of equal protection under the Fifth Amendment.

The case was filed in U.S. District Court, the Southern District of New York, which found in favor of Windsor, stating that discrimination based on sexual orientation was unconstitutional and that the government must show a higher reason for the discrimination. While the case was pending, the Obama administration issued a statement that the U.S. Department of Justice would no longer defend the constitutionality of DOMA's Section 3, the definition of marriage under a Section 530 D letter. The attorney general wrote: "When an Act of Congress is alleged to conflict with the Constitution, it is emphatically the province and duty of the judicial department to stay what the law is" (*Zivotofsky v. Clinton*, 2012). The letter stated that due to a "documented history of discrimination, classifications based on sexual orientation should be subject to a heightened standard of scrutiny." The U.S. Attorney General notified the Speaker of the House of Representatives (28 U.S.C. Section 530D). In response, the Bi-Partisan Legal Advisory Group (BLAG) voted to intervene and defend Section 3 of DOMA. The court granted BLAG status in the case as an interested party (*U.S. v. Windsor*, 2013).

The U.S. Supreme Court ruled 5–4 in Windsor's favor, finding section 3 of DOMA, which defined marriage as between a man and woman, unconstitutional and a violation of liberty in the due process clause of the Fifth Amendment. It states "no person shall be denied life, liberty, or property without due process of law" (U.S. Constitution). In the majority opinion, Justice Kennedy stated, "The Constitution's guarantee of equality "must at the very least mean that a bare congressional desire to harm a politically unpopular group cannot justify disparate treatment of that group'" (*U.S. v. Windsor*, 2013) It is unconstitutional for the federal government to discriminate based on sexual orientation when determining federal benefits. The majority opinion consists of Justices Kennedy, Ginsburg, Breyer, Sotomayor, and Kagan. Chief Justice Roberts and Justices Scalia, Thomas, and Alito wrote dissenting opinions. In writing the opinion for the majority, Justice Kennedy states:

> New York adopted a law to permit same-sex marriage, it sought to eliminate inequality; but DOMA frustrates that objective through a system-wide enactment with no identified connection to any particular area of federal law. DOMA writes inequality into the entire United States Code. . . . DOMA's principle effect is to identify a subset of state-sanctioned, marriages and make them unequal. The principle purpose is to impose inequality, not for other reasons like governmental efficiency. . . . The differentiation demeans the couple, whose moral and sexual choices the Constitution protects . . . The federal statute is invalid, for no legitimate purpose overcomes the purpose and effect to disparage and to injure those whom the State, by its marriage laws sought to protect.
> (*U.S. v. Windsor*, 2013, pp. 20, 22, 25)

It was a landmark ruling for LGBTQ rights, marking the first time the U.S. Supreme Court recognized same-sex marriage as a legal right at the federal level and granted federal benefits. The case was argued on the basis of a tax refund but went beyond to include over 1,000 federally identified benefits for spouses of same-sex married couples. By redefining marriage, same-sex married couples could file joint tax returns and obtain surviving spouse benefits, such as Social Security and veterans' benefits. Prior to the *U.S. v. Windsor* (2013) ruling, gay couples were denied over 1,100 federal provisions enjoyed by married opposite-sex couples. The *Windsor* ruling was limited to same-sex couples who resided in the 11 states and the District of Columbia, where same-sex marriages were legalized. The list of states and years same-sex marriage became legal includes Connecticut (2009), Delaware (2013), District of Columbia (2013), Iowa (2009), Maine (2012), Maryland (2012), Massachusetts (2003), Minnesota (2013), New Hampshire (2012), New York (2013), Rhode Island (2013), and Washington (2012; see *U.S. v. Windsor*, 2013, p. 16 for list of state statutes). It is important to note that in the 39 states that banned same-sex marriages, a same-sex couple would not be eligible for federal benefits. For example, a same-sex couple who married in Delaware then moved to Kentucky would not qualify for federal spousal benefits, creating significant economic disparities for married

Federal Benefits

As a result of the *U.S. v. Windsor* (2013) ruling, Edith Windsor did not have to pay the $363,050 estate tax, which lifted a major economic hardship. In addition, same-sex married couples can now file joint tax returns and, as such, might be taxed at a lower rate and receive a significant tax break on the sale of a residence. In their article "Equal Treatment Under the Law: A Cost Benefit Analysis of Same Sex Benefits Post-Windsor" (Haulsee & Naylor, 2014) highlight the significant tax savings same-sex married couples are eligible to receive on the primary sale of a residence. Prior to the *Windsor* ruling, a same-sex individual would be taxed individually on all profit on the sale of a primary residence over $250,000, and post *Windsor*, they will be taxed on all profit over $500,000, a significant tax break. Married couples only pay taxes on profit over $500,000. This results in a major cost savings for same-sex married homeowners who reside in states that recognize same-sex marriages. It is important because in the U.S. home ownership is the main vehicle for creating long-term wealth.

Social Security Benefits

The U.S. Social Security Act is instrumental in providing economic protection, and for the majority of Americans, it is their only retirement plan. In 2020, the U.S. Social Security Administration will pay out over $1 trillion to 65 million people (U.S. Social Security Administration, n.d.). Of the approximate 65 million people receiving monthly benefits, 46million represent retirees who receive an average monthly check of $1,517.44. Ten million are disabled workers and eligible dependents, 6 million are surviving spouses and children of deceased workers, and 3 million are spouses and children of retired works (U.S. Social Security Administration, 2020). Prior to the *Windsor* (2013) ruling, the Social Security Act defined marriage as husband and wife, excluding same-sex married spouses from social security, widow benefits, and disability benefits. The Old Age Survivors and Disability Insurance program, more commonly known as social security retirement, widow benefits, and Social Security Supplemental Income (SSI) are based on marital status and the amount of income each spouse has earned. For example,

> under SSI, both the level of income to determine eligibility and the level of benefits for those who are eligible differ, depending whether the applicant has an eligible spouse or not. SSI defines "eligible spouse" as an aged, blind, or disabled individual who is the husband or wife of another aged, blind, or disabled individual.
> (U.S. Government Accounting Office, 1997, p. 5)

Post-*Windsor* (2013), the definition of marriage includes sex married couples, and as such, they meet the definition of spousal benefits and can apply and access Social Security spousal benefits.

Family Medical Leave

As a result of the *Windsor* (2013) ruling, same-sex married couples can qualify and benefit from the Family Medical Leave Act (FMLA). The legislation helps workers balance parenting and care-taking responsibilities. The Family Medical Leave Act of 1993 (Pub. L. 103–3) provides 12 weeks of medical leave for employees, who have been employed with the same organization for at least 12 months.

The employer must have at least 50 employees. Medical leave is granted to take care of a spouse, child, or parent. Medical leave can be utilized for the birth of a child, maternity-related disability, adoption or foster care placement, serious health condition of spouse, parent or child, or serious health condition of the employee. The FMLA is critical because it provides job security for employees and working parents. Without it, employees may lose their job if they or a family member faces a crisis or major health issue.

Veteran Spousal Benefits

The *Windsor* ruling ensures benefits to veteran spouses. Regarding veterans' benefits, spousal veteran benefits would be denied to same-sex couples unless their marriage is recognized by the federal government. Veterans spousal benefits include right to burial, death benefits, education assistance, federal employment preference, housing allowance, medical care, and pension (U.S.C. Title 18). These benefits provide a substantial financial benefit to spouses; without these benefits, it can place some military families in poverty.

The federal spousal benefits described earlier serve as examples of the financial hardship placed on same-sex married couples prior to the *Windsor* ruling and the impact of the courts in correcting an economic and social inequality. Post-*Windsor*, same-sex spouses are treated the same as opposite-sex married couples regarding social recognition and federal benefits. Veterans spousal benefits, the FLMA, and Social Security benefits illustrate the types of federal benefits same-sex married couples can apply for and receive. For a complete list of the 1,100 federal statutes and regulations, see the U.S. General Accounting Office's report Defense of Marriage Act: Update to Prior Report (GAO-04–353R, January 23, 2004); also see Haulsee & Naylor, 2014).

Hollingsworth v. Perry *(2013)*

The *Hollingsworth v. Perry* (2013) case, also referred to as Proposition 8, addressed a California state ban on same-sex marriage in the form of a ballot measure. When the California Supreme Court ruled that defining marriage between a man and a woman was unconstitutional, state voters passed a ballot initiative amending the state constitution to define marriage as between a man and a woman, overriding the California Supreme State Court's ruling. State officials refused to enforce the constitutional amendment. There are two legal questions before the U.S. Supreme Court. The first question addresses standing to sue. Do "official proponents of a ballot initiative have authority to assert the State's interest in defending the constitutionality of the initiative when public officials refuse to do so?" (*Hollingsworth v. Perry*, Slip Opinion, 2013, p. 1). The second question is about equal protection: "Does the Equal Protection Clause of the Fourteenth Amendment prohibit the state of California from defining marriage as a union between one man and one woman" (*Hollingsworth v. Perry*, 2013). In a 5–4 decision, the U.S. Supreme Court ruled that supporters of the ballot initiative lacked Article III standing and had no personal stake in the enforcement of the constitutional amendment. The court ruled Proposition 8 was unconstitutional, restoring same-sex marriage in California (see also Wyatt-Nichol & Naylor, 2015; Jurkiewicz, 2014). Chief Justice Roberts wrote the majority opinion. Chief Justice Roberts was joined by Justices Scalia Ginsburg, Breyer, and Kagan. The dissenting opinion includes Justices Kennedy, Thomas, Alito, and Sotomayor. In writing the majority opinion, Chief Justice Roberts opined:

> Article III of the Constitution confines the judicial power of federal courts to deciding actual "Cases" or "Controversies." §2. One essential aspect of this requirement is that

any person invoking the power of a federal court must demonstrate standing to do so. This requires the litigant to prove that he has suffered a concrete and particularized injury that is fairly traceable to the challenged conduct, and is likely to be redressed by a favorable judicial decision. (*Lujan v. Defenders of Wildlife*, 504 U.S. 555–561 1992). In other words, for a federal court to have authority under the Constitution to settle a dispute, the party before it must seek a remedy for a personal and tangible harm. "The presence of a disagreement, however sharp and acrimonious it may be, is insufficient by itself to meet Art. III's requirements." Diamond, supra, at 62. . . . The doctrine of standing, we recently explained, "serves to prevent the judicial process from being used to usurp the powers of the political branches." *Clapper v. Amnesty Int'l USA*, 568 U.S. ___, ___ (2013) (slip op., at 9). In light of this "overriding and time-honored concern about keeping the Judiciary's power within its proper constitutional sphere, we must put aside the natural urge to proceed directly to the merits of [an] important dispute and to 'settle' it for the sake of convenience and efficiency." *Raines v. Byrd*, 521 U.S. 811, 820 (1997). . . . We have never before upheld the standing of a private party to defend the constitutionality of a state statute when state officials have chosen not to. We decline to do so for the first time here.

(*Hollingsworth v. Perry*, 2013, Opinion of the Court)

The Ninth Circuit decision was vacated. Proposition 8 was ruled unconstitutional.

Summary of Rainbow Rulings

The *Hollingsworth v. Perry* (2013) and *U.S. v. Windsor* (2013) rulings reflect the political divide in America. Some states recognized same-sex marriages and domestic unions while other states enforced same-sex marriage bans. At the time of the rulings, 39 states prohibited same-sex marriage (Human Rights Campaign, 2013). Post-Windsor, legal recognition and economic federal benefits for spouses depended on the state a same-sex married couple resided in. For example, a married same-sex couple residing in New York could receive federal tax benefits, but a same-sex married couple residing in North Dakota would not qualify for federal spousal tax benefits. State residence dictated legal rights and economic benefits. If same-sex couples wanted to receive federal benefits, they had to physically move and take up residence in a state that same-sex marriage was legal. In contrast, federal benefits for opposite-sex couples did not depend on the state they resided in; they received the same legal and social recognition and federal benefits in all 50 states. The *Windsor* (2013) ruling highlighted these inequalities. The judicial policy was not sustainable. As a result, additional lawsuits were filed.

Obergefell v. Hodges *(576 U.S. 644 2015)*

The fourth U.S. Supreme Court case, *Obergefell v. Hodges* (2015), legalized same-sex marriage at the federal level. It represented 14 same-sex couples and two men whose spouses passed away. The petitioners were seeking marriage equality. The cases were located in four states that defined marriage as a union between a man and a woman: Kentucky, Michigan, Ohio, and Tennessee. The same-sex couples sued state officials in their capacity to issue marriages licenses, arguing it violated the Fourteenth Amendment to deny gay couples a marriage license. The cases were heard in federal district court in each state. The two central legal questions in the case are, (1) Is a state required to license same-sex marriages? and (2) Is a state required to recognize a same-sex marriage license from another state? The four district courts ruled in favor of the petitioners and the respondents appealed.

The Sixth Circuit Court consolidated the cases and reversed the ruling based on *DeBoer v. Snyder* (2014). Using a rational basis review, the court of appeals ruled that there is no constitutional obligation to recognize or license same-sex marriages. State bans on same-sex marriage furthered the legitimate state interests of upholding morality and tradition while providing am optimal childrearing environment. The case was appealed; writ of certiorari was granted.

The U.S. Supreme Court ruled 5–4 that marriage is a fundamental right and that same-sex couples have a constitutional right to marriage protected under the due process and equal protection clauses of the Fourteenth Amendment (*Obergefell v. Hodges*, 2015). The court

> invoked equal protection principles to invalidate laws imposing sex-based inequality on marriage. . . . The challenged laws burden the liberty of same-sex couples, and they abridge central precepts of equality. Marriage laws at issue are in essence unequal; same-sex couples are denied benefits afforded opposite sex couples and are barred from exercising a fundamental right.
>
> (p. 4)

The court declared state-level bans on same-sex marriage are unconstitutional based on the due process clause of the Fourteenth Amendment. *Baker v. Nelson* (1972), which ruled that marriage equality was not a substantial federal question, was overruled. Justice Kennedy delivered the opinion and was joined by Justices Ginsburg, Breyer, Sotomayor, and Kagan. Chief Justice Roberts and Justices Alito, Scalia, and Thomas dissented.

The court outlined four tenets explaining why "marriage is a fundamental right under the Constitution." First is the liberty of personal choice. Individuals have a right to choose marriage, which is a personal decision. "The right to personal choice regarding marriage is inherent in the concept of individual autonomy" (*Obergefell v. Hodges*, 2015, p. 3). All individuals have a right to marriage. The court guaranteed the right to marry for interracial couples (*Loving v. Virginia*, 1967), prisoners (*Turner v. Safley*, 1987), and men who owe back child support (*Zablocki v. Redhail*, 1978). Second, marriage is an intimate union unlike any other. Married couples have the protected right to use contraception (*Griswold v. Connecticut*, 1965) to prevent them from procreating if they choose. The court argued "same sex couples have the same right as opposite-sex couples to enjoy intimate association, a right extending beyond mere freedom from laws making same-sex intimacy a criminal offense" (*Obergefell v. Hodges*, 2015, p. 3). Third, it safeguards children and families. "Without the recognition, stability, and predictability marriage offers children suffer the stigma of knowing their families are somehow lesser. . . . The marriage laws at issue harm and humiliate the children of same sex couples" (*Obergefell v. Hodges*, 2015, p. 3). Fourth, marriage is a core social institution. The majority opinion also stated the majority of federal case law held it is a violation of the constitution to deny same-sex couples marriage (except for *Citizens for Equal Protection v. Bruning*, 2006). Justice Kennedy opined: "the limitation of marriage to same sex couples may long have seemed natural and just, but its inconsistency with the central meaning of the fundamental right to marry has manifest" (*Obergefell v. Hodges*, 2015).

Based on these reasons, the U.S. Supreme Court granted marriage equality to same-sex couples. They now have the same rights, protections, benefits, and responsibilities as heterosexual married couples. Unlike the *Windsor* (2013) ruling, which only applied to states that legalized same-sex marriage, the *Obergefell v. Hodges* (2015) ruling granted marriage equality in every state across the country; same-sex marriage would be recognized nationwide. Justice Kennedy summarized the decision: "marriage embodies a love that may endure even past death" and that same-sex couples have the right to "equal dignity in the eyes of the law" (*Obergefell v. Hodges*, 2015). The case was a landmark ruling in the LGBTQ rights movement, granting same-sex couples a constitutional right to marriage, recognized in every state across the country.

Defiance

Despite the U.S. Supreme Court's ruling in 2015, there was resistance and defiance in implementing the new judicial policy. Resistance largely took place in southern states. In Alabama, State Supreme Court Chief Justice Ray Moore initially ordered probate justices to defy the *Obergefell v. Hodges* (2015) ruling and not to issue same-sex marriage licenses. At least 13 counties refused to issue marriage licenses to gay couples (Jenkins, January 6, 2016; Margolin, January 6, 2016). Several county clerks in the South resigned their positions rather than issue marriage licenses to gay couples (CBS News, 2015; Solomon, 2015). The most well-known case was in Kentucky, where Rowan County Clerk Kim Davis refused to issue marriage licenses due to religious beliefs. Stating she was "operating under God's authority," Davis denied marriage licenses in her official capacity as county clerk (Blinnder & Perez-Pena, 2015). The couples sued (*Miller v. Davis*, 2015), and Davis was court-ordered to issue marriage licenses. She defied the court order, was arrested, and spent five nights in jail. Davis lost her reelection bid for the county clerk's office in 2018. These cases serve as examples of the ideological divide over same-sex marriage. Over time, resistance to marriage equality decreased. Today, same-sex marriage licenses are issued in all 50 states.

Impact of Ruling

As a result of the two U.S. Supreme Court rulings, *Obergefell v. Hodges* (2015) and *U.S. v. Windsor* (2013), the number of same-sex married couples in the U.S. increased substantially. As illustrated in Figure 2.2, between 2008 and 2013, there was a steady increase of same-sex marriages. In 2008, there were an estimated 142,486 same-sex marriages, and by 2013, the year of the *U.S. v. Windsor* ruling, the number climbed to 230,000. Between 2013 and 2016, which captures the implementation period of both the Windsor and Obergefell rulings, the number of same-sex marriages increased from 230,000 in 2013 to 486,994 in 2015 (U.S. Census, American Community Survey, 2019), an increase of 256,994 same-sex marriages. The number doubled over a period of three years.

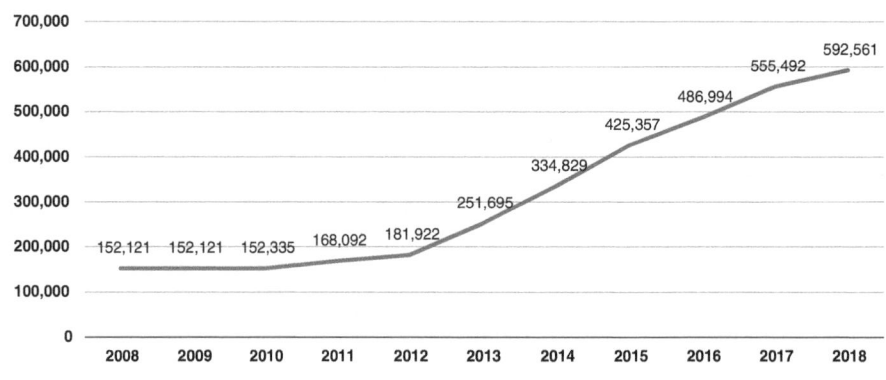

Figure 2.2 Number of Same-Sex Married Couples in the U.S.

Sources: U.S. Census Bureau, Historical Table, Estimates of Same-Sex Couple Households in the American Community Survey (2019); Taylor (2019).

By 2019, the number of same-sex marriages increased to approximately 592,000 (Duffin, 2019; U.S. Population Reference Bureau, 2016). This represents less than 1 percent (0.8) of total married couples in the U.S. (Taylor, 2019) and approximately 20 percent of the total LGBTQ population. For the 20 percent of LGBTQ couples who do marry, they receive all the advantages and privileges of marriage. Same-sex married couples are more likely to have a higher socioeconomic status, more education, both be employed, and higher incomes compared to single LGBTQ people. The higher economic status provides them greater opportunities and privileges than their single LGBTQ counterparts. The substantial increase in same-sex married couples reflects the power of U.S. Supreme Court rulings to quickly effect change. With the new legal rights and economic benefits, the number of same-sex married couples will likely continue to increase, but at a slower rate.

New Benefits

As a result of the *Obergefell v. Hodges* (2015) ruling, same-sex married couples across the country are granted over 1,100 federal benefits. The courts will need to interpret the new benefits as they apply to legally married same-sex couples. Public administrators must ensure social equity by providing same-sex married couples with access, fairness, and due process in the delivery of government benefits and services. This includes over 1,100 federal benefits, with the greatest financial benefits being tax laws and Social Security benefits. Same-sex married couples (and some civil unions and domestic partnerships) are entitled to Social Security benefits, Medicare, and supplemental security income (U.S. Social Security Administration, n.d.).

Class Action Lawsuit

At least one class action lawsuit, *Ely v. Saul* (2020, formerly *Berryhill*), has been brought against the U.S. Social Security Administration for denying spousal benefits to a same-sex couple who was unable to marry due a state marriage ban. In August 2015, Michael Ely applied for spousal benefits with the U.S. Social Security Administration and was denied benefits. He then filed a request for reconsideration, which was denied in October 2015. Ely then filed a request for a hearing. In May 2017, the administrative law judge denied Ely's request based on the nine-month marriage duration requirements not being met (42 U.S.C. 416(g). In 2018, Ely filed a cause of action in court, alleging violation of equal protection and due process (*Ely v. Berryhill*, 2018). Ely and his husband, James Taylor, had been partners for 43 years. From Ely's perspective, it is unconstitutional to deny his same-sex marriage and it is unconstitutional to deny him federal government benefits as a surviving spouse. In 2013, James was diagnosed with cancer and stopped working in January 2014. In 2014, when Arizona legalized same-sex marriage the couple got legally married. Six months later James died of cancer. The U.S District Court of Arizona ruled that the Social Security Administration must waive the nine-month durational requirement of marriage for same-sex spouses to receive surviving spousal benefits. U.S. Magistrate Judge Bruce McDonald wrote that

> [b]ecause same sex marriage is a fundamental right, and the underpinnings of the duration-of-marriage has relied on the unconstitutional ban of that right, it cannot be said to be rationally related to a legitimate interest to a surviving spouse. . . . The unconstitutional infringement on Mr. Ely and Mr. Taylor's fundamental right to marriage is now being perpetuated further by the denial of Mr. Ely to obtain survivor's benefits. For married couples, such as Mr. Ely and Mr. Taylor, who could not meet the durational requirement due to the same-sex marriage ban in their home state, Defendant's decision has

"denied [these] married same-sex couples access to the 'constellation of benefits that the Stat[e] ha[s] linked to marriage." Pavan v. Smith, – U.S. –, 137 S. Ct. 2075, 2078, 198 L. Ed. 2d 636 (2017) (citing *Obergefell*, 135 S. Ct. at 2601).

(*Ely v. Saul*, 2020, p. 16)

The court ruled for the plaintiffs: Ely, putative class members James Obergefell, surviving spouse of John Author, and Anthony Gonzalez, surviving spouse of Mark Johnson. Since the case is a class action lawsuit, the court's decision applies to all same-sex married couples whose marriages were denied due to unconstitutional state marriage bans. The ruling has a direct and quantifiable economic benefit to widowed same-sex spouses. Surviving spousal financial benefits assist individuals with basic necessities to prevent them from living in poverty.

Same-Sex Marriage Polls

In addition to an increase in the number of same-sex marriages, Americans are more accepting of LGBTQ people today than in the past. According to a survey conducted by the Pew Research Center, in 2006, roughly 51 percent of Americans reported that homosexuality should be accepted by society, in 2016 the percentage increased to 63 percent; a 12 percent increase over a 10-year period. The percentages are increasing with millennials; younger Americans tend to be more supportive of LGBTQ rights and even church congregations, which tend to be more conservative. In 2006, 37 percent of congregation leaders reported that gay and lesbians should be full members of the church. In 2012, the percentage increased to 48 percent, and in 2018, it increased to 50 percent. These upward trends in public opinion polls show greater acceptance of gays in society. Similarly, the percentage of people identifying as LGBTQ has also increased. According to the University of California, Los Angeles, Williams Institute (January 2019), in 2006, approximately 3.5 percent of the U.S. adult population identified as LGBTQ, and by 2016, the percentage increased to 4.5 percent (9 million people). As the percentage of Americans supporting LGBTQ people increases, the number of people who openly identify as LGBTQ will likely also increase.

Legal Timeline

As stated in Chapter 1, social equity must be coupled with the rule of law in order to have power and sustainability. Court rulings provide the power and enforcement of law. As illustrated in this chapter, judicial policy can be effective and lead to quick changes. The following is a list of U.S. Supreme Court rulings and federal legislation addressing marriage and sexual privacy.

In 1879, the U.S. Supreme Court ruled it is constitutional to ban polygamy. The First Amendment's free exercise clause protects religious beliefs but not religious activity (*Reynolds v. United States* (1879).

In 1890, the U.S. Supreme Court ruled the Edmunds-Tucker Act of 1887 (Ch. 397, 24 Stat. 635) is constitutional; religious exercise is subordinate to criminal laws *Davis v. Beason* (1890).

In 1942, the U.S. Supreme Court ruled the Oklahoma Habitual Sterilization Act of 1935, which permitted compulsory sterilization of criminals with three convictions, was unconstitutional (*Skinner v. Oklahoma*, 1942).

In 1965, the U.S. Supreme Court ruled 7–2 that the Constitution protects marital privacy against state restrictions on birth control (*Griswold v. Connecticut*, 1965).

In 1972, the U.S. Supreme Court held excluding same-sex couples from marriage was not a substantial federal question (*Baker v. Nelson*, 1972).

In 1986, the U.S. Supreme Court ruled there was no sexual right to privacy; homosexual acts were illegal (*Bowers v. Hardwick*, 1986).

In 1996, Congress passed the Defense of Marriage Act of 1996 (Pub. L. 104–199), which defined marriage as a union between a man and a woman.

In 2003, the U.S. Supreme Court ruled individuals have a right to sexual privacy between consenting adults, invalidating sodomy laws across the country (*Lawrence v. Texas*, 2003), overruling *Bowers v. Hardwick* (1986).

In 2013, the U.S. Supreme Court declared Section 3 of the DOMA unconstitutional, which defined marriage as between a man and a woman (*U.S. v. Windsor*, 2013).

In 2013, the U.S. Supreme Court declared a ballot initiative banning same-sex marriage unconstitutional, restoring marriage equality in California (*Hollingsworth v. Perry*, 2013).

In 2015, U.S. Supreme Court ruled individuals have a fundamental right to marry, granting marriage equality in all 50 states and federal spousal benefits (*Obergefell v. Hodges*, 2015), overruling *Baker v. Nelson* (1972).

In a period of 12 years, from 2003 to 2015, the U.S. Supreme Court made four rulings addressing LGBTQ sexual privacy and marriage rights. The cases are listed by name, year, decision, and court composition of ruling (see Table 2.1).

Although the U.S. Supreme Court ruled 5–4 in favor of same-sex marriage in *Obergefell v. Hodges* (2015), the court composition for the 2019 term is different from the 2014 term. In the marriage equality ruling, Justice Kennedy delivered the majority opinion and was joined by Justices Ginsburg, Breyer, Sotomayor, and Kagan whereas Chief Justice Roberts, and Justices Alito, Scalia,

Table 2.1   Summary of U.S. Supreme Court Cases

Case Name & Year	Decision	Court Composition
Lawrence v. Texas, 2003 Reversed *Bowers v. Hardwick* (1986)	6–3, individuals have a right to sexual privacy under the due process clause of the Fourteenth Amendment. Invalidated sodomy laws in 13 states.	<u>Majority</u>: Kennedy, Stevens, O'Connor, Souter, Ginsburg Breyer Dissenting: Thomas, Scalia, Rehnquist
U.S. v. Windsor, 2013	5–4, Section 3 of the Defense of Marriage Act unconstitutional, violation of liberty based on the due process clause of the Fifth Amendment	<u>Majority</u>: Kennedy, Ginsburg, Breyer, Sotomayor, Kagan Dissenting: Chief Justice Roberts, Scalia, Thomas, Alito
Hollingsworth v. Perry, 2013	5–4, supporters of a ballot initiative lack Article III standing to sue and have no stake in the enforcement of the Constitutional Amendment. Same-sex marriage restored in California.	<u>Majority</u>: Chief Justice Roberts, Scalia, Ginsburg, Breyer, Kagan. Dissenting: Kennedy, Alito, Thomas Sotomayor
Obergefell v. Hodges, 2015	5–4, same-sex marriage is a fundamental right, state-level bans on same-sex marriage are unconstitutional based on the due process clause of the Fourteenth Amendment.	<u>Majority</u>: Kennedy, Ginsburg, Breyer, Sotomayor, Kagan Dissenting: Chief Justice Roberts, Alito, Scalia, Thomas

and Thomas dissented. However, the composition of the U.S. Supreme Court has changed. Justice Kennedy retired in July 2018, and President Trump nominated Brett Kavanaugh. In addition, Justice Scalia passed away in February 2016, and President Trump nominated Neil Gorsuch. Both nominations were confirmed. With the seating of Justice Kavanaugh and Justice Gorsuch, the court is more conservative and less likely to rule in favor of LGBTQ rights.

Conclusion

The past 15 years have generated major legal advancements in LGBTQ rights and civil rights, anchoring the rule of law to LGBTQ rights and social equity. The *Lawrence v. Texas* (2003) ruling grants same-sex couples the right to sexual privacy without being criminalized. The ruling was instrumental in shifting the perception of gays from criminals to citizens. The *U.S. v. Windsor* (2013) case was a watershed moment in the LGBTQ civil rights movement. It overturned DOMA (1996) and redefined marriage at the federal level to include same-sex couples and, as such, granting over 1,100 federal government benefits to same-sex married couples in states that recognized same-sex marriage. The *Obergefell v. Hodges* (2015) ruling was the most expansive granting same-sex couples the constitutional right to marry nationwide with equal recognition and equal protections and benefits. These rulings are monumental, creating federal rights and government benefits (property) for LGBTQ people. The court's decisions reflect significant changes in American society and the institution of marriage. As a result of these rulings, LGBTQ married couples are granted equal treatment and equal status similar to opposite-sex married couples. Justice Kennedy summed up these changes when he stated that

> [t]he history of marriage is one of both continuity and change. Changes, such as the decline of arranged marriages and the abandonment of the law of coverture [wives treated as husband's marital property], have worked [a] deep transformation in the structure of marriage once viewed as essential. These new insights have strengthened, not weakened the institution. Changed understandings of marriage are characteristic of a Nation where new dimensions of freedom become apparent to new generations.
> (*Obergefell v. Hodges*, 2015, p. 2)

Justice Kennedy went on to state:

> No union is more profound than marriage, for it embodies the highest ideals of love, fidelity, devotion, sacrifice, and family. In forming a marital union, two people become something greater than once they were. As some of the petitioners in these cases demonstrate, marriage embodies a love that may endure even past death. It would misunderstand these men and women to say they disrespect the idea of marriage. Their plea is that they do respect it, respect it so deeply that they seek to find its fulfillment for themselves. Their hope is not to be condemned to live in loneliness, excluded from one of civilization's oldest institutions. They ask for equal dignity in the eyes of the law. The Constitution grants them that right.
> (*Obergefell v. Hodges*, Majority Opinion, 2015)

Marriage equality is a new constitutional right and has a direct impact on government and public administration. The *Obergefell v. Hodges* (2015) ruling requires all three levels of government to acknowledge same-sex marriage licenses and provide spousal benefits to same-sex married couples. Public administrators must ensure equity in the delivery of government services, including procedural fairness, distribution of interventions and resources, and access to benefits. With regard to the academic field of public administration, it expands the scholarship and teaching in administrative law and constitutional law, as well as public personnel, human resources, and social equity.

The *Obergefell v. Hodges* (2015) ruling shifts the legal debate from marriage equality to LGBTQ foster parenting and adoption rights. Justice Kennedy identified supporting gay families and children as one of the four tenets for supporting gay marriage (*Obergefell v. Hodges*, 2015). Does this mean that an adoption of a child by a married same-sex couple in one state must be recognized in the other 49 states? Are same-sex married couples entitled to creating families through foster care similar to opposite-sex couples? Will contractors who deliver adoption and foster care services be required to license LGBTQ couples using the same requirements as opposite-sex married couples? These legal questions are the subject of the next chapter.

Resources

American Civil Liberties Union. www.aclu.org
Baehr v. Lewin, 910 P. 2d 112 (Hawaii, 1993).
Baker v. Vermont, 744 A.2d 864 (Vt., 1999).
Edie and Thea: A very long engagement. A documentary video by S. Muska & G. Olfsdottir.
GLAAD. www.glaad.org
International Lesbian, Gay, Bisexual, Trans and Intersex Association (IGLA). (2019). *Sexual orientation laws in the world.* https://ilga.org/maps-sexual-orientation-laws
Kaplan, R., & Dickey, L. (2015). *Then comes marriage.* W.W. Norton & Company.
Lambda Legal. www.lambdalegal.org
Loving. A movie about the 1967 U.S. Supreme Court case *Loving v. Virginia* (1967). Published in 2016.
National Association of Attorney Generals. www.naag.org
National Association of Counties. www.naco.org
Oyez. www.oyez.org
Pavan v. Smith 582 U.S. (2017). https://supreme.justia.com/cases/federal/us/582/16-992/case.pdf
Reynolds v. United States 98 U.S. 145 (1879).
Stonewall National Monument, National Park Service. www.nps.gov/ston/index.htm
U.S. General Accounting Office's report Defense of Marriage Act: Update to Prior Report (GAO-04–353R, January 23, 2004). www.gao.gov/products/GAO-04-353R
USA Gov, Vital Documents, Marriage. www.usa.gov/replace-vital-documents
Williams Institute. (2019, January). *LGBT demographic data interactive.* UCLA School of Law. https://williamsinstitute.law.ucla.edu/visualization/lgbt-stats/?topic=LGBT#economic
Windsor, E., & Lyon, J. (2019). *A wild and precious life: A memoir.* St. Martin's Press.

References

Anderson v. King County, 138 P. 3d 963 (2006).
Anti-Polygamy Act of 1882. (Ch. 47, section 22 stat. 30).
Baker v. Nelson, 409 U.S. 810 (1972).

Bender, A., & Perez-Pena, R. (2015, September 1). Kentucky clerk denies same sex marriage licenses defying court. *New York Times*.
Bowers v. Hardwick, 478 U.S. 186 (1986).
Brause v. Bureau of Vital Statistics, 1998 WL 88743 (Alaska Super. Ct. 1998).
CBS News. (2015, June 30). Arkansas county clerk to resign over same-sex marriage. https://www.cbsnews.com/news/arkansas-county-clerk-to-resign-over-same-sex-marriage/
Citizens for Equal Protection v. Bruning, 455 F.3d 859, 864–868 (CA8 2006).
Davis v. Beason, 133 US 333 (1890).
DeBoer v. Snyder, 772 F. 3d 388 (2014).
De Dsylva v. Ballentine, 351 U.S. 570 (1956).
Defense of Marriage Act of 1996 (Pub. L. 104–199).
Duffin, E. (2019, December 17). Number of U.S. same-sex households in 2018, by marital status. *Statista*. www.statista.com/statistics/325106/total-number-of-same-sex-househlds-in-the-us/
Edmunds-Tucker Act of 1887 (Ch. 397, 24 Stat. 635).
Ely v. Berryhill, 4:18-cv-00557-BPV (Arizona, 2018).
Ely v. Saul (formerly *Ely v. Berryhill*), CV-18–0557-TUC-BGM (Arizona, May 27, 2020).
Eskridge, William N., & Spedale, Darren R. (2006). *Gay marriage: For better or worse? What we've learned from the evidence*. Oxford University Press.
Family Medical Leave Act of 1993 (Pub. L. 103–3).
Goodridge v. Department of Public Health, 798 N.E. 2d 941 (MA, 2003).
Griswold v. Connecticut, 381 US 479 (1965).
Haulsee, J., & Naylor, L. A. (2014). Equal treatment under the law: A cost-benefit analysis of same-sex benefits post-Windsor. *Journal of Health and Human Services Administration*, *37*(2), 207–224. www.jstor.org/stable/24459693
Hernandez v. Robles, 855 N.E. 2d. 1, 7 N.Y.3d 338 (2006).
Hollingsworth v. Perry, 570 U.S. 693 (2013).
Hollingsworth v. Perry, 558 U.S. 183 (2010).
Human Rights Campaign. (2012). www.hrc.org
In Re Marriage Cases, 43 Cal.4th 757, 76 Cal.Rptr.3d 683, 183 P. 3d 384 (2008).
Jenkins, C. (2016, January 6). Alabama chief justice orders halt to same sex marriage license. *Reuters*. www.msnbc.com/msnbc/alabama-chief-justice-orders-halt-to-same-sex-marriage
Kaur, H. (2020, May 11). Pennsylvania has become latest state to ban child marriage – but it's still not fully outlawed in 47 others. *CNN.com*. www.cnn.com/2020/05/11/us/pennsylvania-outlaws-child-marriage-trnd/index.html
Kerrigan v. State Commissioner of Public Health, 289 Conn. 135 (Conn. 2008).
Kettl, Donald F. (2020). *The divided states of America: Why federalism doesn't work*. Princeton University Press.
Lawrence v. Texas, 539 U.S. 558 (2003).
Lewis v. Harris, 908 A. 2d 196 (NJ, 2006).
Loving v. Virginia, 388 U.S. 1 (1967).
Margolin, E. (2016, January 6). Despite order from chief justice, same sex marriage in Alabama lives on. *MSNBC*. www.msnbc.com/msnbc/despite-order-chief-justice-same-sex-marriage-alabama-lives
Maryland Office of the Attorney General. (2015). *The state of marriage equality*. Maryland Office of the Attorney General.
Masci, D., Brown, A., & Kiley, J. (2019, June 24). *5 facts about same sex marriage*. Pew Research Center. www.pewresearch.org/fact-tank/2019/06/24/same-sex-marriage/
Miller v. Davis. 123 F. Supp. 3d 924. (E.D. KY, 2015).
Morrill Act for the Suppression of Polygamy Act of 1862 (Morrill Anti-Bigamy Act) (Ch. 26, Stat. 501).
Obergefell v. Hodges, 576 U.S. 644 (2015).
Ohio ex re. Popovici v. Angler, 280 U.S. 379 (1930).
Oklahoma Habitual Sterilization Act of 1935. Okl. St. Ann. Tit. 57, 171 et seq.: L, 1935, p. 94 et seq.
Perry v. Schwarzenegger, 591 F.3d 1147 (Ninth Circuit, 2010).
Pew Research Center Analysis. (2019). *Gay marriage around the world. Map classifications as of October 2019*. www.pewresearch.org/fact-tank/2019/10/29/global-snapshot-same-sex-marriage/

Raines v. Byrd, 521 U.S. 811 (1997).
Reynolds v. United States, 98 U.S. 145 (1879).
Sigman, Shayna M. (2006). Everything lawyers know about polygamy is wrong. *Cornell Journal of Law and Public Policy, 16*(1), article 3, 118–134. Fall 2016.
Skinner v. Oklahoma, 316 U.S. 535 (1942).
Solomon, D. (2015, July 14). Rusk county clerk resigned rather than issue gay marriage licenses. *The Daily Post*. https://www.texasmonthly.com/the-daily-post/rusk-county-clerk-resigned-rather-than-issue-gay-marriage-licenses/
Sosna v. Iowa, 419 U.S. 393 (1975), p. 404.
Standard v. Superior Court (CA, 2003).
State and Territorial Statutes and Proceedings; Full Faith and Credit (28 U.S.C. Section 1738).
State of Utah. Bigamy Amendments. Senate Bill 102. https://le.utah.gov/~2020/bills/static/SB0102.html
Struening, K. (2009). Looking for liberty and defining marriage in three same-sex marriage cases. In G. A. Babst, E. R. Gill, & J. Pierceson (Eds.), *Moral argument, religion, and same-sex marriage. Advancing the public good* (pp. 19–49). Lexington Books.
Swan, W. (2015). *Gay, lesbian, bisexual, and transgender civil rights: A public policy agenda for uniting a divided America*. CRC Press.
Taylor, D. (2019, September 18). *Male couples make up majority of same-sex households in large cities but not nationwide*. U.S. Census Bureau. www.census.gov/library/stories/2019/09/where-same-sex-couples-live.html
Texas Penal Code. Chapter 21, Section 21. 6(a).
Turner v. Safley, 482 U.S. 78 (1987).
U.S. Census Bureau. (2019). *Historical table, estimates of same-sex couple households in the American Community Survey*. www.census.gov/programs-surveys/acs/
U.S. Constitution (1789).
U.S. General Accounting Office. (1997, January 31). *Defense of marriage act, GAO/OGC-97–16*. Government Printing Office. Barry R. Bedrick. www.gao.gov/assets/230/223674.pdf
U.S. Government Accountability Office. (2004). *Defense of marriage act. GAO 04–353R2004*. Government Printing Office. www.gao.gov/assets/100/92441.pdf
U.S. Population Reference Bureau. (2016, December 7). *Existing data show increase in same sex married couples*. www.prb.org/increase-in-married-same-sex-us-couples/
U.S. Social Security Administration. (2020, August). *Research statistics & policy analysis*. Monthly Statistical Snapshot. Http://www.ssa.gov/policy/docs/quickfacts/stat_snapshot/
U.S. Social Security Administration. (n.d.). *Fact sheet*. Https://www.ssa.gov/news/press/factsheets/basicfact-alt.pdf
U.S. v. Windsor, 570 U.S. 744 (2013).
Varnum v. Brien, 763 n.w.2d 862 (IA, 2009).
Wilkinson, J. (2020, May 12). Polygamy now officially decriminalized in Utah. *New York Daily News*. https://www.nydailynews.com/news/national/ny-polygamy-utah-decriminalized-20200513-64vq5ptw4bf6bi2fkijpfrpchu-story.html
Wyatt-Nichol, H., & Naylor, L. A. (2015). Liberty and equality: In defense of same-sex marriage. *Public Integrity, 17*(2), 117–130. doi:10.1080/10999922.2015.1000108
Wyatt-Nichol, H., & Naylor, L. A. (2013). The policy landscape of sexual orientation. *Journal of Public Management and Policy, 19*(1), 5–18.
Zablocki v. Redhail, 434 US 374 (1978).
Zivotofsky v. Clinton, 566 U.S. 189 (2012).

Chapter 3

Foster Care, Adoption, and Assisted Reproductive Technology

Introduction

In April 2019, Eden Rogers and Brandy Welch, a married lesbian couple with two daughters, decided to become foster parents. The state child welfare agency's policy manual states that prospective families will not be discriminated against based on religion or sexual orientation (DSS Manual, Section 10). The couple submitted an online application and identified themselves as a same-sex married couple who attends the Unitarian Universalist Church, which is nondenominational. The following month the couple received an email from Miracle Hill, a contractor for the state of South Carolina foster care system, denying their request based on faith and sexual orientation. The contractor stated it expects foster parents to "share our beliefs and are active in a Christian Church" and to adhere to the doctrine that "God's design for marriage is the legal joining of one man and one woman." Miracle Hill only serves Evangelical Protestant Christian heterosexual families and asks prospective foster care parents to submit their "personal testimony of [their] faith/salvation in Jesus Christ" (*Rogers v. U.S. DHHS*, 2019, pp. 15–16). It denies services based on religion, including people who are Jewish or Catholic. Miracle Hill argues it has the right to deny Rogers and Welch approval as a result of receiving a federal waiver allowing for religious discrimination. The waiver was granted in January 2019 by the U.S. Department of Health and Human Services (HHS). The couple filed a lawsuit against the HHS and the state of South Carolina in April 2019 (*Rogers v. U.S. DHHS*, 2019). In May 2019, the couple filed a lawsuit alleging the defendant is "unlawfully authorizing state-contracted, government-funded foster care agencies to use religious eligibility criteria to exclude qualified families from fostering children in the public child welfare system . . . on the basis of religion and sexual orientation" (*Rogers v. U.S. DHHS*, 2019, p. 1), which violates the First Amendment establishment clause, the Fifth Amendment equal protection clause, the Fourteenth Amendment due process clause of the Constitution, and 42 U.S.C. section 1983. The defendants filed several motions to dismiss the case. In May 2020, a U.S. District Court, the District of South

Carolina, dismissed the Fourteenth Amendment equal protection claim based on religious discrimination but granted the equal protection claim based on sexual orientation and violation of the establishment clause, moving the case forward. The case is currently pending.

Does a government contractor who receives federal and state funding have a right to deny a same-sex married couple a foster care license based on sexual orientation? Can government contractors use a religious litmus test to withhold government services? Can an evangelical agency refuse services to opposite-sex married Catholic or Jewish couples? This case is an example of the legal challenges same-sex married couples face after the U.S. Supreme Court ruling *Obergefell v Hodges* (2015), which legalized same-sex marriage across the country and granted all rights and responsibilities of marriage including over 1,100 federal benefits, which includes federal foster parent licenses and access to adoption. This chapter explores the legal issues faced by same-sex married couples, post-*Obergefell*, who seek to start or expand their families. Currently, there are approximately 114,000 same-sex couples raising children in the U.S. (Williams Institute, July 2018). For those who wish to expand their families, they can foster, adopt, or utilize assistive reproductive technology, such as surrogacy, which is cost-prohibitive for most people. These options and the legal impediments to creating a family for same-sex couples are described. First, the U.S. Supreme Court case *Obergefell v. Hodges* (2015) and its guidance on families are reviewed, followed by a summary of public opinion polls. Next, foster care, adoption, and assisted reproduction technology (ART), including legal cases, are described.

Marriage Equality and Children

On June 26, 2015, the U.S. Supreme Court delivered a landmark decision in *Obergefell v. Hodges* (2015), granting same-sex couples the right to marriage and full recognition of their marriages. It legalized same-sex marriage across the country. Marriage is a constitutional right, and as such, spouses of same-sex married couples are entitled to the same spousal benefits as opposite-sex married couples, including adoption, health insurance, medical, taxes (estate, property), and retirement benefits, to name a few. For a complete list of federal benefits, see *U.S. v. Windsor* (2013). The court also granted same-sex marriage to ensure children of gay parents grow up with the needed social and legal recognition required for a secure upbringing. Writing for the majority, U.S. Supreme Court Justice Kennedy wrote that a core a reason to protect the right to marriage is to

> safeguard children and families. . . . By giving recognition and legal structure to their parents' relationship, marriage allows children to understand the integrity and closeness of their own family. . . . Marriage also affords the permanency and stability important to children's best interests . . . many same sex couples provide loving and nurturing homes, whether biological or adopted.
>
> (*Obergefell v. Hodges*, 2015)

The U.S. Supreme Court ruled that same-sex couples have a fundamental right to marry and to create a family if they choose. The ruling guarantees that same-sex married couples enjoy the same parenting rights that opposite-sex married couples, including training as foster parents and adoptive parents.

Public Support

Consistent with the U.S. Supreme Court's marriage equality ruling (*Obergefell v. Hodges*, 2015), there's been an increase of support for gay couples adopting children. According to a 2019 Gallup poll, public support of gay adoption increased from a low of 14 percent in 1977 to a high of 75 percent in 2019 (Gallup, n.d.). The 1977 poll is reflective of the antigay crusade led by Anita Bryant of Florida, who was instrumental in securing the first gay adoption ban in the country (Bryant, 1977). However, public opinion has changed drastically over the past 40 years. As of 2019, three-quarters of Americans support adoption by gay people. The increased public support is consistent with the percentage of Americans who know someone who is gay. According to a survey conducted by the Pew Research Center, 63 percent of Americans reported in 2016 that homosexuality should be accepted by society, compared with 51 percent in 2006, a 12-point increase over a 10-year period. In 2013, 75 percent of respondents reported knowing a friend, relative, or coworker who was lesbian, gay, bisexual, and transgender (LGBT) compared to only 24 percent in 1985. This is important because there is a positive relationship between knowing somebody who is gay and increased acceptance of gay people. These national polls reflect changing attitudes in American society. The majority of Americans support adoption by gay couples.

Creating a Family

Despite a significant increase in public support for gays and the U.S. Supreme Court legalizing marriage equality, same-sex married couples still endure legal obstacles in creating families. For gay couples, there are three options for creating a family: (1) biological, (2) foster care and adoption, and (3) ART. Each option has legal challenges and complexities. In the U.S., approximately 114,000 same-sex couples are raising children. According to a study by the University of California, Los Angeles Law School Williams Institute (2018), 68 percent of same-sex couples are raising biological children, 21 percent are raising adopted children, and 3 percent are raising foster children. Compared to opposite-sex couples, same-sex married couples are more likely to adopt (21 percent vs. 3 percent) and more likely to be foster parents (3 percent vs. 0.4 percent). Each of these options is discussed with an emphasis on the U.S. foster care and adoption system, which is funded by the federal government and administered by state governments.

Biological Children

Some same-sex couples or divorced single LGBTQ people may have children from prior marriages and relationships. For example, a spouse of an opposite-sex couple may come to realize over time they are lesbian, gay, bisexual, or transgender, not heterosexual. The individual then gets divorced and later marries a same-sex spouse. The individual may have a biological child or children from a previous marriage or relationship. Having biological children from a previous marriage can create legal impediments regarding birth certificates and legal custody of the child(ren). Since divorce and child custody are within the sphere of individual states and family court, outcomes of cases vary by state. The LGBTQ parent may be treated differently than the heterosexual parent regarding divorce, parental rights, and child custody. Custody battles can be difficult and painful. For example, Paula Overby, a transgender person, describes her painful and heartbreaking story of attempting to gain custody of her son. She chronicles her story in the book *The Transgender Myth: Through the Gender Looking Glass* (2007). The stress from the custody battle drove her nearly to suicidal depression. It serves as an example of the numerous obstacles and hardships LGBTQ individuals can face in trying to raise children and maintain custody.

Gay couples can also become pregnant using ART, such as insemination, which produces a biological child for the gestational mother. This creates legal obstacles for nongestational parents, who are not always recognized by the courts. Court recognition varies by state. ART is discussed fully later in the chapter.

U.S. Foster Care and Adoption

A second option for LGBTQ singles or couples is to become licensed foster parents and adopt children. There are two types of adoptions: (1) domestic and (2) international. Domestic adoption is the most likely path for LGBTQ couples to create a family due to international anti-LGBTQ adoption policies. Regarding domestic adoption, couples can adopt through the U.S. foster care and adoption system, a private adoption agency, or a private attorney. Adoption through private adoption agencies and private attorneys is not addressed here because cases are not funded by or administered by federal, state, or local governments. This section focuses on the U.S. foster care and adoption system since it is funded with federal dollars and administered by state governments. First, a description of how and why children come into the system is provided.

Child Abuse and Neglect

Children come into the child welfare system due to abuse or neglect. According to the HHS, Administration for Children and Families (2018), in 2018, there were 3,534,000 children who received a child abuse and neglect investigation. Of those confirmed, 61 percent are due to neglect, 11 percent due to physical abuse, 7 percent are sexually abused, and 15 percent have dual confirmations such as abuse and neglect. In 2018, approximately 1,770 children were killed due to abuse or neglect. Seventy percent of child fatalities are of children younger than 3 years of age, and approximately one-half of the children are younger than 1 year of age. Of the children killed, the majority (81 percent) are killed by a parent or caregiver.

As a result of abuse and neglect, children are placed in foster care to ensure their safety. There are approximately 417,000 children in foster care and over 107,000 children who are eligible and waiting to be adopted. The average age of a child entering foster care is 7 years old, with the largest percentage of children entering the system being younger than 12 months old. More infants are entering the system due to parental drug abuse and the opioid crisis. This means that the U.S. needs to license close to a half-million foster parents to take care of children in the system whose biological parents or family members are unable to parent them. Without additional foster parents, on average, 20,000 teenagers, ages 18 to 21, age out of the foster care system each year with no adult supervision (U.S. Department of Health and Human Services, 2018). Without parents or adult supervision, these youth are vulnerable and at an increased risk of poverty, homelessness, incarceration, and other negative outcomes (Bilchik, 2006). The U.S. needs more foster and adoptive parents to prevent teenagers from aging out of the system and to provide all children in foster care with a loving, secure home.

The U.S. foster care system operates under a system of federalism. The federal government funds the program and the states administer and manage the program (Kettl, 2020). As such, there are 50 distinct separate state child welfare programs some of which services are privatized. The Social Security Act of 1935 provides the funding for the U.S. child welfare system. Foster care and adoption are funded through Title IV-B and Title IV-E of the Social Security Act (42 U.S.C. §§ 671–679b). In addition, there are numerous federal laws that provide for specific programs and services. The program is composed of child abuse and neglect, foster care, and adoption. A timeline of these laws is provided in the next section. According to federal law, the only population banned from being foster parents is convicted felons. Each state administers its own foster care and adoption program. This means there are 50 individual state child welfare agencies. Foster care and adoption services can be operated by state and local government agencies or contracted out to nonprofit organizations. Contractors are typically nonprofit organizations, which include both secular and religious organizations. Some religious organizations are refusing to serve lesbian and gay couples seeking foster parent licenses and adoption on the basis of religious objections to same-sex marriage and faith. This discrimination has resulted in litigation. These legal cases are addressed later in the chapter.

Timeline of Federal Adoption and Foster Care Laws

The following is a thorough list of key federal adoption and foster care laws. Collectively, these laws form the U.S. adoption and foster care system, also known as the U.S. child welfare system. Although there is no federal law prohibiting LGBTQ people from fostering or adopting children in the 50 states, there are no federal laws requiring states to ensure LGBTQ people are protected from discrimination in pursuing adoption or a foster care license. A federal policy, either from the judicial or the legislative branch, is needed to prohibit discrimination based on sexual orientation or gender identity. Without a legal basis, enforcement is dubious at best.

In 1935, Congress passed the Social Security Act of 1935 (as amended) (Pub. L. 74–271). Title IV-B, Child & Family Services, Stephanie Tubbs Jones Child Welfare System Program, and MaryLee Allen Promoting Safe & Stable Families Program. This section of the law provides for appropriations and allotments to state children welfare agencies and Indian tribal agencies that submit state plans for child welfare services. Title IV-E. Federal Payment for Foster Care, Prevention and Permanency, is the section of the law that appropriates funding to state child welfare agencies for foster care assistance and maintenance, adoption and guardianship assistance, adoption incentives, and independent living for youth 18 to 21 years of age (John H. Chafee program).

In 1965, Congress passed the Immigration and Nationality Act of 1965 (amends the Immigration and Nationality Act). This law exempts children adopted internationally from specific vaccinations.

In 1974, Congress passed the Child Abuse Prevention and Treatment Act (Pub. Law 93–247). This law requires state child welfare agencies to screen, investigate, and prosecute child abuse and neglect.

In 1992, Congress passed the Uniform Adoption Act of 1992 (Pub. L. 115–119 – RAISE Family Caregivers Act).

In 1994, Congress passed the Multi-Ethnic Placement Act of 1994 (Pub. L. 103–382). The purpose is to decrease the time that African American children spend in foster care.

In 1996, Congress passed the Child Abuse Prevention and Treatment Amendments (Pub. L. 104–235).

In 1996, Congress passed the Interethnic Adoption Provisions of the Small Business Job Protection Act of 1996 (Pub. L. 104–188).

In 1997, Congress passed the Adoption and Safe Families Act of 1997 (Pub. L. 105–89).

In 1998, Congress passed the Abandoned Infants Assistance Act of 1998 (Pub. L. 100–505). This policy helps abandoned infants in hospitals, specifically babies with HIV, to find permanent homes.

In 1999, Congress passed the Foster Care Independence Act of 1999 (Pub. L. 106–199).

In 2000, Congress passed the Adoption Awareness Act of 2000 (Pub. L. 106–279). This law directed the HHS (amends the Public Health Services Act) to utilize the internet to help find permanent homes for foster children.

In 2000, Congress passed the Child Abuse Prevention and Enforcement Act of 2000 (Pub. L. 106–177). The purpose of this law is to reduce the incidence of child abuse.

In 2000, Congress passed the Intercountry Adoption Act of 2000 (Pub. L. 106–279). The purpose of this law is to implement the 1993 Hague Convention on Intercountry Adoption.

In 2000, Congress passed the Child Citizen Act of 2000 (Pub. L. 106–395). This law grants automatic citizenship to children adopted internationally.

In 2001, Congress passed the Economic Growth and Tax Relief Reconciliation Act (Pub. L. 107–116). This law provides a $10,000 tax credit for adopting a child with a documented special needs adoption. It helps families offset the cost of adoption.

In 2001, Congress passed the Hope for Children Act (Pub. L. 107–16). The purpose of this law is to offset adoption expenses. It provides a onetime tax credit of $10,000 to families who adopt a child (or children) to assist with the cost of raising children with special needs, and it provides a $10,000 tax exclusion for employer-provided adoption assistance.

In 2001, Congress passed the Promoting Safe and Stable Families Amendments of 2001 (Pub. L. 107–133).

In 2003, Congress passed the Keeping Children and Families Safe Act of 2003 (Pub. L. 108–136). This law reauthorized the Child Abuse and Treatment Act, the Adoption Opportunities Act, the Abandoned Infants Assistance, and the Families Violence Prevention and Services Act.

In 2003, Congress passed the Adoption Promotion Act of 2003 (Pub. L. 108–145). This law reauthorizes adoption incentives under the Adoption and Safe Families Act of 1997 and increases adoption incentives for children 9 years of age and older to prevent them from aging out of foster care.

In 2005, Congress passed the Fair Access Foster Care Act of 2005 (Pub. L. 109–113). This law amends Title IV-E of the Social security Act to allow foster care maintenance payments be made on behalf of eligible foster children to private for-profit organizations. The amendment strikes "nonprofit" from the act.

In 2006, Congress passed the Child and Family Services Improvement Act of 2006 (Pub. L. 109–288). This law altered Title IV of the Social Security Act to limit funding for the Promoting Safe and Stable Families program to not exceed 10 percent of each state's total program expenditure and requires the HHS secretary to set aside $40 million annually to ensure monthly caseworker visits to children in foster care for recruitment, retention, training, and technology.

In 2008, Congress passed Fostering Connections to Success Act of 2008 (Pub. L. 110–351). This law amends part B and E, Title IV of the Social Security Act to support relative caretakers, improve outcomes foster children including adoption access, and promote tribal foster care and adoption access.

In 2011, Congress passed the Child and Family Services Improvement and Innovation Act of 2011 (Pub. L. 112–134). This law extended appropriations for Title IV-B of the Social Security Act until fiscal year 2016 to identify, treat, and monitor emotional trauma of children in care; reduce the length of time of children in foster care who are 5 years of age and younger; and require a caseworker to visit children in foster care a minimum of once per month.

In 2014, Congress passed the Preventing Sex Trafficking and Strengthening Families Act of 2014 (Pub. L. 113–183). The law requires states to develop policies to identify, screen, and provide services to children under the state child welfare system who are at risk of sex trafficking. It also requires state child welfare agencies to report victims of child sex trafficking to law enforcement and the HHS.

In 2018, Congress passed the Family First Prevention Services Act as part of the Bipartisan Budget Act of 2018 (Pub. L. 115–123). The goal of this law is to reform the two federal funding streams (Title IV-B and Title IV-E of the Social Security Act) to focus on preventing children from entering foster care by providing substance abuse treatment, mental health services, and parenting classes.

In 2018, Congress passed the Substance Use Disorder Prevention that Promotes Opioid Recovery and Treatment for Patients and Communities Act or the SUPPORT for Patients and Communities

Act (Pub. L. 115–271). The purpose of the law is to increase access to medical treatment for opioid addiction and to reduce illicit drugs. This law directly impacts foster care children who enter the system due to drug-addicted parents.

In 2019, Congress passed the Victims of Child Abuse Act Reauthorization Act of 2019 (Pub. Law 115–424). This law amends the Child Abuse Prevention and Treatment Act of 1974 (Pub. L. 93–247). It provides federal funding to state child welfare agencies to screen, investigate, and prosecute child abuse and neglect cases.

The federal legislation identified serves as an umbrella of laws comprising the child welfare system. However, none of these federal statutes guarantees the right of LGBTQ people to obtain a foster care license or become adoptive parents of foster children. Without laws to enforce these rights, LGBTQ people can be discriminated against and denied foster care licenses and adoptions.

State Adoption Bans

Having laid the legal framework for the U.S. child welfare system, this section addresses gay adoption bans. The first gay adoption was in 1977 in Florida. Anita Bryant (1977), an antigay crusader, led the movement. Bryant, who was the spokesperson for Florida orange juice, believed adoption by lesbian and gay couples was harmful, although there was no evidence to support her claim. Contrary to her assertions, there is solid research showing that gay couples are equally as good parents as opposite-sex couples. Bilchik (2006) sums up the research on gay parenting as

> in the nearly three decades since the Florida law went into effect, many social science studies have been conducted on the ability of gay people to parent and the development of their children. It has now been established by the research that gay people are just as capable of being good parents as heterosexual or "straight" people, and that their children are just as likely to be healthy and well-adjusted. Not a single reputable study has found that children raised by gay or lesbian parents have been harmed because of their parents' sexual orientation in any way.
>
> (Bilchik, 2006, p. v)

In a report by the American Civil Liberties Union titled "Too High a Price: The Case Against Restricting Gay Parenting," the authors provide strong evidence, based on social science research, that same-sex parents provide loving and supportive families for children, and LGBTQ adoption restrictions hurt children (Cooper & Cates, 2006). A literature review conducted by Inequality at Cornell University found four articles that children raised by gay parents are worse off, and they found 75 academic studies with findings that having a gay or lesbian parent does not harm children and that these children "fare no better or worse than other children" (Inequality Cornell University, 2017, p. 1). The literature review found no significant differences in school outcomes, emotional adjustment, parenting styles, or sexual orientation of the children (Inequality Cornell University, n.d.).

The academic research supporting LGBTQ adoption combined with U.S Supreme Court rulings granting marriage equality (*Obergefell v Hodges*, 2015; *U.S. v. Windsor*, 2013; *Lawrence v. Texas*, 2003) shifted the political debate from anti-LGBTQ stereotypes to religious organizations' rights and freedoms. Current court cases are based on a right to religious expression by adoption service providers. In response to the U.S. Supreme Court ruling *Obergefell v. Hodges* (2015), some state legislatures passed statutes banning gay couples from fostering and adopting children. Either by case law or by statute, these have included permitting religious organizations to discriminate against gay couples, outright state bans on adoptions by gays, and refusal to recognize adoptions by gay couples in other states. In 2018, nine states allowed religiously affiliated adoption agencies to deny gay people a foster care license based on sexual orientation. These include Alabama, Kansas, Michigan, Mississippi, North Dakota, Oklahoma, South Dakota, Texas, and Virginia. Some states had bans simply prohibiting adoption by gays but not fostering a child. In 2015, Mississippi had an adoption ban (Mississippi Code 93–17–3(5)) on same-sex couples that had been in existence for over 20 years. In March 2016, a federal court struck down the Mississippi adoption ban stating it violated the equal protection clause of the U.S. Constitution (*Campaign for Southern Equality v. Mississippi Department of Human Services*, 2016). More recently, in January 2020, the Tennessee Senate passed a bill allowing adoption contractors to deny services and licenses to same-sex couples. This specific bill also protects adoption agencies from discrimination lawsuits. The bill will be voted on by the house (Allison, January 14, 2020). These bans are significant in that the political debate has shifted from the stereotype that LGBTQ harm children (Bryant, 1977) to government contractors have a religious right to deny services based on sexual orientation and faith.

In contrast, nine state legislatures passed laws prohibiting discrimination based on sexual orientation in foster care and adoption agencies. These include California, Maryland, Massachusetts, New Jersey, Nevada, New York, Rhode Island, and Wisconsin. This is important because unless states have antidiscrimination laws in place religious organizations can deny services based on faith and sexual orientation through a federal waiver issued by HHS. Federal waivers have advanced discrimination based on religion by issuing exemptions for contracting with religious organizations that believe marriage is defined by a man and a woman only. The outcome is foster children are denied a permanent family and same-sex married couples are denied a child and services paid for by federal funding. The courts must decide if equal protection of the law is more important than religious objections and what is in the best interest of the children in foster care. In the following sections are legal cases of same-sex married couples alleging discrimination based on sexual orientation and of government contractors using a religious litmus test to deny same-sex couples foster care licenses and adoption.

V.L. v. E.L. *(2016)*

This case involved the state of Alabama's refusal to recognize an adoption from the state of Georgia, which had jurisdiction over the adoption. A lesbian couple, V.L. and E.L., were partners from 1995 to 2011. Through ART, E.L. conceived a child in 2002 and twins in 2004. The couple raised the children together and decided to give V.L. a legal relationship with their three children by filing an adoption petition with the Superior Court in Fulton County, Georgia. E.L., the biological mother, gave consent for her partner, V.L., to adopt the children. The court granted the adoption decree, recognizing both women as legal parents of the children. In 2011, while living in Alabama, the couple's relationship terminated and V.L. sought custody rights. V.L. asked the Circuit Court of Jefferson County, Alabama, to register the Georgia adoption so she could have custody and visitation rights. The initial ruling ordered shared custody, and V.L. received scheduled visitation with their children. E.L. appealed the visitation order with the Alabama Court of Civil Appeals, which ruled the lower court should have conducted an evidentiary hearing. The Alabama State Supreme Court overturned the lower court ruling, stating that the Georgia court had no subject matter jurisdiction and wrongly agreed to V.L.'s adoption of the children. In 2015, the adoptive mother appealed to the U.S. Supreme Court. In 2016, the U.S. Supreme Court unanimously, without hearing oral arguments, reversed the Alabama State Supreme Court for not recognizing a same-sex adoption from another state that had jurisdiction over the adoption (*V.L. v. E.L.*, 2016). The U.S. Supreme Court found in favor of the adoptive mother based on the full faith and credit clause of the U.S. Constitution. It states that "Full Faith and Credit shall be given in each State to the public Acts, Records, and judicial Proceedings of every other State" (U.S. Constitution, Article IV, Section 1). The court described the full faith and credit clause as 'exacting,' citing *Baker v. General Motors Corp* (1998), which states, "A final judgement in one State, if rendered by a court with adjudicatory authority over the subject matter and persons governed by the judgment, qualifies for recognition throughout the land" (p. 233). The court opined that "a State may not disregard the judgment of a sister State because it disagrees with the reasoning underlying the judgment or deems it to be wrong on the merits" (*V.L. v. E.L.*, 2016). In other words, moving across a state line cannot invalidate an adoption or parental rights from another state that had jurisdiction over the matter. Adoption by a same-sex couple in one state is legally recognized by all states across the country.

Fulton v. City of Philadelphia *(2018)*

In *Fulton v. City of Philadelphia* (2018a), Catholic Social Services, a foster care contractor, sued the City of Philadelphia in July 2018 for violating its constitutional right to deny foster care parent placements based on religious beliefs. Specifically, the agency refused to "certify same-sex couples as prospective foster parents" and conduct home study's for same-sex couples seeking to adopt because it went against the teachings of the Catholic Church (*Fulton v. City of Philadelphia*, 2018a). The Department of Human Services (DHS) stopped giving referrals to Catholic Social Services because it discriminated against same-sex couples. DHS and the City of Philadelphia argued Catholic Social Services violated Article XV of the Philadelphia Fair Practices Ordinance outlined in the services contract by refusing to place children with parents with different religious beliefs and sexual orientation. Article XV states:

> Provider shall not discriminate or permit discrimination against any individual because of race, color, religion or national origin. Nor shall Provider discriminate or permit discrimination against individuals in . . . public accommodation practices whether by direct or indirect practice of exclusion, distinction, restriction, segregation limitation, refusal, denial, differentiation ore preference in the treatment of a person on the basis of . . . sexual orientation, gender identity, marital status, familiar [*sic*] status . . . or engage in any other act or practice made unlawful under the Charter . . .
> (*Fulton v. City of Philadelphia*, 2018a, p. 7)

In a similar case in Illinois, *Catholic Charities of the Diocese of Springfield v. Madigan* (2011), the court ruled that even though Catholic Charities had contracted with the state of Illinois for over 40 years providing foster care and adoption services, the organization does "not have a legally recognized protected property interest in the renewal of its contracts for foster care and adoption" (as cited in *Fulton v. City of Philadelphia*, 2018a, p. 16). In the Philadelphia case, Catholic Social Services filed a temporary restraining order and preliminary injunction against the City of Philadelphia and DHS for suspending new foster care referrals and for violating Catholic Social Services' religious and free speech rights. The First Amendment free exercise clause states, "Congress shall make no law . . . prohibiting the free exercise [of religion], which applies to both state and local government under the Fourteenth Amendment" (*Cantwell v. Connecticut*, 1940). "When a challenged law is 'neutral' and 'generally applicable,' and burdens religious conduct only incidentally, the Free Exercise Clause offers no protection" (*Employment Div. v. Smith*, 1990; *Fraternal Order* of Police Newark Lodge No. 12 v. City of Newark, 1999; as cited in *Fulton v. City of Philadelphia*, 2018a, p. 22). The court used the *Smith* framework because the Religious Freedom Restoration Act of 1993 (Pub. L. 103–141) does not apply to state actions: (1) "the term *government* includes a branch, department, agency, instrumentality, and official (or other person acting under color of law) of the United States, a State, or a subdivision of a State; (2) the term 'State' includes the District of Columbia, the Commonwealth of Puerto Rico, and each territory and possession of the United States" (Pub. L. 103–141).

> "The court used a rational basis review in deciding the case. The standard states that [a] statute is presumed constitutional and the burden is on the one attacking the legislative arrangement to negative every conceivable basis which might support it, whether or not that basis has a foundation in the record." . . . The regulation must be reasonable and not arbitrary and it must bear "a rational relationship to a [permissible] state objective."
> (Lighthouse Inst. For Evangelism, Inc. 510 F.3d at 278 as cited in *Fulton v. City of Philadelphia*, 2018a, p. 29)

The judge denied the preliminary injunction and a motion for a temporary restraining order and ruled in favor of the defendant, City of Philadelphia, stating that the city had a legitimate interest in ensuring its contractors adhered to contractual terms and a governmental interest to ensure all qualified parents were licensed. The judge stated that the city has "a legitimate interest in ensuring that the pool of foster parents and resource caregivers is as diverse and broad as the children in need of foster parents and resource caregivers" (p. 63). Referencing *Heart of Atlanta Motel Inc. v. United States* (1964), the judge wrote that "[p]reventing discrimination in the provision of public service is undeniably a legitimate interest" (*Fulton v. City of Philadelphia*, 2018a, p. 64). The ruling was a victory for same-sex couples seeking to become foster parents in Philadelphia. Fulton appealed the ruling. In April 2019, the Third Circuit Court of Eastern Pennsylvania ruled in favor of the City of Philadelphia (No. 2–18-cv-02075, 2018b). In July 2019 Catholic Social Services filed a petition with the U.S. Court of Appeals Third Circuit requesting the U.S. Supreme Court review the case and was granted certiorari in July 2019 (*Fulton v. City of Philadelphia*, 2019). The U.S. Supreme Court is scheduled to make a ruling on the case in the 2020 term (9–123, 140 S. Ct. 1104, 2020). Catholic Social Services is requesting the court answer three legal questions: (1) Can free exercise plaintiffs only succeed by proving a specific type of discrimination claim? (2) Should *Employment Division v. Smith* (1990) be revisited? and (3) Does the government violate the First Amendment by requiring a religious organization's contract to contradict its religious beliefs? (*Fulton v. City of Philadelphia*, 2020).

Dumont v. Gordon *(2017)*

Similar to the *Fulton* case described earlier in *Dumont v. Gordon* (2017), a lesbian couple by the name of Kristy and Dana Dumont was denied a foster care license by St. Vincent Catholic Charities and Bethany Christian Services, which had service contracts with the State of Michigan Department of Health and Human Services. The couple was turned away in 2016 and then in 2017 based on religious objections. The organizations cited religious objections and refused to license the same-sex couple. The couple filed a lawsuit alleging their First and Fourteenth Amendments had been violated by the state contractor. In March 2019, the Michigan attorney general was able to negotiate a settlement agreement with the two parties (*Dumont v. Gordon*, 2019, Settlement Agreement).

It requires all foster care organizations with state contracts to comply with a nondiscrimination requirement and accept all families who qualify as foster parents. Specifically, it states:

> Contracts and the Subcontracts include a non-discrimination provision mandating that contracted Child Placing Agencies (CPAs) comply with the Department's non-discrimination statement prohibiting discrimination "against any individual or group because of race, sex, religion, age, national origin, color, height, weight, marital status, gender identity or expression, sexual orientation, political beliefs, or disability" in the provision of services under contract with the Department" (the "Non-Discrimination Provision"). . . . Examples of Prohibited Discriminatory Conduct include: turning away or referring to another contracted CPA another wise potentially qualified LGBTQ individual or same-sex couple that may be a suitable foster or adoptive family for any child accepted by the CPA for contracted services; refusing to provide orientation or training to an otherwise potentially qualified LGBTQ individual or same-sex couple that may be a suitable foster or adoptive family for any child accepted by the CPA for contracted services; refusing to place a child accepted by the CPA for contracted services with an otherwise qualified LGBTQ individual or same-sex couple suitable as a foster or adoptive family for the child.
>
> (*Dumont v. Gordon*, Settlement Agreement, March 22, 2019, pp. 2, 4, 5)

In response to the settlement agreement, one of the state contractors, St. Vincent Catholic Charities sued the state of Michigan, arguing it is entitled to a state contract under the Constitution entitles it to a contract. In May 2019, the American Civil Liberties Union intervened on behalf of the Dumonts. The case is pending.

Marouf v. Azar *(2018)*

This case addresses alleged discrimination in the federal refugee foster care program. A same-sex married lesbian couple, Fatma Marouf and Bryn Esplin, were denied a foster parent application to foster unaccompanied refugee children by Catholic Charities of Fort Worth, Texas, a subgrantee of the U.S. Conference of Catholic Bishops (USCCB), which is a grantee of HHS (*Marouf v. Azar*, 2018). Catholic Charities denied the application based on "religious beliefs regarding same-sex marriage and raising a child within a traditional family structure" (*Marouf v. Azar*, 2018, p. 2). The couple was denied based on same-sex marriage and that their family structure did not "mirror the holy family" (*Marouf v. Azar*, 2019, p. 6). At the time, Catholic Charities was the only provider of the HHS service in the Fort Worth, Texas area; there was no alternative organization for the couple to apply to foster refugee children. In February 2017, the couple filed a complaint with HHS, Office of Refugee Resettlement (ORR), reporting Catholic Charities for discrimination based on same-sex marital status and, in May 2017, provided the name of the staff person at Catholic Charities. In February 2018, the married couple, Marouf and Esplin, filed a lawsuit against HHS, alleging the agency unconstitutionally awarded grant money to an organization it knew would discriminate against same-sex couples. The plaintiffs assert HHS is violating the Establishment Clause, the Equal Protection Clause, and the deprivation of substantive rights under the Due Process of the U.S. Constitution. The USCCB argues that HHS knew the organization's religious beliefs and stated in both grant applications that federal dollars would be used in accordance with the organization's religious beliefs. Specifically, the USCCB states it "must ensure that services provided under this application are not contrary to the authentic teachings of the Catholic Church, its moral convictions, or religious beliefs" (*Marouf v. Azar*, 6/12/2019, p. 4). The USCCB receives federal funding through the Administration for Children and Families, ORR, which operates the Unaccompanied Refugee Minor Program and the Unaccompanied Alien Child Program. These programs are authorized through two Congressional laws, the William Wilberforce Trafficking Victims Protection Reauthorization Act of 2008 (Pub. L. 110–457) and the Refugee Act of 1980 (Pub. L. 96–212). In June 2019, the court dismissed, in part, and granted, in part, HHS's claim regarding the plaintiffs' standing to bring suit. Citing *Hein v. Freedom from Religion Foundation* (2007), the court dismissed the National LGBT Bar Association for lack of standing to sue under Article III. There are three criteria under Article III, "[a] plaintiff must allege personal injury fairly traceable to the defendant's allegedly unlawful conduct and likely to be redressed by the requested relief" (*Allen v. Wright*, 1984, p. 6; as cited in *Hein v. Freedom from Religion Foundation*, 2007, p. 2).

However, the court did find that Marouf and Esplin have individual standing to sue based on all three causes of action. Judge Metha, U.S. District Court for the District of Columbia, opined that "[ordering the Federal Defendants to develop a system that removes barriers to same-sex couples becoming foster parents and evaluates their eligibility by the same criteria as any heterosexual couple or person will make Plaintiffs whole" (*Marouf v. Azar*, 2019, p. 22) "No speculative inferences are necessary here to conclude that the relief expressed will result in the Plaintiffs receiving dignity and equal treatment they seek" (*Dumont v. Lyon*, 2018, p. 725; as cited in *Marouf v. Azar*, 2019, p. 22). A similar case was filed in South Carolina in which a same-sex married couple was denied a foster parent license based on faith and sexual orientation. This case is described at the beginning of the chapter (*Rogers v. U.S. DHHS*, 2019). Both of these cases are pending.

The preceding cases highlight the legal debate between equal protection and religious objections.

International Adoption

In addition to domestic adoptions through the U.S. foster care and adoption system, International adoption is another pathway to creating a family. According to the most recent report on intercountry adoptions, Americans adopted 4,059 children from 88 countries this past federal fiscal year (U.S. State Department, March 2019). Although it is not possible to know the number of same-sex couples who adopt internationally, there are no U.S. federal laws prohibiting LGBTQ citizens from adopting from a foreign country. The requirements for international adoptions, also known as intercountry adoptions, vary by country. Some countries allow same-sex couples to adopt while other countries do not. For example, China, which is the country where the majority of Americans adopt children, does not allow adoptions by LGBTQ individuals or couples. According to the U.S. State Department website, as of August 2019, Brazil and Mexico City, Mexico, allow LGBT couples to adopt. The Philippines does not recognize same-sex marriage but does not explicitly forbid LGBTQ individuals from applying.

The U.S. State Department, Bureau of Consular Affairs regulates intercountry adoption as set out by the Hague Convention of 1993 on Protection of Children and Cooperation in Respect to Intercountry Adoption (Treaty Doc 105–51, March 31, 1994). The purpose of the treaty is to provide safeguards against child trafficking and to ensure that the best interests of children are served during the adoption process. In regards to adoptive parents, the Hague Treaty requires that the receiving state

> have determined that the prospective adoptive parents are eligible and suited to adopt;
> have ensured that the prospective adoptive parents have been counseled as may be

necessary, and have determined that the child is or will be authorized to enter and reside permanently in that State.

(Chapter II, Article 5)

Except for these requirements, the Hague Convention of 1993 does not address sexual orientation or gender identity of prospective adoptive parents. The U.S. State Department does not place additional requirements on LGBTQ parents.

Intercountry adoption can be an expensive, lengthy process requiring voluminous paperwork, documentation, and apostilles. Typically, international adoptions take longer to finalize than domestic adoptions. Each country has a set of criteria for prospective adoptive parents, which is covered in a home study. Typically, this includes age, criminal background, education, health, mental health, income, marriage/divorce limits, sexual orientation, and residency (time in the adoption country). China also sets a body mass index requirement. Another aspect of intercountry adoption is citizenship. All U.S. families must submit documents to secure their child's U.S. citizenship as required by the Citizen Act of 2000 (Pub. L. 106–395). Intercountry adopted children are automatically granted citizenship by law if they meet the following requirements: (1) they are under age 18, (2) one parent is a U.S. citizen, (3) the child is a permanent resident, (4) the child is in legal and physical custody of a U.S. citizen parent, and (5) the child meets the definition of adoptive child under immigration law (U.S. Department of Justice, Immigration and Naturalization Service, n.d.). If these criteria are met, then the child does not need to apply for citizenship. All adopted children must comport with the citizenship process, regardless of the parent's sexual orientation. International adoption is a lengthy process but a viable option for LGBTQ singles and couples. No additional requirements are made of LGBTQ people unless required by the child's country of origin.

ART

For LGBT parents to establish a legal relationship with their child, which is required for insurance, medical appointments, day care, and school verification, a birth certificate is required. Each state requires a birth certificate for every live birth. Birth certificates are issued by departments of vital statistics in each state. What is automatic for opposite-sex couples who deliver a baby (or babies) can be legally problematic for same-sex married couples. Legal complications occur at both the federal and state levels. Some states do not allow same-sex married couples to be listed on birth certificates, which nullifies the legal parent–child relationship. This issue comes up for same-sex couples who use sperm donors or other forms of ART. Examples of legal cases illustrating this issue are provided next.

Roe v. Patton *(2015)*

This case involves ART and birth certificates. A married same-sex couple, Kami and Angie Roe, a lesbian couple, decided to have a baby using assisted reproduction. Kami conceived using an anonymous donor sperm and delivered a baby girl. The couple wanted both of their names on their daughter's birth certificate. The Utah Office of Vital Records and Statistics refused to recognize her partner, Angie Roe, as the co-parent of their daughter, Lucy. Under the Utah assisted reproduction statute, only males are recognized as nonbiological parents. Specifically, it states, "[i]f a husband provides sperm for, or consents to, assisted reproduction by his wife . . . he is the father of a resulting child born to his wife" (Code Annotated Section 78B-15–701). Because the law does not address same-sex couples (two women), the state does not recognize a second female as a parent.

In April 2015, Kami Roe filed a lawsuit in Utah federal court because under Utah's assisted reproduction statute, only the husband of a women who donated sperm is automatically recognized as a parent. The couple filed a lawsuit alleging violation of the equal protection clause under the Fourteenth Amendment (*Roe v. Patton*, April 2015). "Equal protection requires that same-sex spouses and their children be afforded the same protections [as different sex spouses]" (*Roe v. Patton*, April 2015, p. 2). Angie has parented Lucy since her birth and has an emotional bond with her daughter but is not recognized by Vital Records.

In July 2015, a federal judge ordered the State of Utah, Office of Vital Records and Statistics to recognize Angie Roe as a legal parent and all same-sex couples as legal parents of their children. The Utah assisted reproduction statue must apply equally to same-sex couples as it does to opposite-sex couples since there is no stated governmental interest. The judge stated that

> the court need not decide whether the statutes classify based on sex or sexual orientation and need not decide the applicable level of scrutiny for an Equal Protection analysis because Defendants have not offered a rational basis for the different treatment of male and female spouses of women who give birth through assisted reproduction involving the use of donor sperm.
>
> (*Roe v. Patton*, July 2015)

Pavan v. Smith *(2017)*

This case is similar to *Roe v. Patton* (2015) and addresses the right of same-sex married couples who use ART to conceive to be listed on their child's birth certificates as parents. In 2015, two same-sex married couples conceived using anonymous sperm donors and delivered babies in Arkansas: (1) Leigh and Jana Jacobs, who were married in Iowa in 2010, and (2) Terrah and Marissa Pavan, who were married in New Hampshire in 2011. The two couples completed the required birth certificate paperwork, listing both parents on the birth certificate. The Arkansas State Department of Health denied the request because state law only requires listing the birth mother on the birth certificate. It states, "For the purposes of birth registration the mother is deemed to be the woman who gives birth" (Ark. Code 20–18–401e). "If the mother was married at the time of either conception or birth . . . the name of husband shall be entered on the certificate as the father of the child" (Section 2–18–401 (f)(1)). Regarding artificial insemination, state statute dictates "any child born to a married woman by means of artificial insemination shall be deemed the legitimate natural child of the woman and the woman's husband if the husband consents in writing to the artificial insemination" (Arkansas Code Section 9–10–201(a)(2015). The two couples filed a lawsuit against the Arkansas State Department of Health alleging the birth certificate law violates the U.S. Constitution. The trial court agreed, stating that portions of the Arkansas code are inconsistent with *Obergefell v. Hodges* (2015) and "categorically prohibit every same-sex married couple . . . from enjoying the same spousal benefits which are available to every opposite-sex married couple" (App. to Pet for Cert. 59a' as cited in *Pavan v. Smith*, 2017). In a split decision, the Arkansas State Supreme Court reversed the trial court decision. The plaintiffs appealed and were granted certiorari.

In 2017, the U.S. Supreme Court ruled 6–3 it is unconstitutional for state law to preclude same-sex married couples from being listed as the two parents on the birth certificate (*Pavan v. Smith*, 2017). Chief Justice Roberts and Justices Kennedy, Breyer, Ginsburg, Kagan, and Sotomayor comprised the majority opinion. The per curiam opinion stated that it violated the constitution because "differential treatment infringes *Obergefell's* commitment to provide same-sex couples "the constellation of benefits that the States have linked to marriage" (*Obergefell v. Hodges*, 2015, slip op, at 17). "Same sex parents in Arkansas lack the same rights as opposite-sex parents to be listed on a child's birth certificate, a document often used for important transactions such like making medical decisions and or enrolling a child for school" (*Pavan v. Smith*, 2017, p. 3). The Arkansas State Supreme Court's judgment was reversed. Justices Thomas, Alito, and Gorsuch dissented. In his dissenting opinion, Justice Gorsuch wrote that

> nothing in *Obergefell* spoke (let alone clearly) to the question whether Section 20–18–401 of the Arkansas code, or a state supreme court decision upholding it, must go. The statute in question establishes a set of rules designed to ensure that the biological parents of a child are listed on the child's birth certificate.
>
> (*Pavan v. Smith*, 2017, p. 1)

The U.S. Supreme Court's ruling is a victory for LGBTQ parents who utilize insemination to conceive children, and it is a legal victory for their children. What remains uncertain is whether the same logic will be applied to LGBTQ parents who adopt children (instead of using ART). Will the federal courts require both same-sex parent's names be listed on the birth certificates?

Strickland v. Day *(2018)*

This case addresses ART and child custody rights. Christina and Kimberly Strickland got married in 2009 and decided to use ART. Kimberly served as the gestational mother and delivered the baby in Mississippi. The couple had used an anonymous sperm donor and chose to list only the biological parent on the birth certificate due to Mississippi's adoption ban (same-sex parents were not allowed to adopt). However, when the couple separated and divorced the nonbiological parent was denied parenting rights by the Rankin County Chancery Court. The judge in the divorce ruling found the anonymous sperm donor had parental rights but not Christina Strickland, the nongestational parent, did not. Christina appealed the lower court's decision. The Mississippi State Supreme Court ruled that a nonbiological lesbian parent has the same rights as an opposite-sex married couple with regard to child custody and reproductive technology. The court granted Christina Strickland parental rights and ordered her name on the child's birth certificate as a parent. With her name on the birth certificate as an identified parent, Christina could legally enter the child custody hearing to determine visiting rights with her child (*Strickland v. Day*, 2018).

International Surrogacy and Birthright Citizenship

There are at least four legal cases filed under the birthright citizenship clause of the Immigration and Nationality Act (INA). Under section 301c of the act, children born abroad by parents who are U.S. citizens and have lived in the U.S. prior to the child's birth are automatically U.S. citizens. Specifically, birthright citizenship is granted to

> a person born outside of the United States and its outlying possessions of parents both of whom are citizens of the United States and one of whom has had residence in the United States or one of its outlying possessions, prior to the birth of such person.
>
> (8 U.S.C. Section 1401(c); as cited in *Mize v. Pompeo*, 2019, pp. 6–7)

A biological relationship between the child and both parents is not required under the INA, Section 301. Two of the cases are described next.

Kiviti v. Pompeo *(2019)*

In *Kiviti v. Pompeo* (2019), a gay couple's daughter, Kessem Kiviti, who was conceived using surrogacy in Canada was denied citizenship under the INA (8 U.S.C. Section 1409). The gay couple, Roee and Adiel Kiviti, married in California in 2013. Having used surrogacy to conceive, only Adiel has a biological connection to their daughter. The U.S. State Department does not recognize Roee, the second parent, as a parent because there is no biological connection to the child. Roee and Adiel Kiviti argue the U.S. State Department is treating them as if they are not legally married despite the *Obergefell v. Hodges* (2015) ruling legalizing same-sex marriage with all the benefits and privileges of marriage, including parenting. The couple that alleges the U.S. State Department ignores their legal marriage and misclassifies their daughter, Kessem, as if she was "born out of wedlock," which carries a more stringent residency requirement for the biological parent. Adiel has not lived in the U.S. the past five years, creating a residency requirement. The couple filed a lawsuit against the U.S. State Department alleging their rights are being violated under the (1) INA, (2) due process clause of the Fifth Amendment, (3) equal protection under the due process clause of the Fifth Amendment, and (4) Administrative Procedure Act (APA) (5 U.S.C. Sections 702, 704, 706 and 8 U.S.C. Section 706); action that is arbitrary and capricious. On June 17, 2020, a U.S. district court, the District Court of Maryland, ruled in favor of the plaintiffs, stating their daughter, KRK, is a U.S. citizen by birth and the State Department must issue a passport to KRK. The U.S. State Department's motion to dismiss was granted, in part, dismissing the APA claim, and other three claims were denied. This is a major victory for same-sex married couples utilizing surrogacy to create their families. The *Kiviti* ruling was issued a couple days after the U.S. Supreme Court ruling *Bostock v. Clayton County* (2020), stating that sexual orientation and gender identity were actionable under sex in Title VII of the Civil Rights Law of 1964. The U.S. State Department appealed the ruling in the Fourth Circuit in August 2020 (*Kiviti v. Pompeo*, 2020; Hansler, 2020). A decision has not been issued as of the publication of this book.

Mize v. Pompeo *(2019)*

A similar case was filed in Atlanta, Georgia by a same-sex couple, Derek Mize and Jonathan Gregg, who are both U.S. Citizens (*Mize v. Pompeo*, 2019). Mize and Gregg married in New York in 2015. Their daughter, Simone, was conceived using surrogacy in England, and both fathers are listed on her birth certificate as parents. The U.S. State Department does not recognize their daughter Simone as a U.S. citizen under the INA, stating that the biological father does not meet the five-year residency requirement. The couple filed a lawsuit against the U.S. State Department alleging their rights are being violated under the (1) INA, (2) due process clause of the Fifth Amendment, (3) equal protection under the due process clause of the Fifth Amendment, and (4) the Administrative Procedure Act (5 U.S.C. Sections 702, 704, 706 and 8 U.S.C. Section 706). The case is pending.

In total, there are at least four lawsuits filed by LGBTQ families against the U.S. State Department (Hansler, J., 2020; Immigration Equality). Two of the four cases were described earlier and serve as examples of the legal issues same-sex married couples endure in creating families utilizing international surrogacy. The other two cases include *Blixt v. Tillerson* (2018) and *Dvash-Banks v. Pompeo* (2018). Both are pending. *Dvash-Banks v. Pompeo* (2019, 2018) has been appealed and is pending in the U.S. Court of Appeals, Ninth Circuit.

Summary of Foster Care and Adoption Legal Cases

In sum, there have been numerous lawsuits filed on behalf of same-sex married couples attempting to become foster parents and adoptive parents through the U.S. child welfare system and through ART, both domestic and international surrogacy. Court decisions are pending. At the publication of this book, the U.S. Supreme Court has ruled that states must acknowledge adoptions by same-sex parents from other states (*V.L. v. E.L.* 2016), the state vital statistic department must list both parents names on the baby's birth certificate for same-sex married couples who use ART (*Pavan v. Smith*, 2017; *Strickland v. Day*, 2018; Utah case *Roe v. Patton*, 2015; *Roe and Voe v. Patton*, 2019). It is unclear whether religious contractors can discriminate against same-sex couples based on religious beliefs (*Fulton v. City of Philadelphia*, 2018a, 2018b; *Rogers v. U.S. HHHS & Miracle Hill*, 2019) and against straight opposite-sex married Catholic and Jewish couples (*Rogers. V. U.S. HHS*, 2019). These cases are pending and will be determined by the courts. In addition, the recent U.S. Supreme Court ruling in *Bostock v. Clayton County* (2020), which extends employment protections to gays and transgenders under Title VII, may heavily influence these cases. The U.S. Supreme Court is scheduled to rule on the *Fulton v. City of Philadelphia* (2018b) case in the 2020 term, one year after the *Bostock v. Clayton County* (2020) ruling. Table 3.1 lists the legal cases identified and discussed in this chapter.

Successful Surrogacy

The cases described earlier demonstrate the legal hurdles and battles that LGBTQ couples face when using ART. However, there are also successful cases, albeit of rich and famous people. In 2020, CNN anchor Anderson Cooper, who is openly gay, became a father through surrogacy (Stelter, May 1, 2020). Anderson Cooper and his baby, Wyatt, are featured on the cover of *People* magazine (June 20, 2020), which has a viewership of over 46 million people. The edition focuses on LGBTQ Pride Month, includes the story of Anderson Cooper, and provides pictures of his new son and a picture of him and his mother and American icon, the late Gloria Vanderbilt. In addition, there are stories on Caitlyn Jenner, the most well-known transgender woman in the world, CNN anchor Don Lemmon, who is openly gay, and numerous other LGBTQ people. In 2019, Bravo television host Andy Cohen, who is openly gay, announced the birth of his son, who was conceived through surrogacy. Cohen and his baby boy were on the cover of *People* magazine (February 25, 2019), signaling acceptance of gay parenting in mainstream America. In addition, singer-songwriter Elton John and his partner have two children through surrogacy. These are examples of openly gay men of fame and fortune who have successfully created families through surrogacy. Because surrogacy is expensive it limits the number of people who can access the service. The cost ranges from $100,000 to $200,000 and up. Clearly, it is more difficult for average LGBTQ people without the financial means to pursue surrogacy. However, when celebrities like Anderson Cooper and Don Lemmon openly share their stories with the media, they help pave the way for increased acceptance of LGBTQ parents, making LGBTQ adoption more mainstream and acceptable in American society.

Conclusion

The landmark *Obergefell v. Hodges* (2015) ruling, which legalized same-sex marriage shifted the debate from marriage equality to LGBTQ adoption and parenting rights. LGBTQ couples face

Table 3.1 Foster Care and Adoption Legal Cases

Case Name	Type	Status
V.L. v. E.L. (2016)	Alabama refused to acknowledge adoption by a lesbian couple from Georgia	U.S. Supreme Court ruled 9–0, violation of full faith & credit clause, reversed Alabama Supreme Court ruling
Pavan v. Smith (2017)	Birth certificate for same-sex married couples using assisted reproductive technology (ART)	U.S. Supreme Court ruled 6–3 state must type both parents' names on birth certificate
Fulton v. City of Philadelphia (2020)	Catholic Social Services refuses to serve a gay couple in foster care and adoption	Third Circuit, writ of certiorari filed July 2019, granted by US Supreme Court February 2020.
Rogers v. U.S. HHHS & Miracle Hill (2019)	Foster Parent. Religious agency refuses services based on sexual orientation. Also refuses service to straight Catholic and Jewish couples	Pending in District Court of South Carolina
Marouf v. Azar (2018)	Catholic Charities refuses to serve lesbian couple to foster unaccompanied refugee children	U.S. District Court of D.C., pending.
Roe v. Patton (2015)	Birth certificate for surrogate parents	Federal Utah Court ruled state must acknowledge both surrogate parents on baby's birth certificate. ART statute must apply equally to same-sex married couples.
Strickland v. Day (2018)	ART, child custody rights of nongestational mother	Alabama court ruled nongestational mother's name on birth certificate and granted custody rights
Kiviti v. Pompeo (2020)	International surrogacy by a gay married couple, misclassifies baby as "out of wedlock"	U.S. District Court of Maryland ruled baby is a U.S. citizen by birth
Mize v. Pompeo (2019)	International surrogacy by a gay married couple, misclassifies baby as "out of wedlock"	Case is pending

discrimination when fostering, adopting, and accessing ART. They are denied access to federal foster parenting and adoption programs based on sexual orientation and gender identity. Immediately after the *Obergefell* ruling, roughly 10 state legislatures passed bans on lesbian and gay foster parents and adoption, and an equal number of states passed legislation banning the discrimination of same-sex couples from fostering and adopting reflecting the cultural and political divide in the country. As it stands now, all states must recognize adoptions by other states of same-sex married couples under the full faith and credit clause of the U.S. Constitution (*V.L. v. E.L.*, 2016). Regarding fostering and adopting, the current legal debate is between securing equal protection for LGBTQ people and the religious freedom of government contractors. The ethical issue and moral imperative are ensuring the best interest of children in foster care. Federal laws were created to find permanent homes for children; their needs come first. There are approximately 500,000 children languishing in the U.S. child welfare system waiting to be adopted. Do foster children have to believe in God and attend church to be adopted through a contractor? What if they prefer a secular contractor? What is in the children's best interest? The U.S. child welfare system is based on the philosophy of acting in the best interest of children. Regarding equal treatment, what about opposite-sex couples who are agnostic or atheist? Can they adopt from a religious organization? Will religious objections be applied equally to opposite-sex married couples? What about singles? Can single straight people and single LGBTQ people adopt or only married couples? These legal questions are important and will be determined by the courts.

Resources

AdoptUSKids. www.adoptuskids.org/
American Civil Liberties Union (ACLU). www.aclu.org
Campaign for Children. www.campaignforchildren.org
Child Welfare League of America. www.cwla.org
Congress.Gov. www.congress.gov
Congressional Coalition on Adoption Institute. www.ccainstitute.org/
Family Equality Council. www.familyequality.org
Federal Policy Manual, Foster Care and Adoption. www.acf.hhs.gov/cwpm/public_html/programs/cb/laws_policies/laws/cwpm/policy.jsp?idFlag=3
Gay, Lesbian, and Straight Education Network (GLSEN). www.glsen.org/
Gay, Lesbian, Bisexual and Transgender (GLBT) National Help Center. www.glbthotline.org/
Human Rights Campaign. www.hrc.org/
Immigration Equality. https://immigrationequality.org/
Lambda Legal. www.lambdlegal.com
National Center for Lesbian Rights. www.nclrights.org
National Center or Transgender Equality (NCTE). www.transequality.org/
National Council for Adoption. www.adoptioncouncil.org/
National LGBTQ Task Force. www.thetaskforce.org/
National Safe Haven Alliance. www.nationalsafehavenalliance.org/
Overby, P. M. (2007). *The transgender myth: Through the gender looking glass*. Mirare.
Parents, Families and Friends of Lesbians and Gays (PFLAG). www.pflag.org/
Social Security Act, Compilation of Titles IV-B and IV-E, and Related sections. www.acf.hhs.gov/cb/resource/compilation-of-social-security-act
Social Security Act, Title IV-B. www.ssa.gov/OP_Home/ssact/title04/0400.htm
Social Security Act, Title IV-E. www.ssa.gov/OP_Home/ssact/title04/0400.htm
State Government Resources. www.childwelfare.gov/organizations/
The Trevor Project. www.thetrevorproject.org/
Trans Youth Equality Foundation (TYEF). www.transyouthequality.org/
Trans Youth Family Allies (TYFA). www.imatyfa.org/
True Colors United https://truecolorsunited.org/
U.S. Department of Health and Human Services, Children's Bureau. www.acf.hhs.gov/cb
U.S Record.
U.S. State Department Bureau of Consular Affairs. https://travel.state.gov/content/travel/en/Intercountry-Adoption.html

References

Abandoned Infants Assistance Act of 1998. (Pub. L. 100–505).
Administrative Procedure Act of 1946. (Pub. L. 79–404).
Adoption Awareness Act of 2000. (Pub. L. 106–279).
Adoption Promotion Act of 2003. (Pub. L. 108–145).
Allen v. Wright, 468 U.S. 737 (1984).
Allison, N. (2020, January 14). In first bill of the year, Tennessee Senate passes legislation allowing adoption agencies to deny gay couples. *Nashville Tennessean*. https://www.tennessean.com/story/news/politics/2020/01/14/tennessee-gay-adoption-senate-passes-bill-allowing-agencies-discriminate/4465719002/
Arkansas Code Section 9–10–201(a), 2015.c.
Baker v. General Motors Corp., 522 US 222 (1998).
Bilchik, S. (2006). *Too high a price: The case against restricting lesbian and gay parenting*. Forward (pp. v–vii). American Civil Liberties Union. ACLUA. Lesbian, gay, bisexual, transgender project. ACLU Foundation.
Blitz v. Tillerson 1:18-cv-00124. (USDC, DC, January 22, 2018).
Bostock v. Clayton County 590 U.S. __ (2020).
Bryant, A. (1977). *The Anita Bryant Story: The survival of our nation's families and the threat of militant homosexuality*. Revell.
Campaign for Southern Equality v. Mississippi Department of Human Services, 3:15cv578-DPJ-FKB, March 31, 2016.
Cantwell v. Connecticut, 310 US 296, 303 (1940).
Catholic Charities of the Diocese of Springfield v. Madigan, 11-MR-254, 7th Judicial District Sangamon County, IL (2011).
Child Abuse and Prevention and Treatment Act of 1974. (Pub. L. 93–247).
Child Abuse and Prevention Treatment Amendments. (Pub. L. 104–235).
Child Abuse Prevention and Enforcement Act of 2000. (Pub. L. 106–177).
Child and Family Services Improvement Act of 2011. (Pub. L. 112–134).
Child and Family Services Improvement Act of 2006. (Pub. L. 109–288).
Child Citizen Act of 2000. (Pub. L. 106–395).
Citizen Act of 2000. (Pub. L. 106–395).
Cooper, L., & Cates, P. (2006). *Too high a price: The case against restricting gay parenting* (2nd ed.). American Civil Liberties Union.
Dumont v. Gordon (formerly Lyon). No. 2:17-CV-13080-PDB-EAS (MI, 2017).
Dumont v. Gordon, 2019, Settlement Agreement, No. 2:17-CV-13080-PDB-EAS (MI, March 2019).
Dumont v. Gordon, 341 F. Supp. 3d 722–26) (MI, 2019).
Dumont v. Lyon, 341F. Supp. 3d 706 (E. D. Mich. 2018).
Dvash-Banks v. Pompeo, 2:18-cv-00523-JFW-JC (Ninth Circuit, May 6, 2019).
Dvash-Banks v. Tillerson, 2:18-cv-00523 (USDC, DC, January 22, 2018).
Economic Growth and Tax Relief Reconciliation Act of 2001 (Pub. L. 107–84).
Employment Div. v. Smith, 494 U.S. 872, 879 (1990).
Fair Access Foster Care Act of 2005. (Pub. L. 109–113).
Family First Prevention Services Act of 2018 (Pub. L. 115–123).
Foster Care Independence Act of 1999. (Pub. L. 106–199).
Fostering Connections to Success Act of 2008. (Pub. L. 110–351).
Fraternal Order of Police Newark Lodge No. 12 v. City of Newark, 170 F.3d 359, 364 (3d. Cir. 1999).
Fulton v. City of Philadelphia, No. 19-123 (amicus brief filed, U.S. Supreme Court, Writ of Certiorari granted, August 19, 2020)
Fulton v. City of Philadelphia, No. 18–2574 (3d Cir. 2019).
Fulton v. City of Philadelphia, 2:18-cv-02075. (E.D. Pa. 2018a).
Fulton v. City of Philadelphia, 320 F. Supp. 3d. 661 (E.D. Pa. 2018b).
Gallup. (n.d.). *Gay and lesbian rights. Gallup historical trends report*. https://news.gallup.com/poll/1651/gay-lesbian-rights.aspx

Hague Convention of 29 May 1993 on Protection of Children and Cooperation in Respect to Intercountry Adoption. Multilateral (08–401) Treaty Doc 105–51, 105th Congress, 2d session. Convention by the United States of America and Other Governments. Multilateral Agreement. Signed by the U.S. March 31, 1994. www.state.gov/wp-content/uploads/2019/02/08-401-Multilateral-Consul-Intercount-Adoption.pdf

Hansler, J. (2020, June 19). Judge orders State Department to issue passport to daughter of married same-sex couple. *CNN*. www.cnn.com/2020/06/19/politics/kiviti-same-sex-couple-passport-ruling/index.html

Heart of Atlanta Motel v. United States, 379 U.S. 241 (1964).

Hein v. Freedom from Religion Foundation, Inc, 551 U.S. 587 (2007).

Hope for Children Act. (Pub. L. 107–116).

Immigration and Nationality Act. (8 U.S.C. §1409).

Inequality Cornell University. (2017). *The public policy research portal. What does the scholarly research say about the well-being of children with gay or lesbian parents?* https://whatweknow.inequality.cornell.edu/topics/lgbt-equality/what-does-the-scholarly-research-say-about-the-wellbeing-of-children-with-gay-or-lesbian-parents/

Intercountry Adoption Act of 2000. (Pub. L. 106–279).

Interethnic Adoption Provisions of the Small Business Job Protection Act of 1996. (Pub. L. 104–188).

Keeping Children and Families Safe Act of 2003. (Pub. L. 108–136).

Kettl, Donald F. (2020). *The divided states of America: Why federalism doesn't work*. Princeton University Press.

Kiviti v. Pompeo, 8:19-cv-02665-TDC (Fourth Circuit 2020).

Kiviti v. Pompeo, No. 19–2665 (USDC, DC, District of Maryland, September 19, 2019).

Lawrence v. Texas 539 U.S. 558 (2003).

Lighthouse Inst. For Evangelism, Inc., 510 F.3d at 278 (2007).

Marouf v. Azar, 18-cv-00378 (APM) (USDC DC, 2018).

Marouf v. Azar, 391 F. Supp. 3d 23 (USDC, DC, 2019).

Mississippi, Code 93–17–3(5).

Mize v. Pompeo. (1:19-cv-03331-MLB). (N.D. GA 2019).

Multi-Ethnic Placement Act of 1994 (MEPA) (Pub. L. 103–382).

Obergefell v. Hodges, 576 U.S. 644 (2015).

Overby, P. M. (2007). *The transgender myth: Through the gender looking glass*. Mirare.

Pavan v. Smith, 582 U.S. (2017).

People Magazine. (2020, June 22). People: The pride issue.

People Magazine. (2019, February 25). Andy Cohen.

Preventing Sex Trafficking and Strengthening Families Act of 2014. (Pub. L. 113–183).

Promoting Safe and Stable Families Amendments of 2001. (Pub. L. 107–133).

Refugee Act of 1980. (Pub. L. 96–212).

Religious Freedom Restoration Act of 1993 (Pub. L. 103–141, Section 2; 42 U.S.C. 2000bb). www.govinfo.gov/content/pkg/STATUTE-107/pdf/STATUTE-107-Pg1488.pdf

Roe v. Patton, 2:15-cv-00253-DB (D. Utah, April 13, 2015).

Roe v. Patton, 2:15-cv-00253-DB (D. Utah, July 13, 2015).

Roe & Voe v. Esper, No. 19–1410. (USDC, ED, VA, Alexandria Division. February 15, 2019).

Rogers & Welch v. U.S. Department of Health and Human Services. 6:19-cv-01567-TMC (USDC, Greenville, SC, May 30, 2019).

Social Security Act of 1935. Title IV-B & Title IV-E. (Pub. L. 74–271; 45 CFR Part 1357; USC §§ 671–679b).

Stelter, B. (2020, May 1). "Anderson Cooper announces the birth of his son: Wyatt: Our family continues. *CNN*. www.cnn.com/2020/04/30/media/anderson-cooper-father/index.html

Strickland v. Day, 239 So. 3d 486 (MS Supr. 2018).

Substance Use Disorder Prevention that Promotes Opioid Recovery and Treatment for Patients and Communities Act. (Pub. L. 115–271).

U.S. Department of Health and Human Services, Administration for Children and Families, Administration on Children, Youth and Families, Children's Bureau. (2018). *The adoption and foster care analysis and reporting system (AFCARS) FY 2017 data*. FCARS Report. As of August 10, 2018 – No. 25. Retrieved August 2, 2019, from www.acf.hhs.gov/sites/default/files/cb/afcarsreport25.pdf

U.S. State Department, Bureau of Consular Affairs. (n.d.). *Fact sheet: The child citizenship act of 2000.*
U.S. State Department, Bureau of Consular Affairs. (2019, March). *FY 2018 annual report on intercountry adoption.*
U.S. v. Windsor, 570 U.S. 744 (2013).
Uniform Adoption Act of 1992 (Pub. L. 115–119 – RAISE Family Caregivers Act).
Victims of Child Abuse Re-authorization Act of 2019. (Pub. L. 115–424).
V.L. v. E.L., 577 U.S. __2016).
William Wilberforce Trafficking Victims Protection Reauthorization Act of 2008. (Pub. L. 110–457).
Williams Institute. (2018, July 31). *UCLA School of Law. Same-sex parenting in the U.S.* https://williamsinstutie.law.ucla.edu/press/press-releases/same-sex-parenting/

Chapter 4

LGBTQ Employment Protections

Introduction

Keith Wildhaber, who is gay, was a police sergeant for St. Louis, Missouri. In 2014, he applied for a promotion as a police lieutenant and was informally advised the department had a problem with his sexuality. Specifically, he was told if he wanted a promotion he needed to "tone down his gayness." Wildhaber did not get the promotion and in April 2016 filed a complaint with the U.S. Equal Employment Opportunity Commission (EEOC) and the Missouri Commission on Human Rights alleging violation of the Missouri Human Rights Act. After he filed the complaint, he was reassigned from a day shift close to his home to a night shift about 30 miles from his home. In 2017, he filed a second complaint alleging his department discriminated against him based on his sexual orientation (not fitting the stereotypical male) and unlawful retaliation for filing the first complaint. Wildhaber reported he was turned down 23 times for promotion in a period of 6 years, despite 15 years of service and strong performance reviews. A jury awarded him $20 million to be paid by the St. Louis County Government. He settled for $10.25 million and was promoted to lieutenant in a new Diversity and Inclusion Unit (Holcombe & Alonso, February 16, 2020; *Wildhaber v. St. Louis County Missouri*, 2019).

The Missouri case described is an example of employment discrimination based on sexual orientation and unlawful retaliation. Employment discrimination is wrong. Any type of discrimination whether it takes place in employment, health care, housing, or credit is wrong and should be stopped. Whether it is illegal depends on the protected class and the jurisdiction in which it takes place. Until the U.S. Supreme Court ruling in *Bostock v. Clayton County* (June 15, 2020), there was no federal policy specifically prohibiting lesbian, gay, bisexual, transgender, and queer (LGBTQ) employment discrimination. Title VII of the Civil Rights Act of 1964 (Pub. L. 88–352) identifies five protected groups, stating it is an unlawful employment practice to discriminate because of "race, color, religion, sex or national origin." However, the words *sexual orientation* and *gender identity* are not specifically stated in Title VII, leaving the word *sex* to interpretation. The Trump administration interprets *sex* to not include sexual orientation and gender identity (Executive Order 13782). In contrast, the EEOC interprets *sex* to include sexual orientation and gender identity as actionable under Title VII (*David Baldwin v. Department of Transportation*, 2015; *Macy v. Department of Justice*, EEOC, 2012). At the state level, half of the states across the country passed legislation making it legal to fire an individual based on sexual orientation and gender identity, and the other half bans employment discrimination based on sexual orientation and gender identity. There are also contradictory rulings in the federal courts. The Second and Seventh Circuits held discrimination based on sexual orientation is prohibited under Title VII (*Zarda v. Altitude Express*, 2018; *Hively v. Ivy Tech. Comm. Coll. of Indiana*, 2017). In contrast, the Eleventh Circuit ruled sexual orientation is not actionable under Title VII (*Evans v. Georgia Regional Hospital*, 2017). These conflicting opinions and legal tensions at the federal and state levels created ripeness for the U.S. Supreme Courts to interpret sex in Title VII. In a surprise 6–3 landmark decision delivered by a conservative majority, the court ruled in *Bostock v. Clayton County* (2020), that sex in Title VII includes sexual orientation and gender identity. It is now illegal to fire an individual for being homosexual or transgender. Writing the majority opinion, a conservative appointee of President Trump, Justice Gorsuch states that "an employer who fires an individual merely for being gay or transgender defies the law" [Title VII of the Civil Rights Act of 1964] (*Bostock v. Clayton County*, 2020). Prior to the U.S. Supreme Court ruling in *Bostock v. Clayton County* (2020), a same-sex couple could get legally married under *Obergefell v. Hodges* (2015) and *U.S. v. Windsor* (2013), inform their employer of their marriage, and then be fired from their job based on sexual orientation. LGBTQ activists referred to it as "married on Sunday, fired on Monday" (Barnes, R. 2019). As a result of the *Bostock* ruling, same-sex couples can share their marriages at work with no adverse outcome. The ruling is a sea change in LGBTQ employment discrimination law and civil rights laws. For the past 50 years, the term *sex* under Title VII only applied to biological sex (women and men), and now it also includes protected traits, sexual orientation, and gender identity. This chapter describes and analyzes the legal development of the monumental *Bostock v. Clayton County* (2020) ruling and its implications on LGBTQ employment, health care, housing, public administration, and social equity. First, human rights are discussed, followed by LGBTQ employment discrimination and public opinion data. Next federal legislation on employment discrimination is reviewed, followed by a discussion of state bans on LGBTQ employment discrimination. Last, an analysis of federal and U.S. Supreme Court cases and their impacts on LGBTQ employment rights and other federal laws that prohibit discrimination based on sex is provided.

UN Human Rights

In 1948, the United Nations (UN) General Assembly passed the Universal Declaration of Human Rights. The purpose was to identify an agreed-on set of fundamental human rights. Article I states that "every person is born free and equal in dignity and rights." Article VII states, "All are equal before the law and are entitled without any discrimination to equal protection of the law." This means that every person, regardless of sexual orientation, gender identity, or other status, should has the same rights. Article 23, which is specific to work, states, "Everyone has the right to work, to free choice of employment, to just and favourable conditions of work and to protection against unemployment. Everyone, without any discrimination, has the right to equal pay for equal work" (United

Nations, 1948). These rights, which were created over 70 years ago, are as applicable then as they are today. No one should be discriminated against at work. According to the International, Lesbian, Gay, Bisexual, Trans, and Intersex Association (2019), 77 (or 44 percent) of UN countries prohibit employment discrimination based on sexual orientation. The U.S., which is a UN member, is not listed as one of these countries. Historically, the U.S. has been a world leader in human rights. The recent U.S. Supreme Court ruling, *Bostock v. Clayton County* (2020), extends federal antidiscrimination laws (Title VII of the Civil Rights Act of 1964) to sexual orientation and gender identity, aligning the U.S. with over 70 countries that support fundamental human rights. The ruling elevates the U.S. as a human rights leader on the world stage.

LGBTQ Employment Discrimination

LGBTQ people are discriminated against in the workplace. Discrimination takes place in the form of not being hired, not getting promoted, being fired, enduring poor working conditions, harassment, and violence. According to the National Center for Transgender Equality (2020), sex-based harassment includes jokes or derogatory statements, intentional use of the wrong pronoun, and invasive questions. A survey report by the Center for American Progress (Singh & Durso, 2017) completed in January 2017 found that 25 percent of LGBT people surveyed reported being discriminated at work based on their sexual orientation or gender identity. Twenty-seven percent of transgender people reported being not hired, fired, or denied a promotion the first year due to gender identity. While 11 to 28 percent of LGB respondents reported their sexual orientation cost them a promotion. Roughly 22 percent of LGBT employees report they were not promoted or not paid the same rate as their colleagues. This is significant because discrimination in the form of reduced earnings can have a lasting impact on an individual's finances. Furthermore, due to fear of discrimination, some LGBT people alter their behavior to reduce the likelihood of being "outed" and discriminated against at work, which can lead to being fired. (For example, see *Bostock v. Clayton County*, 2019). Forty-two percent use vague language when discussing relationships, 36 percent hide a relationship, and 24 percent avoid social situations. According to a report by the Human Rights Campaign, approximately 46 percent of LGBTQ workers do not disclose their sexual orientation at work (Fidas & Cooper, 2019). Regarding harassment, 56 percent of LGBT report hearing jokes about sexual orientation and gender identity (Fidas & Cooper, 2019), and roughly 80 percent of transgender people report harassment or mistreatment on the job (James et al., 2016). Workplace discrimination is a well-documented problem for LGBT people and can have a lasting negative impact on mental health, reduced earnings, job prospects, and careers.

If an individual has been discriminated against based on sexual orientation or gender identity, they can start the legal process by filing a complaint with the EEOC and their state human rights commission. EEOC resources are provided at the end of the chapter.

Public Opinion

There is overwhelming public support for LGBT employment protections. A 1998 survey by the Princeton Survey Research Associates (1998) for *Newsweek* found that 83 percent felt that gays and lesbians should have equal rights in obtaining jobs (Newsweek, 1998). A more recent poll completed by Public Religion Research Institute found that 69 percent of Americans support nondiscrimination policies under federal law for LGBT (Fitzsimmons, 2019). What is stunning is that more Americans support nondiscrimination policies (69 percent) than same-sex marriage (58 percent), yet prior to the *Bostock v. Clayton County* (2020) ruling, no federal employment nondiscrimination acts (ENDAs) were passed by Congress. Regarding religious objections, public opinion is split on whether an employer should be able to refuse to hire an LGBT person based on religious reasons; 45 percent favor and 44 percent do not favor. In general, there is strong support from the American public for LGBT nondiscrimination laws. Many private organizations have already passed internal LGBT inclusive policies. For example, over 90 percent of Fortune 500 companies prohibit work discrimination based on sexual orientation and 83 percent have nondiscrimination policies that include gender identity (Human Rights Campaign, n.d.).

Public opinion is important. "Public acceptance is the sine qua non in the creation of formal and informal protections for gays and lesbians. When society is more accepting, gays, lesbians, and bisexuals feel more comfortable being themselves, and when the public demands gay rights laws, government enacts them" (as cited in Riccucci, 2002, p. 135; see also Lewis & Taylor, 2001, 35). However, there is a disconnect between public opinion and federal legislation. Part of the basis for the disconnect is disinformation. In a 2019 poll by Reuters, 45 percent of Americans reported wrongly there is a federal law protecting against discrimination based on sexual orientation, and 31 percent believed there was already a federal law protecting gender identity (Reuters, 2019). This is important because if people believe there is currently a law banning LGBTQ discrimination, it makes it more difficult to get legislation passed. LGBTQ advocates need to counter disinformation campaigns by utilizing public campaigns stating facts.

Federal Legislation

Title VII of the Civil Rights Act of 1964, as amended, is the landmark legislation prohibiting employment discrimination. It grants protections based on race, color, national origin, sex, religion, and disability. The specific language in the law does not include sexual orientation or gender identity. Specifically, the law states:

> It shall be an unlawful employment practice for an employer – (1) to fail or refuse to hire or to discharge any individual, or otherwise to discriminate against any individual with respect to his compensation, terms, conditions, or privileges of employment, because of such individual's race, color, religion, sex, or national origin; or (2) to limit, segregate, or classify his employees or applicants for employment in any way which would deprive or tend to deprive any individual of employment opportunities or otherwise adversely affect his status as an employee, because of such individual's race, color, religion, sex, or national origin.
>
> (Civil Rights Act of 1964 as amended, Section 703e)

Race, color, religion, sex, and national origin are the first five legally protected employment classifications. Title VII applies to employers with 15 or more employees in the private sector, labor organizations, and employment agencies. Title VII was amended in 1972 under the Equal Employment Opportunity Act (Pub. L. 92–261) to cover federal, state, and local government employees and educational institutions. Title VII does not apply to elected officials or political appointees.

Title VII also created the EEOC, which investigates complaints of employment discrimination and instigates litigation on behalf of employees. For the history of the EEOC and its impact on public administration, please see the book *Federal Equal Employment Opportunity: Politics and Public Personnel Administration* (Rosenbloom, 1977). With regard to the impact of Title VII on LGBTQ people, the Obama administration broadened the use of the term *sex* to include sexual orientation as well as gender identity and orientation, but this guidance was eliminated by the Trump administration. Presidential executive orders are covered later in the chapter.

Age, Disability, Genetics, HIV/AIDS, Pregnancy, and Veterans

In addition to the Civil Rights Act of 1964, Congress passed additional laws expanding the list of protected classifications. These include age, disability, pregnancy, veteran status, and genetics. In 1967, Congress passed the Age Discrimination Employment Act (Pub. L. 90–202 and subsequent amendments). It prevents employers from discriminating against workers 40 years of age or older. An individual cannot be fired based on their age in the private sector or public sector (federal, state, and local governments). In, 1973, Congress passed the Vocational Rehabilitation Act, which prohibits federal contractors and the federal government from discriminating against people with disabilities. In 1978, Congress passed the Pregnancy Discrimination Act of 1978 (Pub. L. 95–555), which amends Title VII to prohibit sex discrimination on the basis of pregnancy. The act prevents women from being discriminated against in the workplace for pregnancy, childbirth, or medical conditions related to pregnancy or childbirth. In 1990, Congress passed the American with Disabilities Act (Pub. L. 110–336), which was later amended in 2008 (American Disabilities Amendment Act of 2008). The law prevents employment discrimination based on disability in both the private and public sectors. It applies to employers with 15 or more employees. This policy also includes people with HIV/AIDS, which directly impacts LGBTQ people. According to the U.S. Department of Justice, Office of Civil Rights, an individual has a disability

> if he or she has a physical or mental impairment that substantially limits one or more major life activities, has a record of such impairment, or is regarded as having such impairment. Persons with HIV disease, either symptomatic or asymptomatic, have physical impairments that substantially limit one or more major life activities and thus are protected by the ADA.
>
> (U.S. Department of Justice, n.d.)

Next, in 2008, Congress passed the Genetic Information Nondiscrimination Act of 2008 (Pub. L. 110–233), which makes it illegal to discriminate based on genetic testing. These laws are enforced by the EEOC.

The Civil Service Reform Act of 1978 (Pub. L. 95–454) directly applies to LGBTQ people. The law established the U.S. Office of Personnel Administration, the Merit Systems Protection Board, and the Federal Labor Relations Authority. In addition, it states the federal government is prohibited to "discriminate for or against any employee or applicant for employment on the basis of conduct which does not adversely affect the performance of the employee or applicant or the performance of others" (Chapter 23, section 2302, 10). Historically, the U.S. Office of Personnel Management (2015) has interpreted it to mean it is illegal to discriminate on the basis of sexual orientation. The conduct ban applies to the federal government only, not the private sector. The EEOC, which enforces federal anti-employment discrimination laws, has ruled that discrimination based on sexual orientation (*David Baldwin v. Department of Transportation*, 2015) and gender identity (*Macy v. Department of Justice*, EEOC, 2012) is discrimination based on sex under Title VII of the Civil Rights Act of 1964.

ENDAs

Beginning in 1995, federal ENDAs to protect LGBTQ people were introduced in Congress. Since 2007, there have been at least 13 ENDAs or equality acts introduced in Congress with no success. These include the Employment Non-Discrimination Act of 2007 (H.R. 2015, 110th Congress, 2007), To Prohibit Employment Discrimination Based on Gender Identity (H.R. 3696, 110th Congress 2007), Employment Non-Discrimination Act of 2009 (H.R. 2981, 111th Congress, 2009), Employment Non-Discrimination Act of 2009 (H.R. 3017, 111th Congress, 2009), Employment Non-Discrimination Act of 2009 (S. 1584, 111th Congress, 2009), Employment Non-Discrimination Act of 2011 (H.R. 1397, 112th Congress, 2011), Employment Non-Discrimination Act of 2011 (S. 811, 112th Congress, 2011), Employment Non-Discrimination Act of 2013 (H.R. 1755, 113th Congress, 2013), Employment Non-Discrimination Act of 2013 (S. 815, 113th Congress), Equality Act (H.R. 3185, 114th Congress, 2015), Equality Act (S. 1858, 114th Congress, 2015), Equality Act (H.R. 2282, 115th Congress, 2017), Equality Act (S. 1006, 115th Congress, 2017). (See *R.G. & G.R. Harris Funeral Homes v EEOC*, 2017, p. x.)

As illustrated earlier, despite numerous attempts to pass federal legislation and widespread public support, there was not enough political traction or political will to secure an EDNAs law, making it illegal to discriminate based on sexual orientation or gender identity. This is largely due to the opposition of congressional conservatives who consistently voted against the bills.

Protected Classifications

However, numerous federal laws have been enacted since 1964 to strengthen civil rights and to protect employees from unlawful discrimination. The following classifications are legally protected: age, color, disability, genetics, national origin, pregnancy, race, religion, sex, and veteran status.

A timeline of federal antidiscrimination laws is provided next.

Timeline of Federal Antidiscrimination Employment Laws

In 1935, Congress passed the National Labor Relations Act (Pub. L. 74–198), which gives private-sector employees the right to organize into unions, use collective bargaining, and strike.

In 1938, Congress passed the Fair Labors Standard Act. It sets minimum wage, overtime, record keeping for full-time and part-time employees, and child labor standards. It applies to federal, state, and local governments as well as the private sector.

In 1963, Congress passed the Equal Pay Act (Pub. L. 88–38), which requires employers to pay equal pay for equal work regardless of sex. This means women and men should earn equal pay for comparable work.

In 1964, the Civil Rights Act was passed (Pub. L. 88–352, 78 Stat. 241). Title VII of the law guarantees employment without regard for religion, race, color, sex, and national origin. It also created the EEOC, which oversees employment discrimination complaints.

In 1967, Congress passed the Age Discrimination in Employment Act (Pub. L. 90–202). It prohibits discrimination against individuals 40 years of age in the private sector.

In 1972, Congress passed the Equal Employment Opportunity Act (Pub. L. 92–261). It amends Title VII of the Civil Rights Act of 1964 by extending Title VII protections to include federal, state, and local government employees, and in the private sector, it extends to companies with 15 or more employees. In addition, it requires employers to make reasonable accommodations for employee religious practices.

In 1973, Congress passed the Vocational Rehabilitation Act of 1973 (Pub. L. 114–95). It protects people with disabilities from discrimination by the federal government and by federal contractors. Federal contractors with contracts of $10,000 or more must use affirmative action to hire people with disabilities. It prohibits discrimination of people with disabilities in any federal activity or program. Numerous amendments have been made over the years to strengthen disability protections. It is now referred to as the Rehabilitation Act of 1973.

In 1974, Congress passed the Age Discrimination Act (42 U.S.C. Sections 6101–6107). It prohibits employment discrimination by age (40 years and older) in federal, state, and local government and for any organization receiving federal financial assistance. See 29 U.S.C.A. § 623 et seq. for subsequent amendments.

In 1973, Congress passed the Vietnam Era Veterans' Adjustment Act as amended (38 U.S.C. Section 4212). It prevents the federal government from discriminating against protected veterans.

In 1978, Congress passed the Pregnancy Discrimination Act (Pub. L. 95–555) amends Title VII of the Civil Rights Act of 1964 to prohibit sex discrimination on the basis of pregnancy.

In 1978, Congress passed the Civil Service Reform Act (Pub. L. 95–454). It affirms the merit system and identifies prohibited personnel practices for federal civilian employees.

In 1990, Congress passed the Americans with Disabilities Act of 1990 (Pub. L. 110–336) and amendments). It protects people with disabilities from being discriminated against in all areas including employment.

In 1991, Congress passed the Civil Rights and Women's Equity in Employment Act (Pub. L. 102–166). It increased the penalties for employment discrimination.

In 1993, Congress passed the Family Medical Leave Act (Pub. 103–3). It provides up to 12 weeks unpaid, protected leave per year for people with employers of 50 or more workers.

In 2008, Congress passed the Genetic Information Nondiscrimination Act, which makes it illegal to discriminate based on genetic tests, medical conditions, or disease in employment and health.

In 2009, Congress passed the Lily Ledbetter Fair Pay Act of 2009 (Pub. L. 111–2). It extends the period for filing a complaint for wage discrimination. Each paycheck involving pay discrimination is viewed as a separate violation. It overturned the U.S. Supreme Court ruling in *Ledbetter v. Goodyear Tire & Rubber Co., Inc* (2007).

The federal legislation outlined in this section is critical because it ties employment discrimination to the rule of law. Based on federal statutes, employees have recourse if they are discriminated against. Individuals have recourse with the EEOC and in court if they are discriminated against.

State Bans

Regarding state-level legislation, the country is divided on employment protections based on sexual orientation and gender identity. Prior to the *Bostock v. Clayton County* (2020) ruling, approximately half of the states passed bans on LGBTQ employment discrimination. According to the Movement Advancement Project, as of June 2020, 22 states and 2 U.S. territories prohibit employment

74 ▪ *LGBTQ Employment Protections*

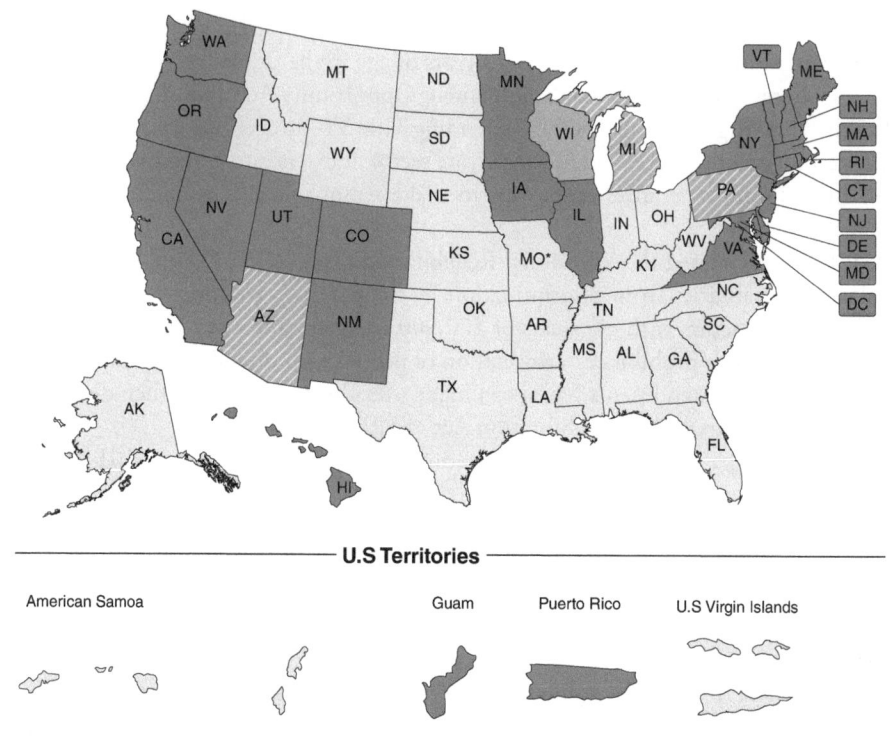

Figure 4.1 U.S. LGBTQ Employment Protections by State

Note: Dark Gray = states that have passed antidiscrimination policies for same sex and gender; light gray = states that have passed antidiscrimination for same-sex people only; gray stripes = states that lack employment protection policies.

discrimination based on sexual orientation and gender identity. These include states mostly on the East and West Coasts, which are typically politically liberal. As illustrated in Figure 4.1, which provides a visual of the political demarcations, they include Washington, Oregon, California, Hawaii, Nevada, Colorado, New Mexico, Minnesota, New York, Pennsylvania, Michigan, Iowa, Illinois, Vermont, New Hampshire, Maine, Massachusetts, Rhode Island, Connecticut, New Jersey, Delaware, Maryland, Virginia, and Washington, D.C. In 2020, the first southern state, Virginia, passed comprehensive LGBTQ protections in employment, housing, credit applications, and public accommodations (Taylor, 2020; VA. Stat. Section 2.2–3904 and Section 36–96.3, as amended by 2020 Va. H.B. 1663 February 27, 2020), creating a path for additional southern states to follow. One state, Wisconsin, prohibits discrimination based only on sexual orientation (not gender identity). States lacking laws prohibiting LGBTQ employment discrimination are located mostly in midwestern and southern states, which are more politically conservative. These include Alaska. Arizona, Texas, Arkansas, Louisiana, Mississippi, Alabaman, Georgia, South Carolina, North Carolina, West Virginia, Ohio, Indians, Kentucky, Tennessee, Missouri, Kansas, Nebraska, South Dakota, North Dakota, Montana, Wyoming, and Idaho. Figure 4.1 illustrates the ideological divide on LGBT employment discrimination and other LGBT issues across the country.

State employment bans, similar to marriage bans, reflect the political divide between LGBTQ rights and religious beliefs. However, with the recent *Bostock v. Clayton County* (2020) ruling, state bans are a moot point.

Executive Orders

In addition to state and federal legislation, presidential executive orders have been issued on employment discrimination and gender identity. Starting in 1965, President Johnson issued Executive Order 11246 which extended Title VII employment protections to government contractors earning $10,000 or more annually (White House, Executive Order 11246). It did not address the sex classification, but it elevated the importance of anti-employment discrimination policy by applying Title VII to government contractors. Executive orders interpreting the sex classification started in the late 1990s. In 1998, President Clinton issued Executive Order 13087, which prohibited discrimination based on sexual orientation in civilian employment (White House, Executive Order 13087). It did not include gender identity. It is significant because it was the first directive by a U.S president protecting sexual orientation as a class. When President Obama took office, he issued several executive orders to expand LGBT discrimination protection in the workplace.

On July 23, 2014, President Obama issued Executive Order 13672, which amended previous executive orders (White House, Executive Order 13672). It added gender identity as a protected class in the civilian workforce (amending Clinton's Executive Order 13087). In addition, Obama prohibited discrimination based on both sexual orientation and gender identity to federal government contractors (amending Johnson's Executive Order 11246). This change in policy is critical because the majority of workers are federal contractors. There are approximately 17 million federal contractors compared to 2 million full-time federal employees (Light, 1999). On December 11, 2014, Obama issued Executive Order 13683 "Fair Pay and Safe Workplaces," which applied Title VII compliance requirements to companies bidding for federal contracts (White House, Executive Order 13683). The executive order was to take effect in 2016; however, a lawsuit delayed implementation of the executive order.

Shortly after President Trump took office, he issued Executive Order 13782, the "Revocation of Federal Contracting Executive Orders" (White House, Executive Order 13782) revoking the compliance requirement of President Obama's 2014 executive order prohibiting federal contractors from employment discrimination based on sexual orientation and gender identity. It revoked Executive Orders 13673 (July 31, 2014), 13683 (section 3, December 11, 2014), and 13738 (August 23, 2016). Obama's "Fair Pay and Safe Workplaces" required companies bidding for federal contracts to prove compliance with federal laws prohibiting discrimination based on sexual orientation and gender identity. Given that the majority of federal government work is completed by contractors the importance of President Trump's executive order cannot be overstated; LGBTQ people have fewer protections under Trump. Executive orders are a powerful tool and can influence the entire executive branch and its contractors. However, as illustrated, a president can revoke a prior president's orders, making the policy short-term. If LGBTQ people are to secure employment rights on a sustainable, long-term basis, employment rights will be granted by the judiciary.

Classifications and Levels of Scrutiny

Equal protection requirements are based on classifications such as race, ethnicity, gender, age and others (Rosenbloom et al., 2019). The courts utilize three levels of scrutiny when determining the constitutionality of a law. The spectrum of scrutiny includes (1) ordinary or rational basis review (least amount of scrutiny), (2) intermediate (moderate scrutiny), and (3) strict scrutiny (the most rigorous scrutiny). Rational basis review is the lowest level of scrutiny. It applies to classifications on age, residency, marital status, and wealth. It requires a governmental interest to be linked to a law.

It asks if there is a rational link between the government's interest, whether it is stated, and the law. The individual challenging the law must prove the government has no interest. The courts typically defer to the government under rational basis review cases.

Intermediate scrutiny is more challenging than rational basis review. It applies to classifications based on gender or sex. The burden of proof is on the government to show the law serves an important governmental objective and is substantially related to achieving that objective. "Classifications based on biological sex are quasi-suspect and face an intermediate test. They must be substantially related to an achievement to important governmental objectives" (Rosenbloom, 2015 p. 45). Whether or not discrimination meets an important objective is determined by the courts. The judiciary is more deferential to it. In *U.S. v. Windsor* (2013) the court found Section 3 of the Defense of Marriage Act unconstitutional and classifications based on sexual orientation require a heightened scrutiny. In *Smithkline Beecham Corporation v. Abbott Laboratories* (2014), an antitrust case involving HIV/AIDS medication, a federal appeals court ruled that as a result of *U.S. v. Windsor* (2013), heightened scrutiny applies to sexual orientation and requires intermediate scrutiny (not rational basis review). As such, "equal protection prohibits peremptory strikes based on sexual orientation" (*Smithkline Beecham Corporation v. Abbott Laboratories*, 2014). As a result of this ruling, attorneys cannot strike jurors from jury service based on sexual orientation.

Strict scrutiny is the highest standard applied by the courts. Classifications based on race and ethnicity receive strict scrutiny due to the equal protection clause. In these cases, the burden of proof is on the government and the judiciary is not deferential. The government must show a compelling governmental interest and that it is narrowly tailored. Precedent was set in *Adarand Constructors v. Pena* (1995). The case involved equal protection violations regarding a federal government contracting policy that used a race classification. To not be liable, the government had to show a compelling governmental interest that was narrowly tailored to the interest with no discriminatory intent (Naylor & Rosenbloom, 2004). Strict scrutiny is also applied to laws involving fundamental rights such as marriage. For example, in *Loving v. Virginia* (1967), the court applied strict scrutiny to a state law banning interracial marriage. In *Obergefell v. Hodges* (2015), the court did not state a level of scrutiny, ruling instead that marriage is a fundamental right and that same-sex couples have a constitutional right to marriage protected under the due process and equal protection clauses of the Fourteenth Amendment. Table 4.1 provides a summary of scrutiny levels by burden of proof, governmental interest, and classification.

Table 4.1 Levels of Judicial Scrutiny by Classification

Level of Scrutiny	Burden of Proof	Governmental Interest	Classifications
Rational Basis Review	Individual	No legitimate interest or rational link	age, disability, wealth, felony status
Intermediate	Government	Important governmental objective & substantially related to the objective	Gender, sex, sexual orientation
Strict	Government	Compelling state interest & narrowly tailored	Race, national origin, fundamental rights

U.S. Supreme Court Cases

Older rulings by the U.S. Supreme Court support LGBTQ discrimination protections. In *Oncale v. Sunflower Offshore Services* (1998), the U.S. Supreme Court ruled 9–0 that same-sex sexual harassment is actionable as sex discrimination under Title VII of the Civil Rights Act of 1964 as amended. In *Romer v. Evans* (1996), the U.S. Supreme Court struck down a Colorado constitutional amendment that invalidated sexual orientation legal protections. The court ruled the amendment violated the equal protection clause because it denied gays the same legal protections that heterosexuals receive. In *Price Waterhouse v. Hopkins* (1989) the court supported the sex stereotyping theory based on gender discrimination. These cases are described next.

Oncale v. Sundowner *(1998)*

Regarding same-sex harassment, the court ruled unanimously in *Oncale v. Sundowner* (1998) that same-sex harassment is actionable under Title VII of the Civil Rights Act of 1964. This case involved Oncale, who was employed as a roustabout by Sundowner on an oil rig in the Gulf of Mexico. Oncale reported he was subjected to sex-related humiliating actions, was physically assaulted, and threated with rape while at work in the middle of the ocean. When he reported the sexual harassment to his supervisor, the supervisor advised that he was also picked on by the same men (as Oncale). Oncale quit his job in fear he would be raped by other men on the oil rig. Oncale filed a complaint against Sundowner in U.S. district court. The court held that a male has no cause of action under Title VII by male co-workers (precedent in *Garcia v. Elf Atochem North America*, 1994). On appeal, the Fifth Circuit held that the *Garcia* ruling was binding. The U.S. Supreme Court ruled unanimously that same-sex harassment in the work place is actionable under Title VII (reversing the Fifth District judgment). Sex protects men as well as women (*Newport News Shipbuilding & Dry Dock Co v. EEOC*, 1983) and race is protected since members of one's own race can discriminate against its own members (*Castaneda v. Partida*, 1977). Justice Scalia, who delivered the court's opinion, stated that "harassing conduct need not be motivated by sexual desire to support an inference of discrimination on the basis of sex." He went on to state that Title VII

> does not reach genuine but innocuous differences in the ways men and women routinely interact with members of the same-sex and of the opposite sex. The prohibition of harassment on the basis of sex requires neither asexuality nor androgyny in the workplace; it forbids only behavior so objectively offensive as to alter conditions of the victim's employment. Conduct that is not severe or pervasive enough to create an objectively hostile or abusive work environment that a reasonable person would find hostile or abusive-is beyond Title VII's purview.
> (*Harris v. Forklift Systems*, 1993 citing *Meritor Savings Bank v. Vinson*, 1986)

Romer v. Evans *(1996)*

In *Romer v. Evans* (1996), the U.S. Supreme Court struck down a Colorado constitutional amendment that invalidated sexual orientation legal protections. The court ruled the amendment violated the Fourteenth Amendment's equal protection clause because in 1992, Colorado voters passed Constitutional Amendment 2 prohibiting all levels of government (state, county, or city) from legally recognizing homosexuals or bisexuals as a protected class. Richard G. Evans, as well as several other individuals and three municipalities, filed a lawsuit. The state trial court entered a permanent injunction. The Colorado State Supreme Court ruled the amendment violated the equal protection clause and, as such, fell under strict scrutiny. Specifically, the amendment prevented gays from participating in the political process; it prevented legislative, executive, or judicial protections. In the majority opinion, U.S. Supreme Court Justice Kennedy wrote that the action did not meet strict scrutiny, nor did it meet the lower requirement of rational basis. The motivation was to harm an unpopular political group, which is not a legitimate governmental interest.

Price Waterhouse v. Hopkins *(1989)*

In *Price Waterhouse v. Hopkins* (1989), the U.S. Supreme Court ruled that employee discrimination based on sex stereotyping is a violation of Title VII. Because sex discrimination is an impermissible motive, which influenced the adverse decision, the employer had to show the same decision would have been made without gender discrimination. This case involved a woman who lost a promotion due to her gender. After five years at Price Waterhouse, an accounting firm, Ann Hopkins was nominated for partnership along with 87 other candidates who were all male: 47 were admitted to partnership, 21 were rejected, and 20, including Hopkins, were held over until next year. Hopkins candidacy was held over despite securing a $25 million contract with the U.S. State Department. Hopkins was advised by a male partner that to improve her chances of partnership she should "walk more femininely, wear make-up, have her hair styled, and wear jewelry" (*Price Waterhouse v. Hopkins*, 1985, 618 F. Supp at 117). The partners later refused to consider her for partnership. Hopkins filed a lawsuit alleging sex discrimination under Title VII. The burden of proof was on Price Waterhouse to show it would have reached the same adverse employment decisions (not promoting Hopkins to partner) if sex discrimination did not occur. The lower courts used the standard of a preponderance of evidence. The U.S. Supreme Court ruled that the standard should have been clear and convincing evidence. A legitimate reason was needed to deny Hopkins partnership. The court ruled in favor of Hopkins.

Federal Case Law

Recent decisions by the U.S. Court of Appeals reflect a divided judiciary on whether sexual orientation is actionable under Title VII of the Civil Rights Act of 1964. The Second and Seventh Circuits hold that sexual orientation is prohibited under Title VII (*Zarda v. Altitude Express*, 2018; *Hively v. Ivy Tech. Comm. Coll. of Indiana*, 2017). In contrast, the 11th Circuit Court ruled sexual orientation is not actionable under Title VII (*Evans v. Georgia Regional Hospital*, 2017). Regarding gender identity, the Sixth Circuit ruled that terminating an employee based on gender transition or transitioning status was sex discrimination under Title VII (*EEOC v. R.G. and G.R. Harris Funeral Homes*, 2018; *Barnes v. City of Cincinnati*, 2005; *Smith v. City of Salem*, 2004). Arguments for three cases were heard on this subject during the U.S. Supreme Court's 2019 term. Two cases focused on sexual orientation under Title VII (*Bostock v. Clayton County* and *Altitude Express v. Zarda*, 2019, No. 17–1618). The third case addresses gender identity under Title VII (*R.G and G.R. Harris Funeral Homes v. EEOC*, 2017). After hearing oral arguments in October 2019 in front of the U.S Supreme Court, the three cases were consolidated into one case, *Bostock v. Clayton County* (2020), to interpret the term *sex* under Title VII of the Civil Rights Act of 1964. These cases are each described next, followed by the U.S. Supreme Court ruling.

Altitude Express v. Zarda *(2018)*

In 2010, Don Zarda was employed as a skydiver instructor for Altitude Express located in Long Island, New York. During tandem jumps, in which clients are strapped by the shoulder and hips to an instructor, Zarda would often share with female clients that he was gay so they would feel comfortable being strapped to him during the dive. A female client alleged Zarda touched her inappropriately during a dive and Zarda tried to cover up his behavior by stating he was gay. As a result of the complaint, Zarda was fired by his employer Altitude Express. Zarda denied inappropriately touching his client. He filed a complaint with the EEOC under Title VII of the Civil Rights Act of 1964 alleging he was fired due to his sexual orientation and not conforming to male stereotypes (*Zarda v. Altitude Express*, 2018). The district court ruled in favor of Altitude Express, stating sexual orientation is not covered under Title VII. In October 2014, Zarda died in a base-jumping accident in Switzerland. His family moved forward with the lawsuit as heirs of his estate (*Altitude Express v. Zarda, et al., Co-Independent Executors of the Estate of Zarda*, No 17–1623). Zarda appealed to the U.S. Court of Appeals, Second Circuit, which ruled for Altitude Express. However, the Second Circuit then overturned two cases *Simonton v. Runyon* (2000) and *Dawson v. Bumble & Bumble* (2005) on sexual orientation. In February 26, 2018, the court ruled that discrimination based on sexual orientation is protected by Title VII under sex. The case, *Altitude Express v. Zarda* (2019, Case No. 17–1623) is consolidated with *Bostock v. Clayton County* (2019, No. 17–1618) and *R.G and G.R. Harris Funeral Homes v. EEOC* (2017). *Bostock v. Clayton County* (2019) is addressed next.

Bostock v. Clayton County *(2019)*

In 2003, Gerald Bostock began employment as a child welfare services coordinator for the Clayton County Juvenile Court in Atlanta, Georgia. His primary responsibility is the Court Appointed Special Advocates (CASA) program. He received good performance evaluations. In addition, under his leadership the program thrived and Bostock was acknowledged by the State of Georgia, as well as the national CASA organization, for his work on behalf of abused and neglected children. In 2013, Bostock joined the "Hotlanta" Softball League, a gay softball group to get back into shape after overcoming prostate cancer. An individual on the Clayton County court system criticized him for being involved in the group and for being gay. In April 2013, Clayton County reported they were doing an audit of the CASA program financials in which he directed. In May 2013, during a CASA advisory board meeting, Bostock was publicly criticized for his participation on "Hotlanta" and his sexual orientation. He was fired on June 2, 2013, for "conduct unbecoming of a county employee" (*Bostock v. Clayton County*, 2020, p. 7). In addition to losing his job, he lost his medical insurance while in recovery from cancer. Bostock filed a complaint with the EEOC. His employer claims he was fired for mismanaging funds. Bostock filed a lawsuit against Clayton County, Georgia, for discrimination based on sexual orientation. The Eleventh Circuit, Southern District of Georgia, heard the appeal and held the lower court's ruling. It ruled that "discrimination based on sexual orientation is not actionable under Title VII" based on the ruling in *Evans v. Georgia Regional Hospital* (2017) and a prior 1979 ruling. Bostock appealed. A writ of certiorari was granted on April 11, 2019, and oral arguments were heard at the U.S. Supreme Court on October 8, 2019.

R.G. and G.R. Harris Funeral Homes v. EEOC *(2017)*

The third case involves a transgender person. In this case, Aimee Stephens began employment in 2007 as the funeral director for Harris Funeral Homes in Michigan. During that time, Stephens presented as a man, and both her driver's license and her funeral director license indicated she was a man. In July 2013, Stephens announced to the funeral home owners she was transgender and would begin living openly as a woman, including dressing like a woman, which was part of the process for sex reassignment surgery. The owners fired Stephens because they did not want a man to dress in a woman's clothes at work because it would distract clients, who were grieving. In addition, it went against the owner's religious beliefs. In September 2013, Stephens filed a complaint with the EEOC alleging sex discrimination. A district court ruled that transgender identity is not a protected class under Title VII, but the sex stereotyping theory based on gender discrimination was supported under the *Price Waterhouse v. Hopkins* (1989) ruling. The Sixth Circuit Court ruled that there is Title VII protection for men to wear women's dresses (*Smith v. City of Salem*, 2004). In the end, the district court ruled in favor of Harris Funeral Home, citing the Religious Freedom Restoration Act (42 U.S.C. 2000bb). Stephens appealed to the Sixth Circuit. The Sixth Circuit Court of Appeals reversed the district court ruling and found for Stephens. It ruled that firing Stephens for not conforming to the dress of stereotypical males and firing Stephens for being a transgender person was a form of sex discrimination and violates Title VII of the Civil Rights Act of 1964. The petitioners argue that the role of the court is "to apply, not amend, the work of the People's representatives" (*Henson v. Santander Consumer USA*, 2017) and that by amending sex to include gender identity, the court usurped the legislative role of Congress. The funeral home owners petition for a writ of certiorari was granted. The case was heard by the U.S. Supreme Court in October 2019. Regretfully, in May 2020, Aimee Stephens passed away from complications of kidney failure (Dwyer &. Svokos, 2020).

U.S. Supreme Court Ruling on Title VII

In U.S. Supreme Court tradition of releasing controversial decisions for the end of the term, the Court made a stunning and historic ruling, on June 15, 2020. The U.S. Supreme Court ruled 6–3 that an "employer who fires a person based on sexual orientation or gender identity is in violation of Title VII" (*Bostock v. Clayton County*, 2020, p. 1). It is illegal to fire an individual because they are homosexual or transgender. The Roberts Court delivered the historic ruling. Chief Justice Roberts and Justice Gorsuch, both conservatives, joined liberal Justices Ruth Bader Ginsburg, Stephen Breyer, Sonia Sotomayor, and Elena Kagan in the majority opinion, a remarkable court composition. Conservative Justices Samuel Alito, Clarence Thomas, and Brett Kavanaugh dissented. In a surprising and unanticipated move, Justice Gorsuch, a conservative appointee of President Trump, sided with the majority and led the court's decision by penning the majority opinion. In a 33-page meticulous opinion, Justice Gorsuch provides a textualist opinion (Primus, 2019) of Title VII and the word *sex*. He opines that "it is impossible to discriminate against a person for being homosexual or transgender without discriminating against that individual based on sex" (p. 9).

> An employer who fires an individual for being homosexual or transgender fires that person for traits or actions it would not have questioned in members of a different sex. Sex plays a necessary and undisguisable role in the decision, exactly what Title II forbids.
> (*Bostock v. Clayton County*, 2020, p. 2)

For example, if a man is fired for having sex with a man in the workplace but a female is not fired for having sex with a man in the workplace, then the man was fired based on sex for having sex. Title VII liability extends beyond an employer treating men and women differently. "The law makes each instance of discrimination against an individual employee because of that individual's sex an independent violation of Title VII" (*Bostock v. Clayton County*, p. 12).

Combining the "but-for-causation" standard (*University of Tex. Southwestern Medical Center v. Nassar*, 2013) to Title VII, which means "a defendant cannot avoid liability just by citing some *other* factor that contributed to its challenged employment action" (*Bostock v. Clayton County*, 2020, p. 2), with disparate treatment, which means "difference in treatment based on sex must be intentional" (*Bostock v. Clayton County*, 2020, p. 2; *Watson v. Fort Worth Bank & Trust*, 1988), the court's ruling states that

> a statutory violation occurs if an employer intentionally relies in part on an individual's employee's sex when deciding to discharge the employee. Because discrimination on the basis of homosexuality or transgender status requires an employer to intentionally treat individual employees differently because of their sex, an employer who intentionally penalizes an employee for being homosexual or transgender also violates Title VII. There is no escaping the role intent plays: Just as sex is necessarily a 'but-for cause' when an employer discriminates against homosexual or transgender employees, an employer who discriminates on these grounds inescapably intends to rely on sex in its decisionmaking
> (*Bostock v. Clayton County*, 2020, pp. 9–10)

For the majority, sexual orientation and gender identity are connected to sex stating "homosexuality and transgender status are inextricably bound up with sex" (*Bostock v. Clayton County*, 2020, p. 10). Citing three precedents, the court asserts it is irrelevant how the employer labels or justifies the discriminatory practice and that "plaintiff's sex need not be the sole or primary cause of the employer's action" (p. 3 slip opinion). In *Los Angeles Department of Water Power v. Manhart* (1978), the discriminatory practice, forcing female employees to make larger pension contributions than male employees, was based on a life expectancy adjustment due to women living longer than men. The employer treated women differently than men were, rationalizing it sought sex equality in pensions. In *Philips v. Martin Marietta* (1971), the discriminatory practice was motherhood: not hiring women who had young children but hiring men who had young children. The employer based the decision on sex (women) and a second factor, young children. It is discrimination to treat female employees differently than male employees. In *Oncale v. Sundowner Offshore Services*, Inc (1998), a male employee on an oil rig claims he was singled out and sexually harassed by male co-workers, a case of same-sex harassment. Although the case did not address the "principal evil Congress was concerned with when it enacted Title VII" (men harassing women), it ruled that same-sex harassment (male to male) is actionable under Title VII (*Oncale v. Sundowner Offshore Services*, p. 79; as cited in *Bostock v. Clayton County*, 2020, p. 14). Oncale alleges the harassment would not have taken place if he were female, which is a Title VII violation. Discrimination is discrimination regardless of the label, rationale, or justification. Regarding discrimination based on sexual orientation and gender identity, Justice Gorsuch writes that

> the employer could easily have pointed to some other, nonprotected trait and insisted it was the more important factor in the adverse employment outcome. Here, too, it is of no significance if another factor, such as the plaintiff's attraction to the same sex or presentation as a different sex from the one assigned at birth, might also be at work, or even play a more important role in the employer's decision. Finally, an employer who intentionally fires an individual homosexual or transgender employee in part because of

that individual's sex violates the law even if the employer is willing to subject all male and female homosexual or transgender employees to the same rule.
>> (*Bostock v. Clayton County*, 2020, pp. 12–15, slip opinion, p. 3)

Justice Gorsuch writes that in determining whether *sex* under Title VII applies to sexual orientation and gender identity the court's charge is to simply determine whether sex is a 'but-for causation.' "A but-for test directs us to change one thing at a time and see if the outcome changes. If it does, we have found a but-for cause" (*Bostock v. Clayton County*, 2020, p. 5). The court went on to point out that the Title VII statue imposes a liability on employers when they "fail or refuse to hire,' 'discharge' or otherwise . . . discriminate against someone because of a statutorily protected characteristic like sex" (p. 7).

The court's decision in *Bostock v. Clayton County* (2020) is momentous and profound. It expands civil rights laws in America to include gay and transgender people, creating a new legal right for LGBTQ people. In response to the majority opinion, Justice Alito wrote a 55-page scathing dissenting opinion, referring to the majority opinion as "preposterous," "arrogant," "wrong," and "irresponsible" (Justice Alito, Dissenting Opinion, *Bostock v. Clayton County*, 2020, pp. 3, 7, 11, and 44). He argues that it was not the intent of Congress in 1964 to include sexual orientation and gender identity in the word sex when Congress wrote the law; the court usurped the power of Congress. Justice Alito opines:

> There is only one word for what the Court has done today: legislation. The document that the Court releases is in the form of a judicial opinion interpreting a statue, but that is deceptive. Title VII of the Civil Rights Act of 1964 prohibits employment discrimination on any of five specified grounds: "race, color, religion, sex, [and] national origin" 42 U.S.C. Section 2000e-2(a)(1). Neither "sexual orientation" nor "gender identity" appears on that list. For the past 45 years, bills have been introduced in Congress to add "sexual orientation' to that list, and in recent years, bills have included 'gender identity' as well. But to date, none has passed both Houses. . . . Title VII prohibition because of "sex," still means what it has always meant. . . . The court tries to convince the readers that it is merely enforcing the terms of statutes, but that is preposterous . . . our duty is to interpret statutory terms to mean what they conveyed to reasonable people at the time they were written.
>> (Justice Alito's Dissenting Opinion, *Bostock v. Clayton County*, 2020, p. 2)

Justice Alito warns that the *Bostock* ruling will have far-reaching implications on over 100 federal laws (Ibid, p. 66), including Title IX, employment by religious organizations, and healthcare. Justice Alito cautions that

> [t]he position that the Court now adopts will threaten freedom of religion, freedom of speech, and personal privacy and safety . . . transgender persons will be able to argue that they are entitled to use a bathroom locker that is reserved for persons of the sex with which they identify, and while the Court does not define what it means by a transgender person, the term may apply to individuals who are gender fluid that is individuals whose gender identity is mixed or changes over time. . . . Thus a person who has not undertaken any physical transitioning may claim the right to use the bathroom or locker room assigned to the sex with which the individuals identifies at the time. The Court provides no clue why a transgender person's claim to such bathroom or locker room access might not succeed. A similar issue has arisen under Title IX, which prohibits sex

discrimination by any elementary or secondary school and any college or university that receives federal financial assistance.

(Ibid, 2020, pp. 45–46)

Justice Alito issues this warning despite the majority opinion stating the *Bostock* ruling only applies to employment discrimination. Justice Gorsuch specifically states that "under Title VII, too, we do not purport to address bathrooms, locker rooms, or anything else of the kind" (*Bostock v. Clayton County*, 2020, p. 31). Regarding sports, Justice Alito advises that the ruling could undermine Title IX by reducing young women's equal opportunity to participate in sports. He states that "it may force a young woman to compete against students who have a very significant biological advantage, including students who have the size and strength of a male but identify as female" (Ibid, 2020, p. 47). Justice Alito also highlights the conflict in employment for religious organizations, stating that "'religious organizations need employees who actually live the faith.' Compelling a religious organization to employ individuals whose conduct flouts the tenets of the organization's faith forces the group to communicate an objectionable message" (p. 49). However, it is important to point out that Title VII provides exemptions for religious organizations and schools with respect to employment (although narrowly applied) similar to Title IX providing religious exemptions to schools, colleges, and universities (see Chapter 6 Public Accommodations for a full discussion).

In summary, the *Bostock* ruling makes firing an individual based on sexual orientation and gender identity a violation under Title VII of the Civil Rights Act of 1964. Being lesbian, gay or transgender is no longer a "fireable offense" (National Center for Lesbian Rights, 2020). The court's decision reverses the judgment of the Eleventh Circuit, Southern District of Georgia (*Bostock v. Clayton County*, 2017, No 17–1618, 723 Fed Appx 964) and affirms judgements in the Second Circuit (No 17–1623, 883 F. 3d 100) and Sixth Circuit (No 18–107 884 F. 3d 560) (*Bostock v. Clayton County*, 2020).

Implications

The court's ruling is a landmark decision on LGBTQ employment protections. It is historic, momentous, and controversial. The ruling expands civil rights laws in America to sexual orientation and gender identity. For the past 50 plus years, "sex" under Title VII has applied to biological sex only (women and men) and pregnancy (Pregnancy Discrimination Act of 1978). Now Title VII under the Civil Rights Act of 1964 includes sexual orientation and gender identity, which are intricately linked to sex (*Bostock v. Clayton County*, 2020). The court's decision extends coverage to LGBTQ people. If they are discriminated against in employment, they can file a complaint with the federal EEOC and state human rights commission. The new employment protections provide solid legal recourse. Gay and transgender people no longer have to live in fear of being fired for their sexual orientation or gender identity. They can now get married on Sunday, go to work on Monday, and announce their marriage with no adverse outcomes. Previously, they could have been fired in half of the states across America. LGBTQ people can exercise their fundamental right to marriage under *Obergefell v. Hodges* (2015) and be protected at work (*Bostock v. Clayton County*, 2020).

In terms of the umbrella of U.S. civil rights laws, there are over 100 federal statutes that prohibit discrimination based on sex in credit, education, employment, equal pay, health care, housing, jury service, military, and a host of other areas. Regarding credit, companies are prohibited to discriminate based on sex in the Equal Credit Opportunity Act (15 U.S.C. Section 1691 (a)(1) and d(a). Sex discrimination is illegal in a lumber of education statutes, including Federal Family Education Loan Program (20 U.S.C. Section 1071), Federal Payments to Reduce Student Interest Costs (20 U.S.C. 1078), Student Loan Marketing Association (20 U.S.C. 1087). Discrimination in Secondary Markets Prohibited (20 U.S.C.1087–4), Discretion of Student Financial Aid Administrators (20 U.S.C. Section 1087), Education Programs (20 U.S.C. Section 1231), Title IV of the Education Amendments of 1972 (20 U.S.C. Section 1681), and Equal Education Opportunities (20 U.S.C. 1701–1702, 1720). The biggest impact and most controversial will be in Title IX. There is currently a pending case in the Fourth Circuit Court of Appeals (Richmond, Virginia) on Title IV and bathroom accommodations for transgender students (see *Grimm v. Gloucester County School Board*, December 2019. A full discussion of this case is included in the next chapter).

Regarding federal government employment, it is illegal to discriminate based on sex in the Merit System Principles (5 U.S.C. Section 2301(b)(2)), Prohibited Personnel Practices (5 U.S.C. Section 2302), Minority Recruitment Program 5 (U.S.C. Section 7201), Discrimination Against United States Personnel (22 U.S.C. Section 2426), and Equal Employment Opportunities (42 U.S.C. Section 2000e). It is also a violation to discriminate based on sex in the Fair Housing Act (12 U.S.C. Section 4545(1); 42 U.S.C. Sections 3604–3606, and 3631) and Equal Pay Act of 1963 (29 U.S.C. Section 206). These public policies are all areas in which LGBTQ people have been discriminated against or harassed. A complete list of federal statutes is provided at the end of the chapter. The biggest impact of the *Bostock* ruling, in terms of scope for LGBTQ protections, will most likely be health care and housing. The implications for these two policy areas are described next.

Health Care

The Patient Protection and Affordable Care Act of 2010 (Pub. L. 111–148), also known as the Affordable Care Act, prohibits discrimination based on sex. Section 1557 of the Affordable Care Act, known as the nondiscrimination provision, prohibits discrimination based on six categories: (1) age, (2) disability, (3) race, (4) color, (5) national origin, and (6) sex. Section 1557 does not include protections for religion. This provision applies to any health program or activity by U.S. Department of Health and Human Services (HHS) administers, any agency receiving HHS funding for health activities or programs, or the health care marketplace (Pub. L. 111–148). The Affordable Care Act is broad-reaching and impacts the majority of Americans. It increases access to health care services by expanding Medicaid coverage for people with incomes 138 percent below the federal poverty line, making health care more affordable; it eliminates lifetime caps on services, which is critical for cancer patients or people with chronic health conditions such as asthma or diabetes, and removes exclusions based on preexisting conditions. People can no longer be denied or dropped from coverage due to health reasons. For example, under the Affordable Care Act people with preexisting conditions, such as HIV/AIDs (and cancer), cannot be denied health care, which is critical for the LGBTQ population, which is disproportionately impacted by HIV/AIDS (U.S. Department of Health and Human Services, HIV, December 19, 2019). Approximately 133 million Americans have preexisting conditions, another 20 million receive health care through the Affordable Care Act's market exchanges and Medicaid expansion (deVogue et al., June 26, 2020). More broadly, the Affordable Care Act builds on civil rights laws including Title VI of the Civil Rights act of 1964 (protects race, color, national origin), Title IX of the Education Amendments of 1972 (protects sex), Section 504 of the Rehabilitation Act of 1973 (protects disability), and the Age Discrimination Act of 1975 (protects people 40 years of age and over). In 2012, the HHS, Office of Civil Rights issued an opinion letter defining sex discrimination to include sexual orientation, sex stereotyping, and gender identity. A final implementing rule was issued by the Obama administration in 2016 (Keith, 2020). Then, in December 2016, a court ruled in *Franciscan Alliance. v. Burwell* (2016) that discrimination on the basis of gender identity and pregnancy termination is not protected under the Affordable Care Act and issued a nationwide injunction. The Franciscan

Alliance argued that the Obama rule violated constitutional and statutory religious freedom protections. The court agreed and cited violations of the Administrative Procedure Act of 1946 (Pub. L. 79–404) and the Religious Freedom Restoration Act of 1993 (Pub. L. 103–141). In November of 2019, HHS announced it would no longer enforce antidiscrimination protections by federal grantees in the delivery of services (Notice of Nonenforcement Refusal to Enforce Health and Human Services Grants Regulations, 2019), which places vulnerable populations such as LGBTQ youth and adults at additional risk (Lambda Legal, March 1, 2020). The announcement results in at least two lawsuits (*DeOtte v. Azar*, 2019; *Family Equality v. Azar*, 2020). Later, on June 12, 2020, the HHS under the direction of the Trump administration issued a new final rule revising the agency's prior interpretation of Section 1557 of the Affordable Care Act (Pub. L. 111–148). The new rule deletes protections based on sex stereotyping and gender identity, and reduces protections for people with disabilities, women, and individuals with limited English proficiency (Keith, 2020). The new Trump rule was a significant blow to the LGBTQ community, dismantling years of advocacy. Then, three days later, on June 15, 2020, the U.S. Supreme Court ruled that sex under Title VII includes sexual orientation and gender identity (*Bostock v. Clayton County*, 2020), creating wide anticipation that the ruling will be applied to the Affordable Care Act, nullifying the Trump administration's new section 1557 rule. At least one lawsuit has been filed against the HHS regarding the new rule after the *Bostock* decision (*Whitman-Walker Clinic v. HHS*, 2020, complaint filed June 22, 2020). The section 1557 rule takes place within the larger political context of the Trump administration's efforts to dismantle the Affordable Care Act. In March 2018, 20 conservative states filed a complaint arguing the Affordable Care Act's individual mandate is unconstitutional (*Texas v. United States*, 2020). In December 2019, the Fifth Circuit Court of Appeals ruled 2–1 the Affordable Care Act's individual mandate is unconstitutional, but the entire law remains in effect. The court sent the case back to the lower court. In March 2020, the U.S. Supreme Court accepted an appeal by 21 state attorney generals from the Fifth Circuit requesting to determine if the Affordable Care Act should remain in effect (*California v. Texas*, 2020). The legal cases reflect the political fault lines in the country; liberal blue states support the Affordable Care Act, and red conservative states want the law gutted (deVogue & Cole, March 2, 2020). The political fighting and mudslinging over the Affordable Care Act (also called Obamacare pejoratively) has been ongoing for the past decade since its inception and has increased due to the 2020 U.S. presidential election. The Affordable Care Act is a centerpiece of Democratic presidential nominee Joe Biden's platform, and Republican president Trump wants it eliminated as part of his political platform. Avoiding the immediate political fight, the U.S. Supreme Court will hear oral arguments in the October 2020 term and release the decision in June 2021, after the presidential election.

If the *Bostock* ruling applies to the Affordable Care Act, section 1557, which is probable, then transgender employees could logically argue that employer health insurance companies should pay for gender dysphoria treatment or sex reassignment surgery. Several district courts have already ruled that under the Affordable Care Act (Pub. L. 111–148), health care providers must provide sex reassignment surgery (*Kadel v. Folwell*, cited in Bostock, 2020, p. 50). The concern is that the U.S. Supreme Court's ruling in *Bostock* will open the floodgates for litigation requiring health care providers (surgeons, physicians, and nurses) and religiously affiliated hospitals to perform sex reassignment surgery or treat gender dysphoria, which may contradict their religious beliefs. Historically, religiously affiliated hospitals have refused to provide a range of reproductive health surgeries related to birth control based on religious beliefs, including abortion, tubal ligation, and vasectomies. It is expected that religiously affiliated hospitals will also refuse to perform sex reassignment surgeries. However, non–religiously affiliated hospitals, health providers, will likely agree to perform sex reassignment surgery. Health insurance companies may refuse due to costs. However, the scope of the *Bostock* impact on health insurance companies is relatively small. The number of transgender people in the U.S. is low (less than 1 percent), and the number of health care claims for gender-affirming surgeries is even lower, having a minimal budget impact for health insurance companies. A recent article titled "Trends in Gender Affirming Surgery in Insured Patients in the United States," published by the *Open Access Journal of the American Society of Plastic Surgeons*, found there were 1,047 gender-affirming surgeries in a period of six years, from 2009 to 2015, in the U.S., and the most common procedure was a mastectomy (Lane et al., 2018). Data findings were generated and analyzed using Truven MarketScan Database, which covers 150 employers and 20 health care plans. The findings, of course, do not include or apply to uninsured transgender people. However, uninsured individuals are less likely to undergo surgery due to the prohibitive costs. Regarding lesbian and gays who are married, they can access employee subsidized/sponsored health insurance as spouses of same-sex couples as a result of *U.S. v. Windsor* (2013) and *Obergefell v. Hodges* (2015). Whether sex reassignment surgery or treatment for gender dysphoria is covered under those plans is determined by the courts.

Even after gaining access to health care insurance, which can be a herculean task, LGBTQ people are still stigmatized and discriminated by health care providers and hospitals with regard to treatment. Transgender people face widespread discrimination in health care, resulting in poor treatment and outcomes. At the extreme, the cases are tragic. For example, a 14-year-old transgender boy was admitted to the hospital for transphobic harassment and suicidal ideation, he was discharged early from the hospital and committed suicide three days later (*Prescott v. Rady Children's Hospital – San Diego* (2017a, 2017b). His mother filed a lawsuit arguing the hospital should have kept her son for the full 72 hours based on his suicidal ideations and respected his gender identity by calling him by his chosen pronoun. In another case, much less severe, a county government employee who is transgender was turned down by the employer-sponsored health insurance companies excluding surgeries to treat gender dysphoria (*Ketcham v. Regence Blue Cross Blue Shield of Oregon*, 2019). In the federal government, an employee was turned down for transition-related care by the federal employee health benefits program (*Koran v. OPM*, EEOC). This case is pending. In contrast, the California Supreme Court ruled that medical providers cannot assert religious objections to discriminate based on sexual orientation and refuse medical care (*Benitize v. North Coast Women's Care Medical Group*, 2008). These cases serve as examples of the legal issues related to disparities in treatment, poor health care outcomes, discrimination, bias, and stigmatization. The next policy area likely to be impacted by the *Bostock v. Clayton County* (2020) ruling is housing.

Housing

Given that federal housing laws protect against discrimination based on sex as defined in Title VII it is probable the U.S. Supreme Court's ruling in *Bostock v. Clayton County* (2020) will be applied to housing and homeless shelters. The *Bostock* ruling will likely impact a proposed rule (June 2020) issued by the U.S. Department of Housing and Urban Development (HUD) that would allow single-sex homeless shelters to discriminate against homeless transgender people. The new rule would allow homeless shelters to base occupancy on biological sex instead of gender identity, denying transgender homeless people shelter. Specifically, the proposed rule states it would allow shelter staff to "determine an individual's sex based on a good faith belief that an individual seeking access . . . is not of the sex, as defined in the single sex facility's policy, which the facility accommodates" (Winfield Cunningham, June 14, 2020). Another component, much larger in scope, is the Fair Housing Act, Title III of the Civil Rights Act of 1968 (42 U.S.C. 3601 et seq.), which prohibits discrimination based on disability, family status, national origin, race, religion, and sex by housing providers, including landlords, financial institutions, mortgage companies, and real estate companies. Individuals who have been discriminated against based on sex (or other protected classifications) can file a complaint with HUD and, if needed, file a criminal complaint with the U.S. Department of Justice. The purpose is to ensure that property owners do not discriminate when selecting renters or buyers; people should be treated fairly and equally. Numerous housing discrimination lawsuits have been filed by LGBTQ people based on sexual orientation and gender identity (*Smith v. Avanti*, 2016; *Walsh v. Friendship Village of South County*, 2018). There are conflicting rulings in the U.S. Court of Appeals. The Eighth Circuit holds that Title VII does not apply to sexual orientation (*Williamson v. A.G. Edwards & Sons, Inc.*, 1989; *Pambianchi v. Arkansas at Tech University*, 2014; also see *Smith v. Mission Associates Ltd. Partnership*, 2002 and *Ordelli v. Mark Farrell & Associates*, 2013). In contrast, the Second Circuit holds that sexual orientation is a form of sex discrimination (*Zarda v. Altitude Express*, 2018) and that sexual orientation is protected under Title VII (*Wetzel v. Glen St. Andrew Living Community*, 2018), and the Seventh Circuit applies sexual orientation to the Fair Housing Act (12 U.S.C. Section 4545) (see *Hively v. Ivy Tech Community College of Indiana*, 7th Cir, 2017). The U.S. Supreme Court's ruling in *Bostock v. Clayton County* (2020) will impact these cases. It is predicted that the term *sex* under the Fair Housing Act and Fair Credit Reporting Act of 1970 (15 U.S.C. § 1681) will be expanded to include sexual orientation and gender identity, protecting LGBTQ people from housing discrimination. An example of a pending housing discrimination case based on sexual orientation is provided next.

Walsh v. Friendship Village of South County *(2018)*

This case is about a married lesbian couple who was denied senior housing based on sexual orientation even though they were financially qualified to live at a retirement community. In the summer of 2016, Mary Walsh and Bev Nance, a married lesbian couple residing in St. Louis, Missouri, decided to downsize and move into a retirement community. The couple, who had been partners for over 35 years, made several visits to Friendship Village of South County and decided to move in. On July 22, 2016, the couple gave a $2,000 deposit and was placed on a waiting list. The property director instructed them to return on July 29, 2016, to sign a residency agreement and pay additional fees, which is common. On July 25, 2016, the property director called Mary Walsh and asked her to clarify her relationship with Bev Nance. Walsh advised that she and Bev Nance were spouses, married in Massachusetts in 2009 (the first state in the country to recognize same-sex marriage – see *Goodridge v. Department of Public Health*, 2003). Two days later, the property director called and informed the couple their application was denied because they are a same-sex couple. On July 29, 2016, the couple received a letter stating their application was denied based on Friendship Village of South County's Cohabitation policy, which states that

> [c]onsistent with its long-standing practice of operating its facilities in accordance with biblical principles and sincerely-held religious standards, that it will permit the cohabitation of resident within a single unit only if those residents, while residing in said unit, are related as spouses by marriage, as parent and child or as siblings. The term 'marriage' as used in this policy means that union of one man and one woman, as marriage is understood in the Bible.
>
> (*Walsh v. Friendship Village of South County*, 2018, Exhibit 2, Cohabitation Policy)

Friendship Village of South County is a continuing care retirement center not affiliated with any religious organization or religion. The retirement center's definition of marriage is similar to Section 3 of the Defense of Marriage Act, which was ruled unconstitutional by the U.S. Supreme Court in *U.S v. Windsor* (2013). In response, the couple filed a housing discrimination complaint with HUD. During the investigation, Friendship Village of South County confirmed it denied the couple housing because they are a same-sex couple. The couple filed a legal complaint alleging that Friendship Village of South County discriminated against them based on sex in violation of the Fair Housing Act (42 U.S.C. 3601 et seq.). In January 2019, the district court dismissed the case and found for Friendship Village of South County. The court stated that same-sex couples are not protected from discrimination under Title VII. In February 2019, the couple filed an appeal with the U.S. Court of Appeals, Eighth Circuit (352 F. Supp. 3d 920, E.D. Mo. 2019). The case is currently pending in the Eighth Circuit Court of Appeals, which holds that Title VII does not apply to sexual orientation (*Williamson v. A.G. Edwards & Sons, Inc.*, 1989, 1990; *Pambianchi v. Arkansas at Tech University*, 2014). The precedent, based on the definition of sex in Title VII, conflicts with the recent U.S. Supreme Court's ruling in *Bostock v. Clayton County* (2020); it is predicted that the precedent will be reversed and the Eighth Circuit will find for the married lesbian couple, Mary Walsh and Bev Nance (*Walsh v. Friendship Valley of South County*, 2020).

In addition to housing and health care, it is anticipated the *Bostock* (2020) ruling will apply to over 100 federal statutes that prohibit discrimination based on sex. These statutes are listed at the end of the chapter. Violations of the statutes of Title VII related to sex are enforceable in all 50 states, impacting employment, health care, housing, and other policy areas nationwide.

For social equity, a pillar of public administration and public service, to be achievable and sustainable, it must be based on the rule of law. As a result of the *Bostock v. Clayton County* (2020) decision, LGBTQ employment protections are now based on the rule of law.

Conclusion

The U.S. Supreme Court *Bostock v. Clayton County* (2020) ruling is historic and far-reaching. After 50 years of interpreting *sex* in Title VII to mean men and women (and pregnancy), it now includes sexual orientation and gender identity as protected traits. It is a monumental ruling for LGBTQ rights by a conservative-majority Court. It is viewed as a pushback against the Trump administration's anti-LBGTQ policies targeting employment, housing, and health care, an attempt to reverse the Obama administration's LGBTQ protections. This chapter describes the legal development and analysis of the landmark ruling *Bostock v. Clayton County* (2020) and its implications on LGBTQ employment and federal antidiscrimination statutes, including housing and health care. The *Bostock v. Clayton County* (2020) ruling connects the law to social equity. It expands employment protections to LGBTQ people and increases the coverage of civil rights in America. As Justice Gorsuch advises, "only the written word is the law, and all persons are entitled to it" (*Bostock v. Clayton County*, 2020, p. 2). To ensure the court's decision is successfully implemented and enforced, it will be imperative to update federal, state, and local statutes; policy manuals; and websites and to require ongoing training and education on LGBTQ inclusiveness to prevent bias, prejudice, and discrimination in all levels of government in personnel administration, human resources, and human rights commissions. It will be important to provide ongoing monitoring of EEOC claims to ensure enforceability and ensure it is implemented in a fair, just, and timely manner to ensure due process. Data will need to be collected, analyzed, and reported to evaluate disparities in LGBTQ employment, housing, health care, and other policies providing protections based on sex and protected traits sexual orientation and gender identity. Funding will need to be allocated to ensure policy compliance.

Antidiscrimination employment laws are critical in preventing discrimination and ensuring a diverse workforce. In American democracy, our goal is for the workforce to mirror its people so that all groups are represented and have a voice in decision-making and, most important, budget allocation. Ideally, government employees at the federal, state, and local levels should look like America's population (Naff, 2001), including race, color, nationality, religion, and sex. This means that 4 percent of federal government employees should identify as LGBTQ. The U.S. Supreme Court's *Bostock* (2020) landmark ruling advances the country several steps forward in securing a representative bureaucracy (Dolan & Rosenbloom, 2003; Krislov & Rosenbloom, 2012). It will also likely expand LGBTQ equal rights and protections in health care, housing, and a host of other federal statutes prohibiting sex discrimination. The next chapter focuses on LGBQ military rights.

Resources

Gay, Lesbian, Bisexual and Transgender (GLBT) National Help Center. www.glbthotline.org/
Human Rights Campaign. www.hrc.org/
Lambda Legal. www.lambdlegal.com
National Center for Lesbian Rights. www.nclrights.org
National Center or Transgender Equality (NCTE). www.transequality.org/
Philadelphia. Movie (1993). TriStar Pictures.
The Trevor Project. www.thetrevorproject.org/
Trans Youth Equality Foundation (TYEF). www.transyouthequality.org/
U.S. Census Bureau. www.census.gov/
U.S. Department of Housing and Urban Development. Website. www.hud.gov/
U.S. Department of Justice. List of State Human Rights Commissions. www.justice.gov/crt/legal info/stateandlocal.php
U.S. Department of Labor. www.dol.gov/
U.S. Equal Employment Opportunity Commission (EEOC). http://eeoc.gov/employees/howto file.cfm
U.S. Supreme Court. Website. www.supremecourt.gov/

References

Adarand Constructors v. Pena, 515 U.S. 200 (1995).
Administrative Procedure Act of 1946 (Pub. L. 79–404).
Age Discrimination Act of 1975 (Pub. L. 94–135).
Age Discrimination in Employment Act of 1967 (ADEA) (Pub. L. 90–202).
Altitude Express v. Zarda, No. 17–1623 (Eleventh Circuit, 2019).
Altitude Express v. Zarda, et al, Co-Independent Executors of the Estate of Zarda, No. 17–1623 (Eleventh Circuit, 2019).
American Disabilities Act of 1990 (Pub. L. 101–336).
American Disabilities Amendment Act of 2008 (Pub. L. 110–325).
Barnes, R. (2019, October 3). Supreme Court term to begin with blockbuster question: Is it legal to fire someone for being gay or transgender? *Washington Post*. https://www.washingtonpost.com/politics/courts_law/

supreme-court-term-to-begin-with-blockbuster-question-is-it-legal-to-fire-someone-for-being-gay-or-transgender/2019/10/03/b3b08a46-e15d-11e9-b199-f638bf2c340f_story.html

Barnes v. City of Cincinnati, 401 F.3d 729 (6th Cir. 2005, March 25).

Benitize v. North Coast Women's Care Medical Group, No. D040094 (Fourth District California, 2008)

Bostock v. Clayton County, Georgia, No. 17–1623 (2019). Retrieved February 23, 2020, from www.supremecourt.gov/DocketPDF/17/17-1618/48357/20180525170054025_36418%20pdf%20Sutherland%20br.pdf

Bostock v. Clayton County, 590 US __ (2020).

California v. Texas, No. 19-840 (2020).

Castaneda v. Partida, 430 US 482, 499 (1977).

City of Los Angeles Dept of Water and Power v. Manhart, 435 US 702 (1978).

Civil Rights Act of 1964 (Pub. L. 88–352). www.eeoc.gov/laws/statutes/titlevii.cfm

Civil Rights and Women's Equity in Employment Act of 1991 (Pub. L. 102–166).

Civil Service Reform Act of 1978 (5 U.S.C. Section 2302(b)(10). www.eeoc.gov/eeoc/history/50th/thelaw/civil_service_reform- 1978.cfm; https://archive.opm.gov/biographyofanideal/PU_CSreform.htm

David Baldwin v. Department of Transportation, Equal Employment Opportunity Commission, Appeal No. 120133080, July 15, 2015.

Dawson v. Bumble & Bumble, 398 F.3d 211 (2d Cir. 2005).

DeOtte v. Azar, 393 F.Supp. 3d 490 (N.D. Tex. 2019).

deVogue, A., & Cole, D. (2020, March 2). Supreme Court will decide the fate of the Affordable Care Act sometime next term, presumably after the election. https://www.cnn.com/2020/03/02/politics/supreme-court-affordable-care-act-case-next-term/index.html

deVogue, A., Luhby, T., & Mucha, S. (2020, June 26). Trump administration asks Supreme Court to invalidate Obamacare. https://www.cnn.com/2020/06/25/politics/trump-administration-obamacare-supreme-court/index.html

Dolan, J., & Rosenbloom, D. H. (2003). *Representative bureaucracy: Classic readings and continuing controversies*. Routledge.

Dwyer, D., & Svokos, A. (June 15, 2020). "Supreme Court makes historic ruling on LGBT employment discrimination. ABC News, Politics.

EEOC v. R.G. and G.R. Harris Funeral Homes, 884 F.3d 560 (6th Cir. 2018).

Employment Non-Discrimination Act of 2007 (H.R. 2015, 110th Congress, 2007).

Equal Employment Opportunity Act of 1972 (Pub. L. 92–261).

Equal Pay Act of 1963 (Pub. L. 88–38).

Evans v. Georgia Regional Hospital, 850 F.3d 1248 (11th Cir. 2017).

Fair Credit Reporting Act of 1970 (15 U.S.C. § 1681).

Fair Housing Act. Title VIII of the Civil Rights Act of 1968 (Pub. L. 90–284). www.justice.gov/crt/fair-housing-act-2

Fair Labors Standard Act of 1938 (29 U.S.C. § 203).

Family Equality v. Azar, 1:20-cv-02403 (S.D. N.Y 2020).

Family Medical Leave Act of 1993 (Pub. L. 103–3).

Fidas, D., & Cooper, L. (2019). *A workplace divided: Understanding the climate for LGBTQ workers nationwide*. Human Rights Campaign. Retrieved February 21, 2020, from www.hrc.org/resources/a-workplace-divided-understanding-the-climate-for-lgbtq-workers-nationwide

Fitzsimmons, T. (2019, March 26). Majority of Americans back LGBTQ protections—But support is sliding. *NBC news*.

Franciscan Alliance. v Burwell, 7:2016-cv-00108 (TX ND) (2016)

Garcia v. Elf Atochem North America, 28 F.3d 446 (Fifth Circuit, 1994)

Genetic Information Nondiscrimination Act of 2008. (122 Stat. 881). Retrieved February 28, 2020, from www.eeoc.gov/laws/statutes/gina.cfm

Goodridge v. Department of Public Health, 798 N.E. 2d 941 (MA, 2003)

Grimm v. Gloucester County Public Schools, WL 3774118 (E.D. Va. 2019).

Harris v. Forklift Systems, Inc., 510 US 21 (1993)

Henson v. Santander Consumer USA, 582 U.S. __ (2017).

Hively v. Ivy Tech. Comm. Coll. of Indiana, 853 F.3d 339, 351–52 (Seventh Circuit, 2017).

Holcombe, M., & Alonso, M. (2020, February 16). A police officer who said he was told to 'tone down your gayness' reaches $10 million settlement and gets promoted. *CNN.com*. Retrieved February 18, 2020, from www.cnn.com/2020/02/13/us/st-louis-county-police-officer-settlement-trnd/index.html

Human Rights Campaign. (n.d.). *LGBTQ equality at the Fortune 500*. Https://hrc.org/resources/lgbt-equality-at-the-fortune-500

International Lesbian, Gay, Bisexual, Trans and Intersex Association. Chiam, Z., Duffy, S., & González, G. M. (2017, November). *Trans legal mapping report 2017: Recognition before the law*. ILGA. Retrieved February 27, 2020, from https://ilga.org/downloads/ILGA_Trans_Legal_Mapping_Report_2017_ENG.pdf

James, S., Herman, J. L., Ranking, S., Keisling, M., Mottet, L., & Anafi, M. (2016). *The report of the 2015 transgender survey* (p. 155). National Center for Transgender Equality. Retrieved February 21, 2020, from www.ustranssurvey.org/reports

Kadel v. Folwell, 1:19CV272 (M.D.N.C., 2020).

Keith, K. Health Affairs. (2020, June 13). HHS strips gender identity, sex stereotyping, language access protections. *Health Affairs*. Retrieved June 22, 2020, from www.healthaffairs.org/do/10.1377/hblog 20200613.671888/full/

Ketchum v. Regence Bluecross Blueshield of Oregon, 19CV31838. www.nclrights.org/wp-content/uploads/2020/01/2019.07.18.-Complaint.pdf

Koran v. OPM. (Washington, DC, EEOC). www.nclrights.org/our-work/cases/koran-v-opm/

Krislov, S., & Rosenbloom, D. H. (2012). *Representative bureaucracy*. Quid Pro Books.

Lambda Legal. (2020, March 19). *Lawsuit: Trump's HHS refuses to enforce anti-discrimination rules, leaving LGBTQ community vulnerable amid COVID-19 pandemic*. www.lambdalegal.org/blog/20200319_lawsuit-trump-hhs-anti-discrimination-lgbtq-covid-19-pandemic

Lane, M., Ives, G., Sluiter, C., Waljee, E. C., Yao, J. F., Tsung-Hung, H., Mei, H., & Kuzon, W. M. (2018, April 16). Trends in gender-affirming surgery in insured patients in the United States. *Open Access Journal of the American Society of Plastic Surgeons*. Published online 2018. doi:10.1097/GOX.0000000000001738. Retrieved June 18, 2020, from www.ncbi.nlm.nih.gov/pmc/articles/PMC5977951/

Ledbetter v. Goodyear Tire & Rubber Co, 550 U.S. 618 (2007).

Lewis, G., & Taylor, H. (2001). Public opinion toward gay and lesbian teachers. *Review of Public Personnel Administration*, 21, 133–151.

Light, P. (1999). *The true size of government*. Brookings Institution Press.

Lily Ledbetter Fair Pay Act of 2009 (Pub. L. 111–2).

Loving v. Virginia, 388 U.S. 1 (1967).

Macy v. Department of Justice. Equal Employment Opportunity Commission, Appeal No. 0120120821. (April 20, 2012).

Meritor Savings Bank v. Vinson, 477 U.S. 57 (1986).

Naff, K. C. (2001). *To look like America: Dismantling barriers for women and minorities in government*. Westview Press.

National Center for Transgender Equality. (2020). *Employment rights*. https://transequality.org/know-your-rights/employment-general

National Labor Relations Act (Pub. L. 74–198).

Naylor, L. A., & Rosenbloom, D. H. (2004). *Adarand, Grutter & Gratz:* Does affirmative Action in federal employment matter? *Review of Public Personnel Administration*, 24(2), 150–174.

Newport News Shipbuilding & Dry Dock Co v. EEOC, 462 U.S. 669 (1983).

Notice of Nonenforcement Refusal to Enforce Health and Human Services Grants Regulations. 84 Fed. Reg. 63809–01. 45 CFR Section 75.300. (2019, November 19).

Obergefell v. Hodges, 576 U.S. 644 (2015).

Oncale v. Sunflower Offshore Services, 523 US 75 (1998).

Ordelli v. Mark Farrell & Associates, 2013 WL 1100811 (D. Or. March 15, 2013).

Pambianchi v. Arkansas at Tech University, WL 11498236, at (E.D. Ark., March 14, 2014).

Patient Protection and Affordable Care Act of 2010 (Pub. L. 111–148). 124 Stat. 119. www.govinfo.gov/content/pkg/PLAW-111publ148/pdf/PLAW-111publ148.pdf

Phillips v. Martin Marietta Corp, 400 U.S. 542 (1971).

Pregnancy Discrimination Act of 1978 (Pub. L. 95–555). Retrieved February 11, 2020, from www.eeoc.gov/laws/statutes/pregnancy.cfm

Prescott v. Rady Children's Hospital, 3:16-cv-02408-BTM-JMA San Diego (2017a). Complaint. www.nclrights.org/wp-content/uploads/2019/07/Prescott-Amended-Complaint.pdf

Prescott v. Rady Children's Hospital, 16-cv-02408-BTMJMA. District Court Order (2017b). www.nclrights.org/wp-content/uploads/2019/07/Prescott-Sept-2017-Order.pdf

Price Waterhouse v. Hopkins, 490 U.S. 228 (1989), pp. 250–251.

Price Waterhouse v. Hopkins, 618 F. Supp at 117 (USDC, DC, 1985).

Primus, R. (2019, October 15). The Supreme Court case testing the limits of Gorsuch's textualism. *Politico Magazine*. www.politico.com/magazine/story/2019/10/15/lgbt-discrimination-supreme-court-gorsuch-textualism-229850

Princeton Research Associates for *Newsweek*, July 30-31, 1999. As cited in Public Perspectives. Considering Alternative Lifestyles. January/February 2000. https://ropercenter.cornell.edu/sites/default/files/2018-07/111024.pdf

Reuters IPSOS Poll Data. (2019, June 6). *Stonewall anniversary poll data*. Retrieved February 21, 2020, from https://static.reuters.com/resources/media/editorial/20190612/StonewallFinalResults.pdf

R. G. and G. R. Harris Funeral Homes v. EEOC, No. 18–107 (E. D. Michigan, 2017).

Riccucci, N. M. (2002). *Managing diversity in public sector work forces: Essentials of public policy and administration* (p. 135). Westview Press.

Romer v. Evans, 517 U.S. 620 (1996).

Rosenbloom, D. H. (2015). *Administrative law for public managers* (2nd ed.). Westview Press.

Rosenbloom, D. H. (1977). *Federal equal employment opportunity: Politics and public personnel administration*. Praeger.

Rosenbloom, D. H., O'Leary, R., & Chanin, J. (2019). *Public administration and law* (3rd ed.). Routledge an imprint of Taylor & Francis group. First issued in hardback 2019.

Section 504 of the Rehabilitation Act of 1973 as amended in 2013. (29 U.S.C. Sec 793; 41 CFR Part 60–741, U.S. Department of Labor).

Simonton v. Runyon, 232 F.3d 33 (2d Cir. 2000).

Singh, S., & Durso, L. E. (2017, May 2). *Widespread discrimination continues to shape LGBT people's lives in both subtle and significant ways*. www.americanprogress.org/issues/lgbtq-rights/news/2017/05/02/429529/widespread-discrimination-continues-shape-lgbt-peoples-lives-subtle-significant-ways/

Smith v. Avanti 1:16-cv-00091 (USDC Colorado, 2016).

Smith v. City of Salem, 378 F.3d 566 (6th Cir. 2004).

Smith v. Mission Associates Ltd. Partnership (2002).

SmithKline Beecham Corporation v. Abbott Laboratories, 740 F.3d 471 (2014).

Taylor, L. (2020, April 11). Gov. Northam signs Va. Values act protections LGBTQ community from discrimination. WSET ABC 13 News. https://wset.com/news/at-the-capitol/virginia-becomes-first-state-in-south-to-provide-anti-discrimination-lgbtq-protections

Texas v. United. States, 19-10011 (Fifth Cir. 2020).

To Prohibit Employment Discrimination Based on Gender Identity (H.R. 3696, 110th Congress 2007).

United Nations. (1948). *Universal Declaration of Human Rights*. New York: United Nations.

University of Tex. Southwestern Medical Center v. Nassar, 570 US 338 (2013).

U.S. Department of Health and Human Services. (2019, December 19). The Affordable Care Act and HIV/AIDS.

U.S. Department of Justice. Civil Rights Division. (n.d.). *ADA/HIV*. Retrieved June 17, 2020, from www.ada.gov/hiv/

U.S. Office of Personnel Management. (2015). *Addressing sexual orientation and gender identity discrimination in federal civilian employment: A guide to employee's rights, protections, and responsibilities*.

U.S. v. Windsor, 570 U.S. 744 (2013).

Va. Stat. §2.2–3904 and §36–96.3 (as amended by 2020 Va. H.B. 1663) (2020, February 27).

Vietnam Era Veterans' Adjustment Act as amended (38 U.S.C. Section 4212).

Vocational Rehabilitation Act of 1973 (Pub. L. 114–95).

Walsh v. Friendship Village of South County (4:18-cv-01222-JCH). (MO, October 5, 2018). www.nclrights.org/wp-content/uploads/2019/07/Walsh-Amended-Complaint.pdf
Walsh v. Friendship Village of South County, No. 19–1395 (Eighth Circuit, 2020).
Walsh v. Friendship Village of South County, 352 F. Supp 3d 920 (E.D. MO, 2019).
Watson v. Fort Worth Bank & Trust, 487 U.S. 977 (1988).
Wetzel v. Glen St. Andrew Living Community, No. 17–1322 (Seventh Circuit, 2018).
White House, Executive Order 11246. U.S. President Lyndon B. Johnson. Retrieved February 22, 2020, from www.eeoc.gov/eeoc/history/35th/thelaw/eo-11246.html
White House, Executive Order 12968. U.S. President Willian Clinton (1995, August 2).
White House, Executive Order 13087. U.S. President William Clinton. Prohibit discrimination based on sexual orientation. Retrieved February 22, 2020, from www.eeoc.gov/laws/executiveorders/13087.cfm
White House, Executive Order 13140, President Clinton (1999).
White House, Executive Order 13672 of July 21, 2014. U.S. President Barack Obama. Amends federal employment protections to cover sexual orientation and gender identity. Retrieved February 22, 2020, from www.eeoc.gov/eeoc/history/50th/thelaw/11478_11246_amend.cfm
White House, Executive Order 13683 of December 11, 2014. U.S. President Barack Obama. Fair pay, safe workplaces. Retrieved February 22, 2020, from www.federalregister.gov/documents/2017/11/06/2017-23588/guidance-for-executive-order-13673-fair-pay-and-safe-workplaces
White House, Executive Order 13738 of August 23, 2016. U.S. President Barack Obama. www.presidency.ucsb.edu/documents/executive-order-13738-amendment-executive-order-13673
White House, Executive Order 13782 of March 27, 2017. U.S. President Donald Trump. Revocation of Federal contracting executive orders. www.federalregister.gov/documents/2017/03/30/2017-06382/revocation-of-federal-contracting-executive-orders
Whitman-Walker Clinic v. HHS, 1:20-cv-01630 (2020).
Wildhaber v. St. Louis County Missouri, 17SL-CC00133 (MO, 2019).
Williamson v. A. G. Edwards & Sons, Inc., 876 F.2d 69, 70 (8th Cir. 1989), cert. denied.
Williamson v. A. G. Edwards & Sons, Inc., 493 U.S. 1089, 110 S. Ct. 1158, 107 L.Ed.2d 1061 (1990).
Winfield Cunningham, P. (2020, June 14). HUD to change transgender rules for single-sex homeless shelters. *Washington Post*. www.washingtonpost.com/politics/hud-to-change-transgender-rules-for-single-sex-homeless-shelters/2020/06/12/d47a5744-ad03–11ea-9063-e69bd6520940_story.html
Zarda v. Altitude Express, 883 F.3d 100 (Second Circuit, 2018).

Chapter 5

LGBT Rights and the U.S. Military Service

Introduction

One of the most important aspects of citizenship is being able to serve one's country. The U.S. military's treatment of lesbian, gay, bisexual, transgender, and queer (LGBTQ) members has been harsh ranging from discrimination and harassment to discharge. Two of the most well-known examples of discrimination based on sexual orientation are Sergeant Leonard Matlovich and Colonel Cammermeyer. Their stories are described along with a historical overview of informal policies to formal policies, including Don't Ask Don't Tell and the Don't Ask Don't Tell Repeal Act of 2010. Since 2010 lesbians, gays, and bisexuals have been legally and openly serving in the U.S. Armed Forces. However, transgender military members were not permitted to openly serve until 2016 under President Obama and the policy was reversed by President Trump. As a result, several lawsuits have been filed against President Trump alleging discrimination and violation of equal rights. These legal cases are analyzed.

Currently, LGB individuals can openly serve in the U.S. Armed Forces. According to the U.S. Department of Defense (DoD), it "recognizes all military and civilian men and women who serve and are part of the LGBT community as equal, contributing members of the total force" (U.S. Department of Defense, June 12, 2017). In 2011, LGB individuals secured the right to 'openly' serve in the military. Since 2011 the DoD has publicly celebrated LGBT Pride Month as a demonstration of its commitment to LGBT service members (U.S. Department of Defense, June 2, 2017 – see Kurtha). Two years later (2013), the Pentagon began recognizing same-sex marriages (SSMs) and providing spousal and family benefits as a result of the U.S. Supreme Court ruling *U.S. v Windsor* (2013). The DoD also has an employee resource group titled the "DoD Association for LGBT," which is a 501(c)(3) nonprofit organization serving DoD family members, servicemembers, contractors, and civilians (DoDPride.org, n.d.). In 2016, President Obama signed an executive order allowing transgender people to openly serve in the military. However, securing the constitutional rights of LGBT citizens in the U.S. Armed Forces has been a long, controversial battle. Historically, the U.S. military, similar to American society, has treated LGBT members distinctly different than heterosexual members and often with severe consequences. Beginning with the American Revolutionary War, homosexual activity was banned in the U.S. military. Members who were caught were involuntary discharged and denied veteran benefits. In addition, gay servicemembers were denied high-level security clearances. This chapter provides an overview of evolving LGBT legal rights in the U.S. military. LGB policies and court cases are discussed first followed by transgender policies.

Lesbians, Gays, and Bisexuals

The U.S. Armed Forces is located in over 100 countries and consists of 2 million members. It is comprised of five branches: Army, Air Force, Navy, Marines, and Coast Guard. The Armed Forces operate under a distinct justice system separate from the U.S. court system. The Uniform Code of Military Justice (UCMJ) (10 Stat. Section 801–896) operationalizes the military justice system and the *Manual for Courts-Martial* consists of regulations on court-martials and punishments for criminal offenses. This is significant because military members charged with homosexual acts (e.g., sodomy) are tried under the military court system, not the U.S. court system.

The U.S. Armed Forces have a small percentage of LGB servicemembers. It is estimated that 2.2 percent of the U.S. military is LGB (Gates, May 2010) compared to 3.0 percent of the general population (National Opinion Research Center, 2017). According to the Williams Institute, there are an estimated 48,500 LGB serving in active duty and ready reserves and an additional 22,500 in the retired reserved forces or standby (Gates, May 2010). Although a small percentage of LGB individuals are service members, the U.S. military (as well as American society in general) has a long history of discriminating against homosexuals. There have been written policies prohibiting homosexuals from serving in the armed forces since World War II (U.S. Government Accounting Office, 1992, p. 2). From 1916 to 1947, gay service members were separated from service through a "blue" administrative discharge, which was code for homosexual (Berube, 1990).

Policy on Homosexuals

Prior to 1942 (World War II), there was no formal written policy banning homosexuals from the U.S. military (U.S. GAO, 1992; Manegold, 1993). However, there were policies prohibiting acts of sodomy. Since the Revolutionary War, sodomy was recognized as a crime. Specifically, the Articles of War of 1806 (revised in 1920, 1916) identified sodomy as a crime (Article 93, 1920). In 1942, military psychiatrists argued that homosexuals were unfit to serve in the military due to "psychopathic personality disorders." Identified homosexuals were discharged and denied veteran benefits (Manegold, 1993; U.S. Naval Institute, Key Dates, n.d.). Gay military servicemembers were labeled "mentally unfit" and given a Section 8 discharge (U.S. Army, Regulation 615–360). From the 1940s to the 1960s, which covers World War II, the Korean War, and Vietnam War, the military defined homosexuality as a mental defect and banned homosexuals from entry. In 1951, the Uniform Code of Military Conduct (UCMC), which applies to all the Armed Forces, was adopted. UCMJ, Article 125 forbids sodomy. It states "any person . . . who engages in unnatural carnal copulation with another person of the same or opposite sex or with an animal is guilty of sodomy" (UCMJ, Article 125) In 1953, President Eisenhower signed Executive Order 10450, which listed sexual perversion (homosexuality) as a security risk and grounds for termination. As a result, homosexuals were denied high-level security clearances. This practice continued for decades. Sodomy (both heterosexual and homosexual) was a felony in every state across the country until 1962. In many ways, U.S. military policy mirrored the discrimination and prejudices against homosexuals that took place in American society. In 1972, the army passed regulation 635–200 which identified homosexual acts as grounds for dismissal. However, when combat arose and personnel needs increased, the military relaxed its screening criteria and allowed homosexuals to serve, then the military discharged them once the conflict decreased (Powers, 2017; Manegold, 1993; Berube, 1990). Following is the story of Sergeant Leonard Matlovich, a celebrated military member who was discharged for being gay.

Sergeant Leonard Matlovich

In 1975, U.S. Air Force Technical Sergeant Leonard Matlovich, led the fight against the military ban on gays and was one of the most visible U.S. gay rights activists in the 1970s and 1980s. After serving his country for 12 years with exemplary service, serving three tours of duty in Vietnam, receiving a Bronze Star Medal, a Purple Heart, two Air Force Commendation Medals, and a Meritorious Service Medal, the U.S. Air Force honorably discharged Sergeant Maklovitch after he told his commanding officer he was gay. Matlovich was officially discharged on September 16, 1975 (*Matlovich v. Secretary of the Air Force*, 1976), for voluntarily acknowledging he is a practicing homosexual. Matlovich filed a complaint in October 1975 and applied for a restraining order to prevent his discharge from the air force. During the appeals process, Matlovich's legal team built a case on a U.S. Air Force exception rule, AFM 39–12, that a homosexual servicemember could be retained under unusual circumstances. It states "where the most unusual circumstances exist and provided that the airman's ability to perform military service has not been compromised" (*Matlovich v. Secretary of Air Force*, 1978, p. 4). The air force acknowledged that it had applied the rule to gay service members before but could not distinguish previous cases from Matlovich's and offered no concrete reason why Matlovich did not qualify as an exemption. During the legal process, Matlovich went from being a closeted military member to one of the leading gay activists in the country. *TIME* magazine ran his picture on the cover with the title "I am a Homosexual: The Gay Drive for Acceptance (TIME, September 8, 1975a). In addition, his story was printed on the front page of the *New York Times* and in numerous articles. NBC broadcast his story on television titled "Sgt. Matlovich v. the Air Force." In 1980, the U.S. Air Force was ordered to give Sergeant Matlovich five years of backpay. He agreed to a $160,000 tax-free settlement from the air force and an honorable discharge. Matlovich continued to advocate for gay rights, was an AIDS activist, and ran for public office. He died from AIDS at the age of 44. Sergeant Matlovich received a 21-gun salute and was laid to rest at Congressional Cemetery in Washington, D.C. The headstone reads: A Gay Vietnam Veteran (Bateman, 2015). Sergeant Matlovich had a major impact on gay rights in the U.S. and, specifically, in the military. He was the first gay service member to publicly acknowledge he was homosexual. He was quoted as saying, "[M]aybe not in my lifetime, but we are going to win in the end" (Bateman, 2015, p. 4).

Formal Policy

In 1982, the Pentagon issued a formal written policy banning gays from military service and cited seven reasons for the ban. It was the policy of the DoD that homosexual behavior by military members would result in a mandatory discharge. The DoD policy directive 1332.14 stated that

> homosexuality is incompatible with military service. The presence in the military environment of persons who engage in homosexual conduct or who, by their statements,

demonstrate a propensity to engage in homosexual conduct, seriously impairs the accomplishment of the military mission. The presence of such members adversely affects the ability of the military services to maintain discipline, good order, and morale; to foster mutual trust and confidence among servicemembers; to ensure the integrity of the system of rank and command; to facilitate assignment and worldwide deployment of servicemembers who frequently must live and work under close conditions affording minimal privacy; to recruit and retain members of the Military Services; to maintain public acceptability of military service; and to prevent breaches of security.

(U.S. GAO, 1992, p. 2)

In addition, the military addressed soldiers with Human Immunodeficiency Virus (HIV). The policy was simple and effective. Soldiers infected with HIV were not allowed to serve in combat (Shilts, 1993). The DoD defines homosexuals as "a person, regardless of sex, who engage in, desires to engage in, or intends to engage in homosexual acts" (U.S. GAO, 1992, p. 2). These acts include "bodily contact, actively undertaken or passively permitted, between members of the same sex for the purpose of satisfying sexual desires" (US, GAO, 1992, p. 2). The policy ban on homosexuals resulted in an estimated 15,000 servicemen and -women being expelled between 1980 and 1990, with the vast majority being enlisted white males (U.S. GAO, 1992, p. 4). Of the U.S. Armed Forces, the navy had the highest percentage of discharges under the separation category of homosexuality. At the time, sodomy was illegal in the majority of states. In 1986, the U.S Supreme Court ruled that homosexual sodomy was not a constitutional right (*Bowers v. Hardwick*, 1986). Sexual privacy did not become a constitutional right until 2003 when the court overturned *Bower* in *Lawrence v. Texas* (2003), invalidating sodomy laws in the remaining 13 states. As of 2003, sexual privacy became a constitutional right for both homosexuals and heterosexuals.

By the late 1980s, attitudes toward homosexuals began to shift. In 1988, a report commissioned by the DoD found that homosexuality did not pose a significant military threat (U.S. Naval Institute, n.d.). In addition, separation from service due to homosexuality was costly. The U.S. General Accounting Office (now known as the Government Accounting Office) issued a report in 1992 stating that the cost of replacing service members discharged for homosexuality was $28,266 for an enlisted member and $120,722 for an officer. Moreover, over 13,000 members were discharged from service due to sexual orientation (Eagan, May 31, 1992). Toward the end of the 1980s, gays and lesbians were becoming more accepted into society as well as the military. Numerous homosexuals service members came out publicly and advocated for gay rights and fought involuntary discharges from the military. See Leonard Matlovich (TIME, 1975b), Joseph Steffan (*Steffan v. Cheney*, 1990; Steffan, 1992) Tracey Thorne, Perry Watkins (*Watkins v. U.S. Army*, 1983; Wyatt-Nichol & Naylor, 2015) and Margarethe Cammermeyer (1994). In addition, U.S. Secretary of Defense Dick Cheney advocated for his press aid Pete Williams when Williams was publicly 'outed' (Hayes, 2007). These individuals led the charge in getting the military ban lifted. The case of Colonel Cammermeyer is described next.

Conduct, Not Status: Serving in Silence

In June 1992, Colonel Margarethe Cammermeyer, a colonel in the Washington National Guard, was involuntarily discharged due to sexual orientation. She had served her country for 30 years and served with distinction. Colonel Cammermeyer was the "highest ranking military officer ever discharged for being homosexual" (*Cammermeyer v. Perry*, 1994; Baldwin, 2013). She was a Vietnam War veteran (served during the Tet Offensive), a Bronze Star recipient (Balzar, 1994), and was selected in 1985 out of 34,000 candidates as the Veteran Administration nurse of the year. In 1989, she applied to the Army War College, and in a top-security clearance interview, Cammermeyer disclosed she was a lesbian. As a result, the army began discharge proceedings (Baldwin, 2013). Cammermeyer fought back and filed a lawsuit in civil court claiming her equal protection rights were violated. Historically, the courts required a rational basis standard of review on the military ban of homosexuals. The DoD argued that homosexuality was considered a security risk and that homosexual behavior was considered misconduct.

Specifically, the Pentagon argued that "counter intelligence agencies target homosexuals" (*High Tech Gays et al. v. Defense Industrial Security Clearance Office*, 1990; Gerstmann, 1999, p. 148). However, the court ruled that it was unconstitutional to discharge Cammermeyer based on sexual orientation because there was no rational relationship between the government's policy and its stated objectives (*Cammermeyer v. Perry*, 1994; Baldwin, 2013; *Meinhold v. Department of Defense*, 1993). In a similar case involving the navy, a judge found that "in the absence of sexual conduct which interferes with the military mission" the DOD's ban on homosexuals is unconstitutional. . . . The DOD's justifications for its policy banning gays and lesbians from military service are based on cultural myths and false stereotypes. These justifications are baseless and very similar to the reasons offered to keep the military racially segregated in the 1940s" (*Meinghold v. DOD*, 1997, 1993). Cammermeyer served for 3 more years, went on to run for U.S. Congress, and was appointed to the Defense Advisory Committee on Women in the Services by the U.S. secretary of defense. Her story (Cammermeyer, 1994) was turned into a movie titled *Serving in Silence: The Colonel Margarethe Cammermeyer Story* (Barwood Films, 1995), which was based on her 1994 autobiography.

Don't Ask, Don't Tell

The assimilation of homosexuals into the military was part of a larger national debate on the worthiness of gays (Manegold, April 18, 1993). Public opinion had begun to change and was more favorable and sympathetic to gays and lesbians. In addition, the murder of gay U.S. Navy Petty Officer Allen Schindler publicly highlighted the military's discriminatory practices against homosexuals (Reza, January 9, 1993). In 1993, the U.S. secretary of defense released a study prepared by the National Defense Research Institute titled *Sexual Orientation and U.S. Military Personnel Policy: Options and Assessment* in which it argued that there would be minimal consequences military recruitment and retention if the gay ban was lifted (The RAND Corporation, 1993). In this political context, President Clinton responded by initiating and signing into law the Don't Ask, Don't Tell Policy (DADT) of 1993 (P. Law 103–160; 10 U.S.C. section 654). The DoD directive 1304.26, issued in December 1993, went into effect on February 28, 1994. In sum, openly homosexual individuals were banned from serving in the military, and closeted gays and bisexuals could serve as long as they did not disclose their sexual orientation or activity. Military members could not be asked about their sexual orientation, nor could they be discharged for identifying as gay. However, they could be discharged for "homosexual conduct," which meant having sexual relations or displaying homosexual overtures. In sum, the DADT prohibited gays from openly serving in the military (Wyatt-Nichol & Naylor, 2013).

Security Clearances

Next, security clearances were addressed. Prior to 1995, gays were denied security clearances, which often meant job loss. The perception was that homosexual behavior made an individual a greater threat to national defense. Specifically, homosexuals were viewed as easy blackmail targets by spies and perceived as more likely to engage in espionage and treason. This belief and practice, barring homosexuals from high-security clearances, date back to the Cold War and the McCarthy era. It applied to all federal employees and military members. The period was known as the lavender scare and impacted military servicemembers as well as intelligence agencies (Gerstmann, 1999). Military members, Foreign Service officers, and Central Intelligence Agency officers were denied clearances and lost their jobs during the McCarthy Red Scare (Harris, 2015). Eventually, the denial of security clearances led to litigation. The most notable of these was *High Tech Gays et al. v. Defense Industrial Security Clearance Office* (1990). The case was based on homosexuality in the military and security clearances. The core issue was whether homosexuals posed an increased threat to security (coercion – blackmail, intimidation, espionage) due to sexual orientation.

In response to this case and others, President Clinton issued Executive Order 12968 in 1995, ending the federal government's ban on denying homosexuals security clearances. The practice of denying security clearances based on sexual orientation was a carryover from the Cold War. Executive Order 12968 states, "The United States Government does not discriminate on the basis of race, color, religion, sex, national origin, disability or sexual orientation in granting access to classified information" (August 2, 1995). The order applies to both government employees and federal government contractors. In addition, the policy prohibits questions inferring suitability for access to information based on sexual orientation. In other words, the federal government cannot ask intrusive questions about sexual orientation. Investigators can ask about concealed activity or conduct that would make them subject to coercion, but they cannot directly ask about sexual orientation. The impact of this policy was monumental in that it ended a 40-year ban on gay's access to high-level security clearances formally instituted by President Eisenhower.

Hate Crimes Added to UCMJ

In 1999, President Clinton signed Executive Order 13140 to amend the UCMJ to include hate-crime evidence in sentencing (Federal Register, October 12, 1999). The executive order was in response to the brutal murder of a gay army soldier named Barry L. Winchell. Private Mitchell was asleep in the barracks at Fort Campbell, Kentucky, when another soldier beat his skull in with a baseball bat. Private Calvin Glover was court-martialed and convicted of premeditated murder (CBS News, December 7, 1999). The murder was a hate crime motivated by Glover's hatred of Winchell's homosexuality. The executive order increased criminal penalties for hate crimes and added hate crimes as admissible to the sentencing authority. Specifically, the executive order states "evidence that the accused intentionally selected any victim or any property as the object of the offense because of the actual or perceived race, color, religion, national origin, ethnicity, gender, disability, or sexual orientation of any person" (White House, Executive Order 13140, Section 1d, p. 55116, October 6, 1999). Although the executive order was signed into law after the sentencing of Glover, Winchell's case solidified opposition to DADT.

DADT Repeal Act of 2010

By 2009, the military ban on homosexuals openly serving in the military became untenable. In addition to Winchell's brutal death, public opinion continued to shift in favor of gays and lesbians in the military; reflecting a change in attitudes and beliefs. In 2010, President Obama signed the DADT Repeal Act (P. Law 111–321), ending the military ban on homosexuals openly serving.

In September 2010, U.S. District Judge Virginia Phillips ruled that the DADT policy was unconstitutional and a month later issued an injunction to stop enforcement of the policy. The policy had been expensive to implement. During the first 10 years of DADT, from 1994 to 2003, approximately 9,682 individuals were discharged at a cost of $22,000 to $43,000 per person (Gates, May 2010). It cost the federal government between $291 million and $552 million to implement President Clinton's DADT policy (Gates, May 2010). Congress repealed DADT in 2011. President Obama signed the appeal and DADT ended in September of 2011, marking the beginning of homosexuals openly serving in the U.S. Armed Forces.

Recognition of Same-Sex Marriages

The remaining wall to fall was same-sex marriage. In 2013, the U.S. Supreme Court struck down the Defense of Marriage Act (DOMA) of 2006 (P. Law 104–199) in *U.S. v. Windsor* (2013). Specifically, the court struck down Section 3 of DOMA, which defined marriage as a relationship between a man and a woman. The court's decision recognized same-sex marriage as a legal right in states that legalized same-sex marriage (13 at the time) and granted federal spousal benefits to same-sex married couples. As a result, in 2013, the DoD began recognizing same-sex marriages of military members if a marriage license was provided as proof (civil unions were not recognized). This meant servicemembers could receive same-sex spousal and family benefits traditionally reserved for heterosexual couples, including health care, basic housing allowance, family separation allowance, dependent identification card, and veteran benefits. Two years later, the U.S. Supreme Court ruled marriage equality was a fundamental right and would be recognized nationwide (*Obergefell v. Hodges*, 2015).

The various changes in military policy on LGB members were a reflection of changing public opinion. Today, gays and bisexuals can openly serve in the U.S. military and are guaranteed constitutional rights in the areas of same-sex marriage, military spousal benefits, hate-crime protection, and security clearance access. The more controversial issue is transgender rights for military members, which is discussed next.

Discrimination Against Women

In addition to discrimination based on sexual orientation, the military has a history of discriminating based on sex. In the book *Women Veterans: Lifting the Veil of Invisibility*, military researchers Harris et al. (2018) describe the routine and systemic marginalization of women in the U.S. military. Discrimination has been sanctioned in both informal and formal policies. When female servicemembers report sexual harassment, rape, or violence, they are often silenced. A tactic known as 'lesbian baiting' is often used to discredit women who report abuse (McClintock, 1996). "Women, straight and gay, are accused as lesbians, when they rebuff the advances by men or report sexual abuse" (Damiano, 1999, p. 501; as cited in Harris et al., 2018). There is also evidence supporting the claim that DADT was used to discharge women from the military. Under DADT, women and minorities were discharged at a higher rate than males. For example, in 2009, women composed 14 percent of the all-volunteer force but accounted for 30 to 39 percent of DADT discharges, and in the army, an astounding 48 percent of discharges under DADT were women (O'Keefe, 2010; as cited in Harris et al., 2018) despite population estimates that 3.5 to 4.5 percent of the U.S. population is lesbian or gay (Trotta, 2019; Williams Institute, 2019). Equally important, Pentagon data reveal that "black women were three times more likely than any demographic in the military to have been charged for violations under the policy" (Harris et al., 2018, p. 15; Holloway, 2010), which is astonishing given that the black population (both male and female) composes only 13 percent of the U.S. population.

Regarding formal policies, the U.S. Supreme Court has ruled that military policies have treated women servicemembers differently than males. For example, in *Frontierro v. Richardson* (1973) the U.S. Supreme Court ruled that the air force's employee benefit policy discriminated against female servicemembers' spouses. They were treated distinctly different than male service member spouses with regard to employee benefits. In addition, women have been excluded from combat and the selective service. Beginning in 1948, women were excluded from direct ground combat under the Women's Armed Forces Integration Act of 1948 (Pub. L. 80–645; 62 Stat. 356). The combat exclusion policy was enforced for approximately 50 years. It was not until the 1990s that women combat restrictions were slowly lifted. In 1994, the DoD issued a "Direct Ground Combat Definition and Assignment Rule," which relaxed restrictions. It states, in part, "Service members are eligible to be assigned to all positions for which they are qualified, except that women shall be excluded from assignment to units below the brigade level whose primary mission is to engage in direct combat on the ground" (U.S. Army, Vergun, D., February 7, 2013). Later, in 2013, U.S. Secretary of Defense Leon Panetta and the Joint Chiefs of Staff made a monumental shift by rescinding the DoD's 1994 Direct Ground Combat Definition and Assignment Rule, thus ending the women combat exclusion policy. The DoD is "paving the way for more women to serve in direct combat roles and in more military occupational specialties that are now open only to males" U.S. Army, Vergun, D., February 7, 2013). By ending the women combat exclusion policy, the remaining policy that discriminates against women is the U.S. Selective Service, which gives the president the power to draft male citizens during time of war (Selective Service System, 2017a, 2017b). Currently, women are excluded from the Selective Service. Harris et al. (2018) argue that for women to be treated equally in the military, they must be granted full citizenship and full agency, which includes the 2013 combat exclusion repeal, drafting women in the Selective Service, and additional measures to ensure women are welcomed and embraced in the military. For example, white women attrition in the military outpaces recruitment and retention rates (Harris et al., 2018, p. 93) due to a perceived hostile environment. Approximately 50 percent of women report some form of harassment (Harris et al., 2018, p. 4). The DoD has made significant positive changes in its treatment of women in the military but additional policies are needed to ensure equal treatment.

Transgender People

In the military, transgender people are treated distinctly different than LGB military members (similar to American society). This section describes the number of transgender people, discusses transgender prohibition policies and rights, followed by legal cases. According to the Williams Institute, approximately 150,000 transgender individuals have served in the U.S. military. Currently, there are approximately 15,500 transgender military members serving on active duty, in the guard or reserve forces (8,800 active duty and 6,700 guard or reserve; Gates & Herman, May 2014). In addition, there are an estimated 134,300 transgender individuals who are veterans and retired guard or reserve forces for a total of 149,800 transgender individuals who have served or who are currently serving in the U.S. military. Historically, transgenders have not been able to openly serve in the military. There service as a transgender military member has been hidden, similar to homosexual military members. Until June 2016, it was the policy of the U.S. military to prohibit "openly transgender individuals from accession into the military and authorized the discharge of such individuals" (White House, Presidential Memorandum, August 25, 2017).

Prohibition of Transgender People

In 2011, the DADT policy (10 U.S.C. Section 654) was repealed, ending the military ban on gays, lesbian, and bisexuals. However, DADT did not address transgender individuals (Kerrigan, 2011). The prohibition of transgender individuals was not based on federal legislation or an executive order but based on medical military code (Harrison-Quintana & Herman, 2013). The U.S. Military Medical Code considered transgender individuals to suffer from psychosexual disorders such as transsexualism, cross-dressing, or gender transition (Witten, 2007). As such, transgender military members could be discharged if suspected or if they 'come out.' It has been argued that the military has a disproportionate number of transgender members. A study by Klasfeld (2012) reveals that male-to-female transgender identity is twice as high among the military than the general population. Of military members who transition from male-to-female some are motivated to join the military based on a "flight into hypermasculinity" in which to correct feelings of incongruence (Brown, 1988), which can create medical issues. Historically, transgender people have been formally prohibited from serving in the U.S. military. The DoD Directive 332.38 "prohibited transgender people from openly serving in the U.S. military" (*Stone v. Trump*, 2017, p. 15).

Rights of Transgender People

The formal right for transgenders to openly serve in the U.S. Armed Forces began under the Obama administration. On July 1, 2016, U.S. Defense Secretary Ash Carter lifted the transgender ban allowing transgender people to serve in the military. This meant military members identified or diagnosed with transgender identity or gender dysphoria could not be legally discharged from the military. In the past, sex reassignment surgery could not be performed or funded by the Veterans Health Administration or Veterans Administration (U.S. Department of Veterans Affairs, 2013, 2011). However, this policy was changed by President Obama. Under the Obama administration, the military authorized resources for sex reassignment procedures and granted permission of accession of transgender individuals to the military. A Rand study prepared for the U.S. Secretary of Defense Ash Carter, titled "Impact of Transgender Personnel on Readiness and Health Care Cost in the U. S. Military Likely to Be Small" (2016), stated that lifting the ban on transgenders would involve a small percentage of the armed forces and have a minimal impact on the military (Rand Corporation, 2016). The military was required to accommodate transgender troops over the next year. "Transgender recruits had to undergo a set of vigorous physical and mental tests order to join. This meant a medical provider had to certify they've been clinically stable in their preferred sex for 18 months [for those on hormone therapy] and are free of significant distress or impairment" (Baldor, December 11, 2017). Under DoD directive 1300.28, section 1.2(a) "transgender persons . . . are subject to the same standards and procedures as other members with regard to their medical fitness for duty, physical fitness, uniform and grooming standards, deployability, and retention" (*Stone v. Trump*, 2017). Based on the directive, transgender people were able to openly serve in the armed forces sharing with military personnel they were transgender and seeking medical treatment in the military for gender dysphoria and for transitioning.

Policy Reversal

However, the policy was short-lived. The policy was reversed under President Trump. On August 25, 2017, President Trump reversed President Obama's order and issued a transgender ban (after military members came out and stated they were transgender to military personnel). The Presidential Memorandum on Military Service by Transgender Individuals states:

> Until June 2016, the Department of Defense (DoD) and the Department of Homeland Security (DHS) (collectively, the Departments) generally prohibited openly transgender individuals from accession into the United States military and authorized the discharge of such individuals. Shortly before President Obama left office, however, his Administration dismantled the Departments' established framework by permitting transgender individuals to serve openly in the military, authorizing the use of the Departments' resources to fund sex-reassignment surgical procedures, and permitting accession of such individuals after July 1, 2017. . . . Accordingly, by the authority vested in me as President and as Commander in Chief of the Armed Forces of the United States under the Constitution and the laws of the United States of America, including Article II of the Constitution, I am directing the Secretary of Defense, and the Secretary of Homeland Security with respect to the U.S. Coast Guard, to return to the longstanding policy and practice on military service by transgender individuals that was in place prior to June 2016 until such time as a sufficient basis exists upon which to conclude that terminating that policy and practice would not have the negative effects discussed above. The Secretary of Defense, after consulting with the Secretary of Homeland Security, may advise me at any time, in writing, that a change to this policy is warranted . . . halt all use of DoD or DHS resources to fund sex reassignment surgical procedures for military personnel, except to the extent necessary to protect the health of an individual who has already begun a course of treatment to reassign his or her sex.
> (White House, Presidential Memoranda, National Security & Defense, August 25, 2017)

The new transgender policy became effective January 1, 2018. It prevents openly transgender individuals from joining the military and stops military resources for sex reassignment surgical procedures for current military members (unless in the middle of medical treatment). President Trump's rationale for reversing the policy is that it could "hinder military effectiveness and lethality, disrupt unit cohesion, or tax military resources" (White House, Presidential Memorandum, August 25, 2017, p. 1). In response to Trump's anti-transgender policy, at least four lawsuits have been filed alleging that banning transgender individuals from the military is a violation of the U.S. Constitution: *Doe v. Trump* (2017), *Karnoski v. Trump* (2017), *Stockman v. Trump* (2017), and *Stone v. Trump* (2017). The *Stone v. Trump* (2017) case is described next.

Stone v. Trump *(2017)*

This case involves six U.S. military members alleging President Trump violated their constitutional rights by enforcing a military transgender ban, dismissing transgender members, banning required medical treatment, and banning enlistment of transgenders. The case was filed in the U.S. District Court of Maryland in April 2017 with six plaintiffs. They include five named military members and one anonymous member: Petty Officer Brock, Staff Sergeant Kate Cole, Senior Airman John Doe, Airman First Class Seven Ero George, Petty Officer First Class Teagan Gilbert, and Technical Sergeant Tommie Parker. Petty Officer Brock Stone is an 11-year veteran of the U.S. Navy who served a nine-month deployment to Afghanistan and received an achievement medal for his deployment. In June 2016, he shared with military personnel he was transgender after the issuance of the Open

Service Directive. He is undergoing hormone therapy as part of his gender transition. Staff Sergeant Kate Cole has served in the U.S. Army for approximately a decade, including a one-year deployment to Afghanistan. She revealed her transgender status after the issuance of the Open Service Directive. Senior Airman John Doe has served in the U.S. Airforce for over six years and received "Airman of the Year" for his flight. Doe completed a six-month deployment to Qatar. He is undergoing hormone therapy for gender transition. Airman First Class Seven Ero George serves in the Air National Guard and is a member of the Honor Guard. He also shared that he was transgender on a reliance of the Open Service Directive. He is undergoing hormone therapy as part of his gender transition. Petty Officer First Class Teagan Gilbert is a reservist who served 13 years in the U.S. Navy and a one-year deployment to Afghanistan. She revealed she was transgender under the Open Service Directive. She is undergoing hormone therapy as part of her gender transition. Technical Sergeant Tommie Parker has served in the U.S. Marine Corps for 4 years and the Air National Guard for over 26 years. She shared with military personnel she was transgender under the 2016 Open Service Directive. The Open Service Directive was issued by U.S. Secretary of Defense Ash Carter under the Obama administration on June 30, 2016, stating,

> Effective immediately, no otherwise qualified Service member may be involuntarily separated, discharged or denied re-enlistment or continuation of service, solely on the basis of their gender identity. Transgender service members will be subjected to the same standards as any other Service member of the same gender. A service member's whose ability to serve is adversely affected by a medical condition or medical treatment related to their gender identity should be treated, for purpose of separation and retention, in a manner consistent with a Service member whose ability to serve is similarly affected for reasons unrelated to gender identity or gender transition.
>
> (as cited in *Stone v. Trump*, 2017)

In addition to the directive, in September 2016, the DoD produced a transgender handbook titled *Transgender Service in the U.S. Military: An Implementation Handbook*, signaling to service members it was permissible to be openly transgender in the military. Less than a year later, on July 26, 2017, President Trump announced a transgender ban on Twitter. The plaintiffs allege they are being discriminated against on the basis of sex which is a violation of the due process clause of the Fifth Amendment of the U.S. Constitution, a violation of their fundamental right to liberty under the due process clause of the Fifth Amendment, and a violation of equal process (*Stone v. Trump*, 2017; *Doe v. Trump*, 2017). It is estimated to cost $960 million to implement the transgender ban (Belkin et al., August 2017). Three federal courts (D.C., Maryland, and Washington) stopped the transgender military ban. The U.S. Court of Appeals for the Fourth Circuit denied the Trump administration's request to delay the January 1, 2018, enlistment date. The U.S. Department of Justice advised it would not intervene to prevent transgender individuals from entering the military (ACLU.org January 2, 2018) and petitioned the U.S. Supreme Court to review the federal district court's ruling preventing the implementation of Trump's transgender military ban. Then in February 2018, U.S. Secretary of Defense James Mattis delivered a report to President Trump recommending a transgender ban in the military (Mattis, February 22, 2018). On January 22, 2019, in an unsigned 5–4 order, the U.S. Supreme Court lifted the injunction until the cases are decided (deVogue & Cohen, January 22, 2019). This gives the military authority to discharge openly transgender members and stop enlistment of transgender people in the military until decisions are made in the lower court cases. The court also denied Tramp's request for a review of lower court decisions (before the appellate courts had ruled). The majority opinion consisting of Chief Justice Roberts and Justices Alito,

Thomas, Kavanaugh, and Gorsuch. Justices Ginsburg, Breyer, Sotomayor, and Kagan dissenting. As of April 12, 2019, except for limited exceptions, transgender individuals are banned from serving in the U.S. military. In June 2019, the Ninth Circuit ruled that the Trump administration's ban on transgenders discriminates against transgenders, treating them differently than other people, requiring a heightened level of scrutiny. The government must show that the policy is based on a compelling governmental interest (*Karnoski v. Trump*, 2019). The other court cases are pending. The transgender ban is considered a major defeat for the LGBTQ community.

Public Opinion on Transgender Military Members

The military transgender ban contradicts public opinion surveys. A 2017 public opinion survey shows that 63 percent of Americans favor transgender people serving in the military (Greenberg et al., 2019). A more recent Gallup poll (2019) shows the percentage has increased to 71 percent of Americans supporting transgenders serving in the military (McCarthy, June 20, 2019). Based on current polls, a majority of Americans support transgender people serving in the military. The issue is a lack of political support. The same 2019 Gallup poll found that of those surveyed, 44 percent of Republicans do not support transgender people serving in the military, compared to 88 percent of Democrats who support transgender people serving in the military. Conservatives and evangelicals are opposed to transgenders serving in the military.

Conclusion

The U.S. military, one of the largest organizations in the world is composed of more than 2 million members. Its members span 100 countries and 6 continents. Its mission is to protect the U.S. In addition to its mission of maintaining national defense, it is also charged with reflecting its citizenry, public opinion, and demographic changes. This means the U.S. Armed Forces must adapt their domestic policies, similar to modifying their foreign policies to remain strong. This includes changes in recruitment, personnel, and human resources. Since 2010, lesbians, gays, and bisexuals have been legally and openly serving in the U.S. Armed Forces (Don't Ask Don't Tell Repeal Act of 2010). However, transgender military members were not permitted to openly serve until 2016 under President Obama. Under Obama, transgenders could openly serve and receive military medical benefits for gender dysphoria and transition. After transgender members 'came out' to military personnel, the directive/policy was reversed by President Trump in 2017. Although policy reversals are within the legal scope of presidential executive policies, this specific policy has the appearance of a 'bait and switch' tactic. If military members openly state they are transgender, then the military will provide free medical care. However, after transgender military members came out, the policy changed, and now those identified as transgender are subject to stigma, prejudice, bias, and dismissal, leaving them exposed and without employment. As described in previous chapters, presidential policy reversal is not new; it has been utilized for decades. However, the transgender ban and its adverse outcomes on military members and their careers highlight the need for a sustainable, long-term policy on transgender military service. In January 2019, the U.S. Supreme Court decided in *Stone v. Trump* (2019) to lift the injunction until the cases are decided in the lower courts (deVogue & Cohen, January 22, 2019). In June 2020, the Ninth Circuit ruled that the Trump administration's military ban targets transgenders and that the government must show how the ban meets a compelling governmental purpose (*Kanoski v. Trump*, 2019). The other three cases are pending. As of the publication of this book, the military transgender ban remains in effect.

Resources

American Civil Liberties Union. www.aclu.org
American Military Partner Association. www.modernmilitary.org
Department of Defense Association of LGBT. www.DoDPride.org
Gender Justice League. www.genderjusticeleague.org/
GLBTQ Legal Advocates and Defenders (GLAD).
Human Rights Campaign. www.hrc.org
Lambda Legal. www.lambdalegal.org/
Modern Military Association of America. www.modernmilitary.org
National Center for Lesbian Rights. www.nclr.org
OutServe-SLDN. www.outserve-sldn.org
U.S. Department of Defense. Transgender Service in the U.S. Military: An Implementation Handbook. September 30, 2016. https://dod.defense.gov/Portals/1/features/2016/0616_policy/DoDTGHandbook_093016.pdf

References

American Civil Liberties Union. (2018, January 2). *Trump administration will not ask Supreme Court to halt trans military recruits*. www.aclu.org/press-releases/trump-administration-will-not-ask-supreme-court-halt-trans-military-recruits
Articles of War of 1806. (Revised in 1916, 1920). Article 93.
Baldor, L. (2017, December 11). Pentagon says transgender people can enlist starting Jan. 1 *Associated Press News*.
Baldwin, H. (2013). Don't ask, don't tell: Lesbians challenge the new military policy. *Berkeley Journal of Gender, Law & Justice, 10*(1), 148–155.
Balzar, J. (1994, June 2). Lesbian Army officer wins battle in court: Military federal judge orders reinstatement of Col. Margarethe Cammermeyer. Ruling raises questions about 'don't ask, don't tell' policy. *New York Times*.
Barwood Films. (1995). *Serving in silence: The Colonel Margarethe Cammermeyer story*.
Bateman, G. W. (2015). Matlovich, L., & Leonard, P., Jr. (1943–1988). *GLBTQ encyclopedia entry*. www.glbtq.com
Belkin, A., Barrett, F., Eitelberg, M. J., & Ventresca, M. J. (2017, August). *Discharging transgender troops would cost $960 million*. Palm Center Blueprints for Sound Public Policy. Palm Center.
Berube, A. (1990). *Coming out under fire: The history of gay men and women during World War II*. The Free Press.
Bowers v. Hardwick, 478 U.S. 186 (1986).
Brown, G. R. (1988). Transsexuals in the military: Flight into hypermasculinity. *Archives of Sexual Behavior, 17*(6), 527–537.
Cammermeyer, M. (1994). *Serving in silence*. Viking.
Cammermeyer v. Perry, Nos. 94-35600, 94-35674 (Ninth Circuit, 1994).
CBS News. (1999, December 7). Army private guilty of murder.
Damiano, C. L. (1999). Lesbian baiting in the military: Institutionalized sexual harassment under "Don't Tell Don't Tell, Don't Pursue". *Journal of Gender, Social Policy & the Law, 7*(3), Article 4, 500–505.
deVogue, A., & Cohen, Z. (2019, January 22). Supreme Court allows transgender military ban to go into effect. *CNN*. www.cnn.com/2019/01/22/politics/scotus-transgender-ban/index.html
DoDPride. Department of Defense. (n.d.). *Association of lesbian, gay, bisexual, and transgender employees and allies*. https://dodpride.org/
Doe v. Trump, 288 F. Supp. 3d 1045 (WD, Washington at Seattle, 2017).
Don't Ask Don't Tell Act of 1993. (Pub. L. 103–160).
Don't Ask Don't Tell (DADT) Repeal Act. (Pub. L. 111–321).
Eagan, T. (1992, May 31). Dismissed from Army as lesbian, colonel will fight homosexual ban. *New York Times*.
Eagan, T. (2011, September 4). Discharged for being gay, many seek to re-enlist. *New York Times*.

Federal Register. Section 1d. RCM 1001(b) (4), Vol 64, No. 196 Tuesday, October 12, 1999. Presidential Documents.

Frontiero v. Richardson, 411 US 677 (1973).

Gates, G. J. (2010, May). *Lesbian, gay, and bisexual men and women in the US military: Updated estimates.* Executive Summary. The Williams Institute, School of Law, University of California.

Gates, G. J., & Herman, J. L. (2014, May). *Transgender military service in the United States.* The Williams Institute, School of Law, University of California.

Gerstmann, E. (1999). *The Constitutional underclass: Gays, lesbians, and the failure of class-based equal protection.* University of Chicago Press.

Greenberg, D., Najle, M. J., Bola, N., & Jones, R. P. (2019). *America's growing support for transgender rights.* Public Religion Research Institute (PPRI). www.prri.org/research/americas-growing-support-for-transgender-rights/Achieving

Harris, G. L. A., Sumner, R. F., & Gonzalez-Pratz, M. C. (2018). *Women Veterans: Lifting the veil of invisibility.* Routledge.

Harris, S. (2015, July 31). One less secret: How the CIA came out of the closet. *The Daily Beast.* www.thedailybeast.com/how-the-cia-came-out-of-the-closet

Harrison-Quintana, J., & Herman, J. L. (2013). Still serving in silence: Transgender service members and veterans in the National Transgender Discrimination Survey. *LGBTQ Public Policy Journal, 3*, 1–13.

Hayes, S. F. (2007). *Cheney: The untold story of American's most powerful and controversial vice president.* HarperCollins.

High Tech Gays v. Defense Industrial Security Clearance Office, 895 F. 2nd 563 (Ninth Circuit, 1990).

Holloway, L. (2010, October 6). *Don't ask don't tell hurts African American the most.* www.theroot.com

Karnoski v. Trump, 2:17-cv-01297-MJP (USDC, WA, September 14, 2019).

Karnoski v. Trump, 2:17-cv-01297 (USDC, WA, 2017).

Kerrigan, M. F. (2011). Transgender discrimination in the military: The new don't ask don't tell. *Psychology, Public Policy, and Law, 18*(3), 500–518.

Klasfeld, A. (2012, July 24). Transgenderism more likely in the military, study finds. *Courthouse News Service.*

Lawrence v. Texas, 539 U.S. 558 (2003).

Manegold, C. S. (1993, April 18). The odd place of homosexuality in the military. *The New York Times.*

Matlovich v. Secretary of the Air Force, Civ. A. No. 75–1750 (1976, February 2).

Matlovich v. Secretary of the Air Force and Colonel Thogersen, 591 F.2d 852 (D.C. Circuit. 1978).

Mattis, J., U.S. Secretary of Defense of February 22, 2018. Memorandum for the President. Department of defense report and recommendations on military service by transgender persons. https://media.defense.gov/2018/Mar/23/2001894037/-1/-1/0/military-service-by-transgender-individuals.pdf

McCarthy, J. (2019, June 20). In U.S., 71 percent support transgender people serving in the military. *Gallup News.* https://news.gallup.com/poll/258521/support-transgender-people-serving-military.aspx

McClintock, M. (1996). Lesbian baiting hurts all women. In *Women's voices in experiential education.* Https://files.eric.ed.gov/fulltext/ED412049.pdf

Meinhold v. U.S. Department of Defense, 808 F. Supp 1455, 1458 (C.D. Cal. 1993).

Meinhold v. U.S. Department of Defense, No. 96–56094 (9th Cir. 1997).

National Opinion Research Center. (2017). *General social survey. Proportion of Americans identifying as lesbian, gay or bisexual, 2008–2016.* University of Chicago.

Obergefell v. Hodges, 576 U.S. 644 (2015).

O'Keefe, E. (2010, August 17). Minorities disproportionately discharged for don't ask don't tell violations. *Washington Post.*

Powers, R. (2017, December 22). *Policies concerning homosexuals in the military. The balance.* US Military Careers.

Rand Corporation. (2016, June 13). *Impact of transgender personnel on readiness and health care cost in the U. S military likely to be small.* Prepared for the U.S. Secretary of Defense. Conducted by the Forces and Resources Policy Center, National Defense Research Institute. www.rand.org/news/press/2016/06/30.html

Rand Corporation. (1993). *Sexual orientation and U.S. military personnel policy.* National Defense Research Institute. Prepared for the Office of Secretary of Defense. www.rand.org/content/dam/rand/pubs/monographs/2010/RAND_MG1056.pdf

Reza, H. G. (1993, January 9). Homosexual sailor beaten to death, Navy confirms crime: Gay-bashing may be motive, activists and family members say. They charge cover-up by military. *Los Angeles Times.*
Selective Service System. (2017a). "Who must register?"
Selective Service System. (2017b). State/Commonwealth and territory legislation.
Shilts, R. (1993). *Conduct unbecoming: Gays & lesbians in the U.S. military.* St. Martin's Press.
Steffan, J. (1992). *Honor bound: A gay American fights for the right to serve his country.* Avon Books.
Steffan v. Cheney, 920 F.2d 74 (D.C. Cir. 1990).
Stockman v. Trump, 2:17-cv-06516 (USDC, CA, September 5, 2017).
Stone v. Trump, WL 5697228 (D. MD 2019).
Stone v. Trump, 1:17-cv-02459-MJG (USDC MD, August 28, 2017).
TIME Magazine. (1975a, September 8). I am a homosexual: The gay drive for acceptance.
TIME Magazine. (1975b, September 8). The sexes: The Sergeant v. The Air Force.
Uniform Code of Military Justice (UCMJ). (10 Stat. Section 801–896, Article 145).
U.S. Army News Service. (2013, February 7). *Secretary of defense rescinds 'direct ground combat definition and assignment rule*. Vergun, David. www.army.mil/article/94932/secretary_of_defense_rescinds_direct_ground_combat_definition_and_assignment_rule#:~:text=The%20memo%20rescinds%20the%201994,primary%20mission%20is%20to%20engage
U.S. Census Bureau. (2018).
U.S. Department of Defense. (2017, June 12). *DoD news, defense media activity.* Pentagon Celebrates Diversity at Annual LGBT Pride Event, by Terri Moon Cronk.
U.S. Department of Defense. (2017, June 2). Office of the Under Secretary of Defense. Personnel and Readiness. Subject: Department of Defense 2017 Lesbian, Gay, Bisexual and Transgender Pride Month. Signed by A. M. Kurta.
U.S. Department of Veterans Affairs, Veterans Health Administration (VHA). (2013). *VHA Directive 2013–003: Providing health care for transgender and intersex veterans.* Washington, DC.
U.S. Department of Veterans Affairs, Veterans Health Administration (VHA). (2011, June 9). *VHA Directive 2011–024: Providing health care for transgender and intersex veterans.* Washington, DC.
U.S. General Accounting Office. (1992, June). *Report to congressional requestors. Defense force management. DOD's policy on homosexuality. GAO/NSIAD-92-98.* Washington, DC. www.gao.gov/assets/160/151963.pdf
U.S. Naval Institute. (n.d.). *Key dates in U.S. policy on gay men and women in military service.* www.usni.org/news-and-features/dont-ask-donttell/timeline
U.S. v. Windsor, 570 U.S. 744 (2013).
Watkins v. U.S. Army (1983).
White House, Executive Order 13140. October 6, 1999. President Clinton.
White House, Executive Order 12968. August 2, 1995. President Clinton.
White House, Presidential Memorandum, National Security & Defense, August 25, 2017. Presidential Memorandum for the Secretary of Defense and the Secretary of Homeland Security. Subject: Military Service by Transgender Individuals.
Williams Institute. (2019, January). *LGBT demographic data interactive.* UCLA School of Law. https://williamsinstitute.law.ucla.edu/visualization/lgbt-stats/?topic=LGBT#economic
Witten, T. M. (February 2007). *Gender identity and the military – Transgender, transsexual, and intersex identified individuals in the U.S. Armed Forces.* Michael D. Palm Center. www.palmcenter.org/wp-content/uploads/2007/05/TransMilitary2007.pdf
Women's Armed Forces Integration Act of 1948 (Pub. L. 80–645; 62 Stat. 356).
Wyatt-Nichol, H., & Naylor, L. A. (2015). Liberty and equality: In defense of same-sex marriage. *Public Integrity, 17*(2), 117–130. doi:10.1080/10999922.2015.1000108
Wyatt-Nichol, H., & Naylor, L. A. (2013). The policy landscape of sexual orientation. *Journal of Public Management and Policy, 19*(1), 5–18.

Chapter 6
Public Accommodations, Title IX, and Government ID

Introduction

In April 2011, Chrissy Polis, an adult transgender woman was beaten by two teenage girls in a McDonald's bathroom outside Baltimore, Maryland. The beating was taped by a McDonald's employee and posted on YouTube. The video, which showed the teenagers kicking and hitting Polis until she had seizures, went viral. The beating made national headlines and served as a rallying point for transgender protections. The 19-year-old teenager, Teonna Monae Brown, pled guilty to one count of first-degree assault and one hate crime; she received a five-year sentence. The 14-year-old was not sentenced (Siegel, February 10, 2011). Polis, whose birth gender was male, used the women's bathroom based on her gender identity, which is female. This is a criminal and a civil case involving public accommodations. Do transgender individuals have the right to use bathrooms and other public facilities based on gender identity or biological sex?

Public Accommodations

Social equity is concerned about fair and equal treatment. This includes equal treatment in public accommodations such as the case described in the introduction. Public accommodations include both private businesses and government offices that people enter to engage in commerce or to apply for services. Most businesses and government agencies provide bathrooms for public use and some retail businesses provide dressing rooms. Before the passage of the Civil Rights Act of 1964 (Pub. L. 88–352), bathrooms were racially segregated, one for blacks and one for whites. Today, the majority of restrooms are segregated by sex, one designated for women and one for men. There are a few exceptions such as Starbucks, which offers unisex bathrooms, and the transportation sector. For example, it is not logistically feasible to designate sex-specific bathrooms for 300 people at

35,000 feet in the air on a commercial jet. As such, unisex bathrooms for transportation (jets, buses) are viewed as reasonable and acceptable by the American public. With regard to dressing rooms, most retail stores provide dressing rooms for customers. Are transgender people supposed to use the dressing room based on birth sex or gender identity? What if a transgender person has their birth certificate changed to match their gender identity, then what? Should retail stores require customers to produce a birth certificate to enter a dressing room? Stores such as Target, and others, designate unisex dressing rooms in remodeled stores, so it is a moot point for most Target customers. But what does this mean for Walmart customers and other stores? For stores that have traditional male and female dressing rooms and bathrooms, it is problematic for transgender people because it can lead to discrimination, harassment, and violence.

This chapter focuses on public accommodations, such as bathroom bills, and government identification documents (ID) for transgender people. First, federal legislation on public accommodations is reviewed, followed by presidential directives, and court cases. This chapter traces the shift in policy from federal protections based on race to protections based on disabilities, setting the policy stage for transgender protections. Last, legal issues pertaining to government ID (driver's license, passports, etc.) for transgender people is described.

U.S. Transgender Population

According to the Williams Institute at the University of California, 0.06 percent, or roughly 1.4 million of the U.S. adult population, identifies as transgender people (Flores et al., 2016). The majority are in the 18–25 age group. Transgender people compose a smaller percentage of the population than gays and lesbians. As such, it has fewer people to mobilize and less political power.

Legislative History

Having provided an overview of gender terms and their relevance to public policy in Chapter 1, this chapter provides the federal legislative history on public accommodations. In the U.S., laws on public accommodations fall under the umbrella of civil rights. Americans have the right to use public accommodations including public transportation without discrimination based on race, national origin, religion, and disability. As of 2020, there are no federal laws that prohibit discrimination in public accommodations based on sex, sexual orientation, or gender identity. This increases the likelihood that transgender people will be discriminated against in public accommodations, such as bathrooms, dressing rooms, gyms, or other public facilities. This can result in physical harm, violence, and sometimes death. According to the U.S. Federal Bureau of Investigation (2018), approximately 25 transgender people are murdered annually. This section provides an overview of federal legislation that addresses public accommodations for transgender people. A table summarizing federal legislation is provided at the end.

Civil Rights Act of 1964

The legal foundation for public accommodations is based on the landmark legislation the Civil Rights Act of 1964 (Pub. L. 88–352). The law addresses voting rights, equal employment, and desegregation of public schools and public accommodations. It is the first federal law prohibiting discrimination by public accommodations. It includes race, color, religion, and national origin.

However, it does not include sex. The law was created in the 1960s to end racial segregation and Jim Crow laws, which prohibited blacks from voting and using white facilities. Regarding equal access, the law states that

> all persons shall be entitled to the full and equal enjoyment of the goods, services, facilities, privileges, advantages, and accommodations of any place of public accommodation, as defined in this section, without discrimination or segregation on the ground of race, color, religion, or national origin.
>
> (Civil Rights Act of 1964)

Equal access is guaranteed if the public accommodations is engaged or operates in commerce, which includes "lodgings; facilities principally engaged in selling food for consumption on the premises; gasoline stations; places of exhibition or entertainment; other covered establishments" (Ibid).

The basis of public accommodations is the U.S. Constitution's commerce clause. The commerce clause grants Congress the authority "to regulate commerce with foreign Nations and among the several States including Indian tribes" (Article I, Section VIII, Clause 3). Any business that is engaged in commerce is covered under the policy. As such, the term *public accommodation* includes both private businesses and government facilities. It includes sports arenas, hotels, restaurants, movie theaters, and so on. And it includes government offices where citizens apply for services and benefits. However, it does not apply to private clubs, such as country clubs, fraternities, or sororities that require members to pay dues. Nor does it cover religious organizations, such as churches, unless the space is rented out for nonreligious purposes. Public accommodations include businesses and government offices that are open to the general public. It applies to race, color, religion, and national origin but not sex. This is significant because gender identity (and sexual orientation) falls under the category of sex in Title VII of the Civil Rights Act of 1964 (*Bostock v. Clayton County*, 2020). As such, there are no federal laws protecting transgender people in public accommodations.

Title IX of the Educational Amendments of 1972

The Educational Amendments of 1972 (Public Law No. 92-318) were designed as part of the larger umbrella of civil rights laws created in 1964. Title IX, which is well known for its impact on high school and collegiate athletics, makes it illegal to discriminate based on sex in any federally funded educational program or activity. Title IX states: "No person in the United States shall, on the basis of sex, be excluded from participation in, be denied the benefits of, or be subjected to discrimination under any education program or activity receiving Federal financial assistance" (Pub. L. 92-318). According to the U.S. Department of Justice (DOJ), the main objective is to "avoid the use of federal money to support sex discrimination in education programs and to provide individual citizens effective protection against those practices" (U.S. DOJ, n.d.). Under the law, sexual harassment and assault are forms of sexual discrimination. The goal of the policy is to promote gender equity in education.

With regard to college admissions, there is a distinction between public and private colleges. According to the U.S. Department of Education,

> Title IX's prohibition on discrimination in admissions applies only to institutions of vocational education, professional education, and graduate higher education, and to public institutions of undergraduate higher education. 20 U.S.C. § 1681(a)(1); 34 C.F.R. § 106.15. The prohibition on discrimination in admissions does not apply to

private undergraduate colleges. All other programs and activities of private undergraduate colleges (including single-sex colleges) are governed by Title IX if the college receives any Federal financial assistance.

(U.S. Department of Education, Office of Civil Rights, n.d.)

Private schools controlled by religious organizations are exempt: "Title IX does not apply to an educational institution that is controlled by a religious organization to the extent that application of Title IX would be inconsistent with the religious tenets of the organization" (20 U.S.C. § 1681(a)(3); 34 C.F.R. § 106.12).

Title IX does apply to honor societies and professional service societies, and professional fraternities and sororities (34 C.F.R. § 106.31(b)(7). These groups cannot exclude people who apply for membership based on sex. Nor does Title IV apply to the membership practices of social fraternities or sororities at institutions of higher education if the fraternity or sorority has a U.S. Internal Revenue Service, 501(c)(3) tax status. This permits fraternities and sororities at college campuses to base membership on sex (as well as single-sex living arrangements). Assigning students to dormitories, fraternities, and sororities based on sex is a historically accepted practice. Title IX does not apply to the membership practices of the Young Men's Christian Association (YMCA), the Young Women's Christian Association (YWCA), Boy Scouts, Girl Scouts, Camp Fire Girls, voluntary youth service organizations (20 U.S.C. § 1681(a)(6)(B), or the American Legion or its Boy State or Nation Conference or Girl State or Nation Conferences (20 U.S.C. § 1681(a)(7). This means that women can join the local YMCA and men can join the local YWCA. However, Title IV does apply to other activities or programs within these organizations that receive federal funding, such as day care, subsidized meals, sports, and so on.

Over 40 years after the passage of the law, the White House began interpreting and defining Title IX. Under the Obama administration, transgender students were included under Title IX protections. Specifically, the DOJ issued a 2016 letter stating that "schools receiving federal money may not discriminate based on a student's sex, including a student's transgender status. The guidance makes clear that both federal agencies treat the student's gender identity as the student's sex for purposes of enforcing Title IX" (May 16, 2016). In a nine-page letter titled "Dear Colleagues Letter," the Obama administration provided guidance for transgender students to use the bathrooms and locker rooms consistent with their gender identity, not birth sex (Lhamon & Gupta, 2016; U.S. Department of Education, 2016; White House, Presidential Memorandum, 2016). In response to the Obama directive, a group of 13 states filed a lawsuit for injunctive relief against the U.S. Department of Education (*Texas v. United States of America*, 2016). The federal district judge ruled that the U.S. Department of Education's policy was unenforceable and questioned its interpretation of the word *sex* (201 F. Supp. 3d 810). Next, in February 2017, the Trump administration issued an opposing interpretation, rescinding Obama's directive (DeVos, 2017); transgender access to bathrooms and locker rooms are to be determined by the courts, not the executive branch. According to U.S. Education Secretary DeVos, transgender students will continue to be protected from harassment and bullying under Title IX but not physically accommodated. Students must use the bathroom matching their biological sex.

Opponents argue that not physically accommodating students in bathrooms and locker rooms can lead to increased bullying, discrimination, and harm to transgender students, including suicide (Haas et al., 2014). Transgender youth have a prevalence of suicide attempts of 41 percent compared to 4.6 percent of the general population (Ibid). Waiting on the courts to interpret the word *sex* is problematic for two reasons. First, students will likely graduate before the U.S. Supreme Court decides on the matter, leaving the issue unresolved and determined by state policy, which varies across the country. Second, presidential directives lack sustainability. Each president can rescind a prior president's directive, which creates instability for schools and students. Opposing executive directives from President Obama (D) and President Trump (R) point to the need for Congress to define *sex* or the U.S. Supreme Court to interpret Title IX as it relates to transgender public accommodations.

Religious Exemptions to Title IX

The U.S. Department of Education permits religious exemptions to Title IX of the Educational Amendments of 1972 (20 U.S.C. § 1681). Regarding the process or steps for applying for religious exemptions, it is based largely on the "Smith Memo" and "Singleton Memo." A 1989 memo by Smith, who was the Acting Assistant Secretary for Civil Rights, wrote the "Smith Memo," which identifies the provisions for applying for religious exemptions. It states that

> [u]nder 34 C.F.R. § 106.12 of Title IX Regulation, institutions controlled by a religious organization are exempt from those sections of the regulation that conflict with the organization's religious tents. Under 106.12(b), "an education institution which wishes to claim exemption should submit a written statement to the Assistant Secretary identifying the sections of the regulation that conflict with specific tenets."
> (U.S. Department of Education, Smith Memo, October 11, 1989)

A previous memo, written by Assistant Secretary for Civil Rights Harry Singleton, also provides guidance on how to submit an exemption request (U.S. Department of Education, Singleton Memo, February 19, 1985).

Regarding public elementary and high schools,

> Title IX's prohibition on discrimination in admissions applies only to institutions of vocational education, professional education, and graduate higher education, and to public institutions of undergraduate higher education. 20 U.S.C. § 1681(a)(1); 34 C.F.R. § 106.15. A public school district therefore may offer a nonvocational single-sex school so long as it provides a substantially equal school to students of the excluded sex. All other programs and activities of public schools (including single-sex schools) are governed by Title IX if the school district receives any Federal financial assistance. . . . Public elementary and secondary schools are also subject to the sex discrimination prohibitions of the Equal Protection Clause of the U.S. Constitution and the requirements of the Equal Educational Opportunities Act of 1974.
> (U.S. Department of Education, Office of Civil Rights, n.d.)

A number of small private colleges have recently applied for religious exemptions to Title IX regarding sexual orientation and gender identity. These include small private undergraduate colleges that are controlled by religious organizations. According to the U.S. Department of Education website, "[t]he prohibition on discrimination in admissions does not apply to private undergraduate colleges. All other programs and activities of private undergraduate colleges (including single-sex colleges) are governed by Title IX if the college receives any Federal financial assistance" (U.S. Department of Education, Office of Civil Rights, Website, n.d.). Private undergraduate colleges that applied between 2017 to 2019 for religious exemptions include Appalachian Bible College, Arlington Baptist College, Asbury Theological Seminary, Baptist Missionary Association Theological Seminary,

Berea College, Bethany Global University, Bob Jones University, Boston Baptist College, Cairn University, Cedarville University, Central Christian College of the Bible, Charlotte Christian College and Theological Seminary, College of Biblical Studies, College of the Ozarks, Columbia International University, Compass College of the Cinematic Arts, Crown College, Dallas Baptist University, Elm Bible Institute and College, Emmanuel College, Erskine College, Evangel University, Faith Baptist Bible College and Theological Seminary, Family of Faith Christian University, Florida College, Grace Bible College, Harding University, Heartland Baptist Bible Colle, Houston Baptist University, Judson University, Kentucky Mountain Bible Collee, Life Pacific College, Lutheran Brethren Seminary, Native American Christina Academy, North Carolina School of Biblical studies, Oak Hills Christian College, Oral Roberts University, Randall University, Shepherds Theological Seminary, Sterling College, Taylor University, The Masters University, Trinity Baptist College, University of Dallas, and Vanguard University (U.S. Department of Education, Office of Civil Rights, n.d.). The list is not exhaustive but provides examples of the institutions seeking religious exemptions based on the mission of the college; these are mostly religious colleges and seminaries. The U.S. Department of Education, Office of Civil Rights, maintains a public list on its website of religious exemption requests: https://www2.ed.gov/about/offices/list/ocr/docs/t9-rel-exempt/index.html. The majority of the requests are related to sexual orientation and gender identity. One example from the website is an approved exemption from Central Christian College of the Bible, located in Moberly, Missouri. In the correspondence, the U.S. Department of Education, informs the college that

> Title IX and its implementing regulation at 34 C.F.R. § 106.12 provide that Title IX does not apply to an educational institution that is controlled by a religious organization to the extent that the application of Title IX would be inconsistent with the controlling organization's religious tenets. Therefore, such educational institutions may request an exemption from Title IX by identifying the provisions of Title IX that conflict with a specific tenet of the religious organization. The request must identify the religious organization that controls the educational institution and specify the tenets of that organization and the provisions of the law or regulation that conflict with those tenets.
> (U.S. Department of Education, correspondence dated January 18, 2018)

The letter identifies the requested religious needs and exemptions:

> Your request letter states that the College is controlled by the Independent Christian Churches and "exists to develop servant-leaders for the church." Your letter explains that the College is governed by a Board of Directors, all of whom must be members of the independent Christian Churches. The letter also states that College faculty members must agree to abide by certain theological affirmations and College employees "are expected to participate in a Restoration Movement (Independent Christian/Church of Christ) Church." Your letter requests exemption from certain provisions of Title IX and its implementing regulations to the extent they "would violate the sincerely held religious beliefs of Central Christian College of the Bible and the Christian Churches." In support of this request, your letter cites the College's Bylaws, which "reiterate [the College's] Biblical stance and core religious beliefs," including with respect to gender and sexuality, the sanctity of human life, and marriage. The letter further explains that the College's beliefs include that "God wonderfully and immutably creates each person as male or female" and that "rejection of one's genetic gender is a rejection of the

image of God within that person," that "all human life is sacred and created by God in His image," and that the term 'marriage' only refers to the united of one man and one woman in a single, exclusive union as delineated in Scripture. . . . The College is exempt from these provisions to the extent that compliance would conflict with the controlling organization's religious tenets.

The preceding paragraph serves as an example of the type of religious exemptions under Title IX. The next piece of legislation addressing public accommodations is Section 504 of the Rehabilitation Act of 1973.

Section 504 of the Rehabilitation Act of 1973

Section 504 of the Rehabilitation Act of 1973 (Public Law 93–112; 29 U.S.C. Section 794) prohibits discrimination based on disability by federal agencies. Specifically, it states:

> No otherwise qualified individual with a disability in the United States shall, solely by reason of her or his disability, be excluded from participation in, be denied the benefits of, or be subjected to discrimination under any program, service or activity receiving federal financial assistance or under any program or activity conducted by any Executive agency or by the United States Postal Service.
>
> (Section 504)

It expanded the Civil Rights Law of 1964 by adding disabilities to the list of classes protected from discrimination by federal agencies. Later in 2013, Section 504 of the Rehabilitation Act of 1973 was amended to include federal contractors and subcontractors who receive $10,000 or more in federal funding (29 U.S.C. Sec 793; 41 CFR Part 60–741). In addition, federal contractors and subcontractors must comply with the American Disabilities Act Amendments of 2008 and provide accommodations to individuals with disabilities in their workplace. The amendment was made by the U.S. Department of Labor as an administrative rule, which went into effect March 2014. The amendment strengthens affirmative action and diversity, which are core components of social equity.

Civil Rights Restoration Act of 1987

The Civil Rights Restoration Act of 1987 (Pub. L. 100–259) was passed by Congress after overriding President Reagan's veto. The policy was created to clarify the application of civil rights legislation, including Title IX of the Education Amendments of 1972, Section 504 of the Rehabilitation Act of 1973, the Age Discrimination Act of 1975, and Title VI of the Civil Rights Act of 1964. Section 2 states:

> The Congress finds that (1) certain aspects of recent decisions and opinions of the Supreme Court have unduly narrowed or cast doubt upon the broad application of title IX of the Education Amendments of 1972, section 504 of the Rehabilitation Act of 1973, the Age Discrimination Act of 1975, and title VI of the Civil Rights Act of 1964; and (2) legislative action is necessary to restore the prior consistent and long-standing executive branch interpretation and broad, institution-wide application of those laws as previously administered.
>
> (Civil Rights Restoration Act of 1987, Pub. L. 100–259, p. 1)

Specifically, it provides an interpretation of the words "program and activity" by stating the definition for Title IX of the Education Amendments of 1972, Section 504 of the Rehabilitation Act of 1973, the Age Discrimination Act of 1975, and Title VI of the Civil Rights Act of 1964. It states that

> the term 'program or activity' and 'program' mean all of the operations of – (1)(A) a department, agency, special purpose district, or other instrumentality of a State or of a local government; or(B) the entity of such State or local government that distributes such assistance and each such department or agency (and each other State or local government entity) to which the assistance is extended, in the case of assistance to a State or local government; (2)(A) a college, university, or other postsecondary institution, or a public system of higher education; or (B) a local educational agency (as defined in section 198(a)(10) of the Elementary and Secondary Education Act of 1965), system of vocational education, or other school system; (3)(A) an entire corporation, partnership, or other private organization, or an entire sole proprietorship – if assistance is extended to such corporation, partnership, private organization, or sole proprietorship as a whole; or (ii) which is principally engaged in the business of providing education, health care, housing, social services, or parks and recreation; or (B) the entire plant or other comparable, geographically separate facility to which Federal financial assistance is extended, in the case of any other corporation, partnership, private organization, or sole proprietorship; or (4) any other entity which is established by two or more of the entities described in paragraph (1), (2), or (3); any part of which is extended Federal financial assistance, except that such term does not include any operation of an entity which is controlled by a religious organization if the application of section 901 to such operation would not be consistent with the religious tenets of such organization.
> (Civil Rights Restoration Act of 1987, Section 908)

The law provided clarification on two terms, *programs* and *activities*, to prevent misinterpretation.

American Disabilities Act of 1990

Building on Section 504, the American Disabilities Act (ADA) of 1990 (Pub. Law 110–325) was passed to prohibit discrimination based on disability as well as HIV/AIDS. The act was modeled after the Civil Rights Act of 1964 (Pub. L. 88–352) and seeks to ensure equality for people with disabilities. Its goal is to guarantee that people with disabilities have the same access as people without disabilities. It prohibits discrimination in four areas: (1) telecommunications, (2) employment, (3) public accommodations, and (4) transportation. In the area of employment, covered employers are required to make "reasonable accommodations," which can include providing interpreters, making workstations accessible, and modifying equipment. Covered employers include state and local governments, private businesses with 15 or more employees, labor unions, and employment agencies.

In the area of transportation, people with disabilities must be accommodated on commuter rail and public transit buses. With regard to public accommodations, all hotels, restaurants, sports arenas, grocery stores, and retail stores must provide access for people with disabilities. Existing construction must modify and remove barriers to access. All new construction must be designed to accommodate people with disabilities including wheel chair ramps. No person can be denied services based on their disability. The U.S. Access Board provides ADA Access guidelines to meet compliance with standards. Access designs include detailed technical specifications and requirements for ramps, stairs, elevators, dressing rooms, and so forth (American Disabilities Act, n.d.). Section II of the ADA ensures that people with disabilities have an equal opportunity to vote (see

Section II). According to the ADA Checklist for Polling Places provided by the U.S. Department of Justice (June 2016), this includes building entrances, lifts and elevators, parking, passenger drop-offs, ramps, and voting areas to ensure voting access for people with disabilities.

The act was later amended by Congress in response to two U.S. Supreme Court rulings that used a narrow interpretation of the term *disability* (see *Sutton v. United Air Lines, Inc.*, 1999; *Toyota Motor Manufacturing, Kentucky, Inc. v. Williams*, 2002). The American Disability Act Amendment (ADAA) of 2008 was amended to broaden the definition of *disability* and expand coverage in both the ADA as well as Section 504 of the Rehabilitation Act of 1973. This is important because in 2008, only 28 percent of polling places were accessible to people with disabilities (U.S. Government Accountability Office, 2009), signaling additional measures were needed to ensure people with disabilities are accommodated at the polls and can exercise their right to vote.

U.S. Department of Homeland Security

Although not based on federal legislation the U.S. Department of Homeland Security (DHS), which ensures national security and operates the Transportation Security Administration (TSA), issued an internal agency policy on airport screening to prohibit discrimination based on sex and gender identity. It applies directly to transgender people. Specifically, it states:

> TSA recognizes the concerns that some members of the transgender community may have with certain security screening procedures at the nation's security checkpoints. TSA is committed to ensuring all travelers are treated with respect and courtesy. Screening is conducted without regard to a person's race, color, sex, gender identity, national origin, religion or disability.
>
> (U.S. Department of Homeland Security, TSA, n.d.)

Screening can include physical pat downs by TSA agents. Transgender people are allowed to have someone of their choice with them during the pat down. Pat downs are significant because they can result in transgender people being publicly "outed," which can lead to harassment or physical violence. Because it involves direct human contact it has a direct impact on transgender people.

In total, there are six federal legislative policies, two conflicting executive policies, and one federal internal agency policy (DHS) that define the parameters of public accommodations. These laws and executive directives potentially lay the foundation for prohibiting discrimination of transgender people in public accommodations. As of 2020, it is illegal to discriminate in public accommodations and transportation based on race, color, national origin, religion, and disability. However, there is no federal legislation prohibiting discrimination based on sex or gender identity in public accommodations. These federal policies are summarized in Table 6.1.

Bathroom Bills

Lacking a consistent and sustainable federal policy on transgender public accommodations, state legislatures across the country took up the initiative. At the state level, the policy initiative is known as bathroom bills. Proponents of bathroom restrictions argue for public safety and protecting women and children from predators. They view transgender people as a potential physical and sexual threat to children. Opponents argue bathroom restrictions are discriminatory and, in some cases, criminalize transgender people (Rushin & Carroll, 2017). According to the National Conference of State Legislatures, between 2013 and 2016, approximately 24 states sought to restrict access to sex-segregated

Table 6.1 Federal Policy by Protected Class

Public Law Name & Number	Type & Protection	Demographic Categories
Civil Rights Act of 1964	Public accommodations, transportation	Race, color, religion, or national origin
Title IX of the Educational Amendments of 1972	Public schools, universities & colleges	Sex (as of 2017, it means male or female)
Section 504 of the Rehabilitation Act of 1973	Protected by federal agencies, contractors & subcontractors	Disability
Civil Rights Restoration Act of 1987	Defines program or activity for four civil rights acts.	Title VI, Civil Rights Act of 1964, Title IX, Rehabilitation Act of 1987, Age Discrimination Act of 1975
American Disabilities Act of 1990	Public accommodations, employment, transportation, telecommunications	Disability
ADA Amendment of 2008	Broadened definition of *disability*	Disability, state and local government, private sector. and unions with 15 or more employees
Obama, U.S. Department of Education, May 2016.	Title IX, transgender protections for bathrooms, lockers, same-sex schools	Gender identity
Trump, Devos, U.S. Department of Education, February 2017 Directive	Rescinded Obama directive. Courts decide bathroom & locker room usage	Sex (male, female only)
U.S. Department of Homeland Security, Transportation Safety Association (TSA; internal policy)	TSA airport screening	Race, color, sex, gender identity, national origin, religion, or disability.

facilities in the form of bathroom bills (2017). The purpose was to make access based on birth or biological sex, not gender identity. In 2016, North Carolina passed a law requiring people to use the sex listed on birth certificates. The law restricted bathroom access, preempting municipal- and county-level antidiscrimination laws. In response, a lawsuit was filed challenging the constitutionality of the bathroom law (*Carcano v. McCrory*, 2016). In addition, the National Collegiate Athletic Association threatened to stop holding sporting events in North Carolina, and some corporations publicly opposed the law, putting economic pressure on the state legislature. In the end, North Carolina revoked the law (Blinder, 2017). In contrast to North Carolina, the state of California passed a law giving transgender people the legal right to use bathrooms based on gender identity, not birth sex (California Fair Employment & Housing Council, 2017), and single-sex bathrooms were labeled gender-neutral (California Assembly Bill No. 1732, 2016). These two contradictory state laws on public accommodations represent the political and cultural division within the country.

An equal concern is the potential criminalizing of transgender people. In a law review article titled "Bathroom Laws as Status Crimes," Rushin and Carroll (2017) argue that "by effectively criminalizing noncriminal conduct so inextricably linked to the status of being trans, some proposed bathroom laws may violate the Eighth Amendment's bar on cruel and unusual punishment" (2017, page 1). Citing *Robinson v. California* (370 U.S. 660, 1962), states can regulate behavior, but the Eighth Amendment prevents states' from criminalizing a person's status. Regulating an individual's bodily functions or bowel movements arguably criminalizes a person's status. Two examples include Indiana and Florida. In 2016, Indiana attempted to make it a criminal offense to use bathrooms based on gender identity. Specifically, Senate Bill No. 35 stated it would make it a Class A misdemeanor, which could result in up to one-year incarceration and up to a $5,000 fine (Indiana Code Annotated Section 35-50-3-2). In Florida, House Bill 83 considered using a bathroom based on gender identity a misdemeanor of the second degree, which included up to 60 days in jail and a $500 fine. Not only do bathroom laws potentially criminalize transgender people, but they also enlist law enforcement to monitor restroom use. Should police officers be monitoring bathrooms?

It is not only 'bathroom bills' that limit the lives of transgender people. Discrimination also applies to a wide range of daily activities from going to the grocery store, accessing the gym, and going to and from work. Most recently, it has been applied to organized sports:

> Gov. Brad Little (Idaho) signed two bills into law . . . that limit the rights of transgender people. One measure bans transgender girls from playing on girls' and women's sports teams, while the other prohibits transgender people from changing their gender on Idaho birth certificates.
>
> (Rose & Silverman, March 3, 2020)

As described earlier, bathroom bills are complex and divisive in nature. These bills reflect and represent the wide array of values, morals, and religious beliefs across the country set against the larger economic engine of capitalism and shrinking government budgets. The flurry of bathroom bills waned in 2018, and states shifted focus to more achievable policy outcomes, leaving the larger legal decision of transgender use of public accommodations to the courts.

U.S. Supreme Court Rulings

Public accommodations (bathrooms and dressing rooms) involve commerce activity. Federal legislation prohibiting discrimination in public accommodations is based on the U.S. Constitution's (1789) commerce clause, which grants Congress the authority to "regulate commerce with foreign Nations and among the several States including Indian tribes" (Article I, Section 8, Clause 3). As stated in the Civil Rights Act of 1964, "equal access is guaranteed if the public accommodations is engaged or operates in commerce, which includes "lodgings; facilities principally engaged in selling food for consumption on the premises; gasoline stations; places of exhibition or entertainment; other covered establishments" (Pub. L. 88–352). For a thorough discussion on the commerce clause, see Rosenbloom (2015, pp. 36–40). Regarding transgender public accommodations, at least one legal case advanced to the U.S. Supreme Court. It is discussed next.

Gloucester County School Board v. G.G. *(2017)*

In August 2014, transgender teen Gavin Grimm and his mom met with his school counselor to inform his high school Gavin would be attending as a boy. In addition, they provided a treatment letter for gender dysphoria from his psychologist. Initially, the school agreed that Gavin would be called by his new legal name, which was a male pronoun. For restrooms, he would use an alternate private facility by the school nurse's office or teachers' lounge. However, once school started, Gavin felt stigmatized and singled out because his teacher publicly stated in class that it took him a long time to use the restroom, which was the result of using an alternate bathroom. Gavin and his mother met with the school principal and requested that Gavin be allowed to use the boys' restroom to avoid being humiliated in class. The principal agreed. However, a parent found out that a transgender student was using the boys' bathroom and complained about privacy rights to the local school board. In December 2014, the Gloucester County School Board released a new policy to install unisex restrooms. In addition, the school board decided that Gavin could no longer use the boys' bathroom.

Gavin and his family filed a lawsuit against Gloucester Public Schools which is located about 45 minutes from Williamsburg, Virginia. The plaintiffs argue prohibiting bathroom access violates the Fourteenth Amendment Equal Protection Clause of the U.S. Constitution and Title IX of the Educational Amendments of 1972. Gavin had been excluded from participation in a federally funded school program because of sex and the exclusion caused him harm. At the time, the Obama administration defined *sex* to include gender identity (Lhamon & Gupta, 2016; U.S. Department of Education, 2016). In 2016, the U.S. Supreme Court agreed to hear the case (*Gloucester County School Board v. GG* (137 S. Ct. 369, 2016; 822 F.3d 709, 4th Cir., 2016, cert granted). However, in February 2017, the Trump administration revoked the Obama's administration's policy that defined *sex* in Title IX to include gender identity. Shortly thereafter, the U.S. Solicitor General sent a letter to the U.S Supreme Court advising of the reversal in federal executive policy. On March 6, 2017, the U.S. Supreme Court vacated the judgment and sent the case back to the Fourth Circuit in Richmond, Virginia, for review. Gavin graduated in June 2017 without access to the boys' bathroom, although he had a court order and birth certificate stating his male gender. In August 2019, a U.S. district court, the Eastern District of Virginia, ruled in favor of student Gavin Grimm, stating the local school board's bathroom policy and refusal to change his gender to male on school transcripts violates his rights under Title IX of the Educational Amendments of 1972 and the U.S. Constitution's Fourteenth Amendment. The court issued a permanent injunction requiring the school board to update his school transcript to male (U.S. district court, Eastern District of Virginia). In December 2019, the Gloucester School Board appealed the decision (*Grimm v. Gloucester County School Board*, 2019). The case is pending.

Impact of Bathroom Bills

The average person uses the bathroom 4 to 10 times per day. Students use locker rooms several times per week for physical education classes and sports. As such, lacking access to restrooms and locker rooms can negatively impact transgender students in public K–12 schools (*Grimm v. Gloucester County School Board*, 2019) as well as universities (*Johnston v. University of Pittsburgh*, 2015). Not accommodating students in bathrooms and locker rooms can lead to isolation. In turn, this can create more discrimination and harm to transgender students, including suicide (Haas et al., 2014). Transgender youth have a prevalence of suicide attempts of 41 percent compared to 4.6 percent of the general population (Ibid). As such, it is critical that the court clarify and define Title IX policy as it relates to transgender students and adults in a timely manner.

Government Identity Documents

It is important for all people, including transgender people, to easily access public accommodations. Another component of access is government identification. This section of the chapter addresses government identification documents (IDs), which are critical to daily life in the same way public accommodations are critical to daily life. A government ID is required to drive vehicles, board commercial planes, start employment, enter government buildings, purchase a house, open banking accounts, and so on. Government IDs includes U.S. passports, military ID, driver's licenses, and vital statistics documents, such as birth, marriage, and death certificates. For transgender people, government ID takes on an elevated role because they need ID to prove their gender identity, which is different from the birth sex listed on the original birth certificate. Transgender people must change their name and gender marker to match their identity records. Federal government–issued IDs includes a U.S. passport, military ID, and federal employment cards. State-government ID includes driver's licenses, all vital statistics certificates (birth, marriage, and death), and voter registration cards. State policy on gender ID requirements varies by state. For example, sex surgery might be required in one state to update a birth certificate but only hormone therapy in another state to update a birth certificate, creating unequal treatment and costs across states. Without a federal policy on gender identity, the process is dictated by each state creating unequal treatment for transgender people.

As a result, a lawsuit was filed in 2015 by six transgender people in Michigan alleging that their constitutional privacy was violated by the Michigan secretary of state (*Love v. Johnson*, 2016). The state would not change the gender marker on a government-issued ID unless the birth certificate gender marker was also changed. To change the birth certificate gender marker the state requires sex confirmation surgery, which is expensive and risky. Only 25 to 30 percent of transgender individuals complete the surgery due to risks. Second, transgender transitioning is a long process that requires hormone therapy, psychological therapy, and, for some, sex reassignment surgery. It can take years to transition completely. People don't have time to wait; they need government ID to drive, apply for jobs, and so forth. Third, a transgender person begins the process by petitioning the district court for a name change, which is time-consuming and expensive. Once the person has a certified copy of the court order, then they can begin to change federal, state, and local gender identity records. Having accurate ID records is important. According to the National Center for Transgender Society Equality (2019), having identity documents that do not match can lead to harassment, discrimination, and violence for transgender people. There are some private businesses, such as United Airlines that accept a nonbinary gender marker (The Guardian, 2019).

Federal REAL ID

In 2005, Congress passed the REAL ID Act (Pub. L. 109–13). The policy was in response to the September 11, 2001, terrorist attacks. The policy gives the DHS authority to regulate state driver's licenses to ensure national security. This includes participating in a national database, requiring specific information, and using encoding technology on the card. Each state is required to submit all driver's licenses in a national database known as the American Association of Motor Vehicle Administrators. Beginning October 1, 2020, individuals must present a REAL-ID compliant license, passport, or U.S. military ID to enter a federal facility, nuclear power plant, or board a commercial flight. The DHS requires states to ensure documentation for citizenship, residency, address, gender, and Social Security numbers. According to Section 202 of the Real ID Act (Pub. L. 109–13), each state driver's license must have the following information on the license and be verified by written documentation: full legal name, date of birth, gender, driver's license number, photograph, address of residence, signature, and physical security to prevent fraud. Gender on driver's licenses varies by state law. Some states allow a gender-neutral marker known as X while other states use the traditional binary marker: male or female. Over 7,200 gender X state IDs have been issued

(Lam, August 31, 2019). According to the Lambda Legal, Movement Advancement Map (February 17, 2020), which tracks nonbinary markers on state driver's licenses, 16 states and the District of Columbia provide a third gender option, X. These include Arkansas, California, Colorado, Connecticut, Indiana, Maryland, Minnesota, Maine, Massachusetts, Nevada, New Hampshire, New York, Oregon, Utah, Vermont, and Washington. The X option is viewed as a major win for transgender rights. Nine states require sex reassignment surgery to change the gender marker on birth certificates. This includes federal law requiring gender on state-issued driver's licenses; however, each state defines the term *gender*. States that do not allow a third gender option are mostly located in the Midwest and South.

- 16 states + D.C. allows residents to mark M, F, or X on their driver's license
- 18 states + D.C. uses easy to understand form and does not require provider certification
- 10 states, 1 territory uses easy to understand form and requires provider certification (accepted from wide range of professionals)
- 3 states uses easy to understand form and requires provider certification (accepted from limited range of professionals)
- 6 states has no form. No court order or proof of surgery required, but burdensome process requirements and/or provider certification required from limited range of professionals
- 4 states, 2 territories has unclear, unknown or unwritten policy regarding gender marker changes
- 9 states, 2 territories requires proof of surgery, court order, or amended birth certificate
(www.lgbtmap.org/equality-maps/identity_document_laws)

Federal government–issued ID cards include U.S passports, consular report of birth abroad, and Social Security cards. Name changes are allowed on all federal identity records. This is to accommodate marriages, divorces, and adoptions (domestic and international, see Intercountry Adoption Act of 2000, Pub. L. 106-279). However, sex or gender marker changes are determined by each federal agency.

U.S. Passport

A U.S. passport is a federal ID issued by the U.S. State Department to U.S. citizens and nationals. It allows people to enter and exit other countries around the globe (with the exception of North Korea) (8 U.S.C. § 1185(b). The U.S. passport provides identity and shows an allegiance to the U.S. (*Haig v. Agee*, 1981). The passport represents country, citizenship, and loyalty. According to the U.S. State Department (n.d.), in 2019, there were approximately 146,775,089 valid U.S. passports in circulation. Roughly 42 percent of Americans hold passports compared to 66 percent in Canada and 76 percent in the U.K. (McCarthy, January 11, 2018). The U.S. passport application allows for name changes but does not permit a gender-neutral marker (as of February 17, 2020). The passport application uses the binary marker: male or female, which is problematic for individuals who are intersex or do not associate with either sex (nonbinary).

Zzyym v. Pompeo

In 2015, navy veteran and intersex citizen Dana Zzyym filed a federal discrimination lawsuit against the U.S. State Department for not allowing Dana to use a gender-neutral marker on a U.S. passport application (*Zzyym v. Pompeo*, 2015). Specifically, Dana alleges violation of due process and equal protection of the U.S. Constitution as well as violation of the federal Administrative Procedure Act (5 U.S.C. § 706). The case was filed in the U.S. district court in Colorado. Dana was born with ambiguous sex characteristics, and her birth certificate states "unknown" for sex. This is important because a first-time application for a passport requires a birth certificate and the gender identity must match other ID. After undergoing numerous sex operations Dana has concluded that her sex is intersex and that she wants her U.S. passport to reflect a gender-neutral marker. Dana serves as an associate director for the Organization Intersex International. She has been unable to fly to other countries for work due to a lack of a passport. The court ruled in favor of Zzyym on November 22, 2016, and September 9, 2018 (*Zzyym v. Pompeo*, 2018). However, the U.S. State Department refuses to issue Zzyym a passport with a gender X marker. In 2020, the case was opened in the U.S. Court of Appeals for the Tenth Circuit (*Zzyym v. Pompeo*, 2020). On May 12, 2020, the Tenth Circuit ruled that three of the five rationales given by the U.S. State Department for denying Zzyym a passport matching her gender were not legitimate and that the State Department acted arbitrary and capricious when it denied Zzyym the passport. According to the State Department, "some individuals are born neither male nor female. Forcing these individuals to pick a gender thus injects inaccuracy into the data. A chef might label a jar of salt a jar of sugar, but the label does not make the salt any sweeter. Nor does requiring intersex people to mark 'male' or 'female' on an application make the passport any more accurate" (p. 15). The court overturned the district court ruling and advised the State Department to reconsider Zzyymm's passport request (*Zzyym v. Pompeo*, 2020). The State Department has utilized a binary sex policy (male, female) on passports for 39 years and has not updated its passport policy to include intersex to maintain accurate records.

The United Nation's agency on travel, the International Civil Aviation Organization, recognizes the X gender marker on passports; specifically, it states: "Sex of the holder, to be specified by use of the single initial commonly used in the language of the State where the document is issued and, if translation into English, French or Spanish is necessary, followed by an oblique and the capital letter F for female, M for male, or X for unspecified" (International Civil Aviation Organization, 2015, p. 14). According to a report issued by the International Lesbian, Gay, Bisexual, Trans and Intersex Association (see Holzer, 2018), at least 10 countries provide the option of gender-neutral marker X on passports: Australia, Bangladesh, Canada, Denmark, Germany, India, Malta, Nepal, New Zealand, and Pakistan. Individuals with passports from these 10 countries with gender-neutral X on the passport can enter the United States. As of publication of this book, the U.S. State Department does not allow X as an unspecified gender marker on the passport.

Other Federal ID

The U.S. State Department also issues a consular report of birth abroad documents. These are used when U.S. residents deliver a biological child outside of the U.S. For example, a military family might deliver a baby overseas while on duty. A name change can be made for a fee. A name change requires a marriage certificate or court order (U.S. State Department, Birth of U.S. Citizens Abroad, n.d.). No information regarding sex marker change is available on the State Department website for consular report of birth abroad.

The U.S. Social Security Administration (SSA) issues social security cards with a name and social security number. It does not have a gender marker on the card. As such, there is no gender marker to be changed on the card for transgender people. According to the SSA, a name can be changed by submitting a driver's license, court order, or U.S. passport (U.S. Social Security Administration, n.d.). No information regarding sex marker change is available on the SSA website.

State Identity Records

State government-issued ID records include driver's licenses and vital statistics, such as birth, marriage, and death certificates. An office of vital statistics in each state is responsible for these records. Typically, these are located in the state health department or social services. The U.S. Centers for Disease Control and Prevention, National Center for Health Statistics compiles state-level data on vital statistics. However, state governments make laws regarding changes in name and sex marker on the birth certificate, not the federal government. As such, these laws vary by state. For transgender people, birth certificates present the biggest challenge in the changing of a name and sex marker. For example, some states require a sex change operation before a gender marker can be changed. According to the Intersex & Gender Queer Recognition Project (n.d.), which tracks state-level legislation on ID documents, there are currently eight states and New York City that recognize nonbinary gender on the birth certificate. These include California, Colorado, Connecticut, Michigan New Hampshire, New Jersey, New York City, Oregon, and Washington. It is commonly referred to as gender x, intersex, or nonbinary category. Some states label it "unspecified." Seven states prohibit sex marker changes on the birth certificate. These include Kansas, North Carolina, Ohio, South Carolina, Tennessee, and Texas. The remaining states allow for gender change from male to female only on the birth certificate. Some states require affidavits, court orders, or letters from physicians confirming the gender change. This varies by state. According to the Lambda Legal, Movement Advancement Map (February 17, 2020), which tracks nonbinary markers on state driver's licenses, 16 states and the District of Columbia provide a third gender option, X. These include Arkansas, California, Colorado, Connecticut, Indiana, Maryland, Minnesota, Maine, Massachusetts, Nevada, New Hampshire, New York, Oregon, Utah, Vermont, and Washington.

Marriage certificates are issued by the state but take place at the local level in the form of a marriage license, which is later converted into a marriage certificate. Most states will not change a name on a marriage certificate without a court order. Requirements for the driver's license are similar. They are issued by state governments at the local department of motor vehicles. The driver's license includes both a name and gender marker. Laws for changing a name and sex marker vary by state. (Refer to the Intersex & Gender Queer Recognition Project website listed in resources, which tracks state-level legislation on government ID cards.)

Voter Registration Cards

Regarding voter registration cards, states administer elections, not the federal government. As such, state legislatures determine policies on name change and gender marker change. Each state (including D.C. and five U.S. Territories) is different with regard to voter registration application, cards, and changes in demographic information. The Help America Vote Act of 2002 (Pub. L. 107–252, Section 15403e) requires each state to designate a "chief election official" to coordinate elections as defined by the National Voter Registration Act of 1993 (42 U.S.C. 1973). In some states, elections are administered by the secretary of state while in other states administration falls under the director of the state board of election. According to the National Association of State Secretaries (n.d.), there are 40 chief election officials who are secretaries of state. The remaining are state board of election directors or a variation thereof. Most voter registration cards provide information on name, address, gender, political party, and voting place. To change voter information, an individual would need to contact the office of the chief election officer in their state or local board of elections.

Accurate voting cards are important because states with strict voter ID requirements demand a government-issued ID card. For transgender people whose government-issued ID may not match their gender identity, this is problematic because it takes time and money to update ID cards. Potentially, a transgender person could be denied the right to vote without an updated birth certificate that requires sex surgery. Moreover, transgender people with inaccurate identification can face voter suppression and harassment (Herman, 2015). At the federal level, the U.S. Election Commission does not provide guidance on LGBTQ issues since elections are administered by the states. However, there is an organization, Election Protection, that provides a telephone number for assistance if transgender people are intimidated or denied the right to vote at the polls (Election Protection 866, n.d.).

Local Government ID

Local government–issued ID cards include employment and allow for name changes on employment cards. The rules for making name changes, as well as gender identity marker changes, vary by jurisdiction. According to the U.S. Census, there are approximately 39,000 local governments across the country, which include townships (16,000), municipalities (19,500) and counties (3,000). A transgender individual would need to check with their local government on requirements for name changes and gender marker changes.

This section provided a review of key government ID cards issued by federal, state, and local governments. These records are important because they impact an individual's daily life, and for transgender people, they require extra costs in terms of money and time. Table 6.2 summarizes key ID records by level of government.

Conclusion

Securing legal rights for transgender people has been a long, protracted fight. The battle for transgender rights has been tougher than securing LGB. As of today, there is no uniform federal definition of

Table 6.2 Identity Record by Government Level, Demographics, and Cost

ID Card Type	Level of Govt & Agency	Demographic Information	Cost
Consular Report of Birth Abroad	Federal, State Department	Name, gender marker	$50
Military ID	Federal, military branch	Name	
Social Security	Federal, Social Security Administration	Name	Free
U.S. Passport	Federal, State Department	Name, gender marker	$110 + $35 fee = $145
Birth Certificate	State, Vital Statistics	Name, gender marker	Varies
Driver's License	State, Motor Vehicles Administration	Name, gender marker	Varies
Marriage Certificate	State, Vital Statistics	Name	Varies
Voter Registration	State chief election officer	Name, gender marker	Free

gender. Sex under Title VII of the Civil Rights Law of 1964 has recently been expanded to include sexual orientation and gender identity (*Bostock v. Clayton County*, 2020). The federal Real ID Act of 2005 requires each state to verify and document specific variables on driver's licenses, but it does not define gender. As such, each state defines gender, which creates variation across the country. Regarding U.S. passports, thus far, the U.S. State Department (n.d.) has refused to issue gender-neutral passports, despite being ordered to do so (*Zzyym v. Pompeo*, 2018; *Zzyym v. Pompeo*, 2019) and encouraged to do so by the Tenth Circuit (*Zzymm v. Pompeo*, 2020). Similarly, as of the publication of this book, the U.S. Supreme Court has not ruled on the Title IX definition of *sex* regarding public accommodations, but the U.S. Supreme Court's ruling in *Bostock v. Clayton County* (2020) may apply to Title IV public accommodations. Without federal legislation or court rulings, the country will continue to be split on these issues: Southern states and some midwestern states will deny transgender people rights while the East and West Coast states will pass transgender protections. This will mean that the rights of transgender people will vary by state creating unequal treatment and discrimination.

Resources

interACT: Advocates for Intersex Youth. https://interactadvocates.org/
Intersex and Genderqueer Project (IGRP). www.intersexrecognition.org/
Lambda Legal. www.lambdalegal.org/
National Association of Secretaries of State. https://nass.org
National Association of State Election Directors. https://nased.org
National Center for Transgender Equality. https://transequality.org/
National Constitutional Center. https://constitutioncenter.org/interactive-constitution/preamble
National Gay and Lesbian Task Force. www.thetaskforce.org/
The Trevor Project. www.thetrevorproject.org/
The Williams Institute. School of Law. University of California, Los Angeles.
Trans Youth Equality Foundation. www.transyouthequality.org/
Transgender Law Center. www.thetaskforce.org/
U.S. Department of Education, Office for Civil Rights. https://www2.ed.gov/about/offices/list/ocr/index.html
U.S. Department of Education, Office for Civil Rights. Religious Exemptions. https://www2.ed.gov/about/offices/list/ocr/correspondence/other.html
U.S. Equal Employment Commission. Disability Discrimination. www.eeoc.gov/laws/types/disability.cfm
U.S. Social Security Administration. http://www.ssa.gov
U.S. State Department. http://www.state.gov
U.S. State Department, Bureau of Consular Affairs. Passports. Change of Sex Marker. (n.d.). https://travel.state.gov/content/travel/en/passports/apply-renew-passport/change-of-sex-marker.html
Vital Statistics. U.S. Centers for Disease Control and Prevention. National Center for Health Statistics. www.cdc.gov/nchs/nvss/index.htm

References

American Disabilities Act. (n.d.). *Accessibility guidelines for buildings and facilities*. U.S. Architectural and Transportation Barriers. Washington, DC. www.access-board.gov/attachments/article/1350/adaag.pdf
American Disabilities Act of 1990 (Pub. L. 101–336).
American Disabilities Amendment Act of 2008 (Pub. L. 110–325).

Age Discrimination Act of 1975 (Pub. L. 94–135).
Blinder, A. (2017, November 4). An embattled North Carolina seeks to outrun a law's bitter legacy. *New York Times*.
Bostock v. Clayton County 590 U.S. _ (2020)
California, Assembly Bill No. 1732 (2016).
California, Fair Employment & Housing Council. (2017).
Carcano v. McCrory, No. 1:16-cv-236 (North Carolina, 2016)
Civil Rights Act of 1964 (Pub. L. 88–352).
Civil Rights Restoration Act of 1987. (Pub. L. 100–259).
DeVos, Betsy. (2017, February 22). *U.S. Secretary Betsy DeVos issues statement on new Title IX*. https://www2.ed.gov/about/offices/list/ocr/letters/colleague-201605-title-ix-transgender.pdf
Educational Amendments of 1972 (Pub. L. 92–318).
Election Protection 866. (n.d.). https://866ourvote.org
Flores, A. F., Herman, J. L., Gates, G. L., & Brown, T. N. (2016). *How many adults identify as transgender in the United States?* The Williams Institute. Law School. UCLA. http://williamsinstitute.law.ucla.edu/wp-content/uploads/How-Many-Adults-Identify-as-Transgender-in-the-United-States.pdf
Gloucester County School Board v. GG, 137 U.S. 369 (2016).
Gloucester County School Board v. GG, 822 F.3d 709 (Fourth Circuit, 2016).
Grimm v. Gloucester County School Board, Appeal, 19–1952 (Fourth Circuit, December 9, 2019).
Grimm v. Gloucester County School Board, 4:15cv54 (USDC, ED, VA, August 9, 2019).
Haig v. Agee, 453 U.S. 280, 293 (1981).
Hass, A. P., Rodgers, P. L., & Herman, J. L. (2014, January). *Suicide attempts by transgender and gender non-confirming adults*. The Williams Institute. Law School, UCLA. http://williamsinstitute.law.ucla.edu/wp-content/uploads/AFSP-Williams-Suicide-Report-Final.pdf
Help America Vote Act of 2002 (Pub. L. 107–252). www.doj.gov/crt/center-146-election-admnistration-improvement
Herman, J. (2015). *The potential impact of voter identification laws on transgender voters in the 2014 general election*. The Williams Institute, Law School, UCLA. https://williamsinstitute.law.ucla.edu/wp-content/uploads/voter-id-laws-september-2014.pdf
Holzer, L. (2018). *2018 Non-binary gender registration models in Europe. Report on third gender marker options*. International Lesbian, Gay, Bisexual, Trans and Intersex Association (ILGA) Europe. www.ilga-europe.org/sites/default/files/non-binary_gender_registration_models_in_europe_0.pdf
Indiana Code Annotated Section 35-50-3-2.
Intercountry Adoption Act of 2000 (Pub. L. 106–279). www.govinfo.gov/content/pkg/PLAW-106publ279/pdf/PLAW-106publ279.pdf
International Civil Aviation Organization. (2015). *Doc. 9303. Machine readable travel documents* (7th ed.). Part 4: Specifications for Machine Readable Passports and other TD3 size MRTDs. P. 14. Approved by the U.N. Secretary General. Montreal, Canada. Retrieved February 17, 2020, from www.icao.int/publications/Documents/9303_p4_cons_en.pdf
Intersex and Genderqueer Project. (n.d.). www.intersexrecognition.org/
Johnston v. University of Pittsburgh, 3:2013cv00213 (W.D. PA 2015).
Lam, K. (2019, August 31). More than 7,000 Americans have gender X IDs, a victory for transgender rights. Is it a safety risk, too? *USA Today*. www.usatoday.com/story/news/nation/2019/08/08/nonbinary-gender-ids-momentum-intersex-state-driver-licenses/1802059001/
Lambda Legal. (n.d.). *Movement advancement map. X gender markers by state*. www.lambdalegal.org/map/x-markers
Lhamon, C. E., & Gupta, V. (2016, May 13). *Joint letter by the U.S. Department of Education and U.S. Department of Justice*. Dear Colleague Letter on Transgender Students. https://www2.ed.gov/about/offices/list/ocr/letters/colleague-201605-title-ix-transgender.pdf
Love v. Johnson, 15–11834 (ED, MI, August 23, 2016).
McCarthy, N. (2018, January 11). The share of Americans holding a passport has increased dramatically in recent years. *Forbes*. www.forbes.com/sites/niallmccarthy/2018/01/11/the-share-of-americans-holding-a-passport-has-increased-dramatically-in-recent-years-infographic/#31868a883c16

National Association of State Secretaries. (n.d.). *Roster of secretaries of state/lieutenant governors*. https://www.nass.org/membership

National Center for Transgender Equality (2019).

National Conference of State Legislators (2017). www.ncsl.org

National Voter Registration Act of 1993. (42 U.S.C. 1973).

Robinson v. California, 392 U.S. 514. Part III.A (1962)

Rose, A., & Silverman, H. (2020, March 3). Idaho governor signs two bills that limits the right of transgender people. *CNN*. www.cnn.com/2020/03/31/us/idaho-transgender-bills/index.html

Rosenbloom, D. H. (2015). *Administrative law for public managers* (2nd ed.). Westview Press.

Rushin, S., & Carroll, J. (2017). Bathroom laws as status crimes. *Fordham Law Review, 86*(1), Article 11. http://ir.lawnet.foundation.edu/flr/vol86/iss1/11

Section 504 of the Rehabilitation Act of 1973 as amended in 2013. (29 U.S.C. Sec 793; 41 CFR Part 60–741, U.S. Department of Labor).

Siegel, A. (2011, September 13). Teen gets 5 years for attack on transgender woman at McDonalds. *Baltimore Sun*. www.baltimoresun.com/news/maryland/baltimore-county/bs-md-co-mcdonalds-sentencing-20110913-story.html

Sutton v. United Air Lines, 527 U.S. 471 (1999).

Texas v. United States of America, 7:16 -cv-00054 (2016, August 26).

The Guardian. (2019). *United becomes first airline to introduce non-binary gender option on bookings*. https://www.theguardian.com/travel/2019/mar/27/united-becomes-first-airline-to-introduce-non-binary-gender-option-on-bookings

Toyota Motor Manufacturing, Kentucky v. Williams, 534 U.S. 184 (2002).

Trotta, D. (2019, March 5). Some 4.5 percent of U.S. adults identify as LGBT. *Reuters*.

U.S. Census Bureau. (2018). *Number of cities, townships, and counties*. www.census.gov

U.S. Constitution. 1789.

U.S. Department of Education. (2018). *National center on education statistics*. https://nces.ed.gov/fastfacts/display.asp?id=84

U.S. Department of Education. (2016, May). *Office of elementary and secondary education, office of safe and healthy students. Examples of policies and emerging practices for supporting transgender students*. https://www2.ed.gov/about/offices/list/oese/oshs/emergingpractices.pdf

U.S. Department of Education, Connecticut Interscholastic Athletic Conference. (2020, May 15). *Memo*. www.adfmedia.org/files/SouleDOEImpendingEnforcementLetter.pdf

U.S. Department of Education, Office of Civil Rights. (2018, January 18). *Correspondence to Central Christian College of the Bible*. https://www2.ed.gov/about/offices/list/ocr/docs/t9-rel-exempt/central-christian-college-of-the-bible-response-01182017.pdf

U.S. Department of Education, Office of Civil Rights. (n.d.). https://www2.ed.gov/about/offices/list/ocr/docs/t9-rel-exempt/index.html

U.S. Department of Education. Singleton Memo. (February 19, 1985). https://www2.ed.gov/about/offices/list/ocr/docs/singleton-memo-19850219.pdf

U.S. Department of Education. Smith Memo. (1989, October 11). https://www2.ed.gov/about/offices/list/ocr/docs/smith-memo-19891011.pdf

U.S. Department of Homeland Security. (2005, May 11). REAL ID Act. (Pub. L. 109–13). 119 STAT. 231 109th Congress. www.govinfo.gov/content/pkg/STATUTE-119/pdf/STATUTE-119-Pg231.pdf#page=72

U.S. Department of Homeland Security, TSA. (n.d.). www.tsa.gov/transgender-passengers

U.S. Department of Justice. (n.d.). *Overview of Title IX of the Educational Amendments of 1972*. www.justice.gov/crt/fcs/TitleIX-SexDiscrimination

U.S. Department of Justice. Civil Rights Division. Disability Rights Section. Report. American with Disabilities Act: ADA Checklist for Polling Places. (2016, June). www.ada.gov/votingchecklist.pdf

U.S. Federal Bureau of Investigation. (2018). Hate crimes report.

U.S. Government Accountability Office. (2009). *Voters with disabilities; Additional monitoring of polling places could further improve accessibility*. Washington, DC.

U.S. Social Security Administration. (n.d.). www.ssa.gov/people/same-sexcouples/

U.S. State Department, Bureau of Consular Affairs. Travel. Reports and Statistics. U.S. Passports. (n.d.). *Fiscal year 2019 table valid passports in circulation.* https://travel.state.gov/content/travel/en/about-us/reports-and-statistics.html

U.S. State Department, International Travel. Birth of U.S. Citizens Abroad. (n.d.). https://travel.state.gov/content/travel/en/international-travel/while-abroad/birth-abroad/replace-amend-CRBA.html

White House, Presidential Memorandum. (2016). Dear Colleagues Letter. Obama Administration.

Williams Institute. UCLA School of Law. (2019, January). *LGBT data and demographics.* https://williamsinstitute.law.ucla.edu/visualization/lgbt-stats/?topic=LGBT&area=28#density

Zzyym v. Kerry, 15-cv-02362-RBJ (D. CO, 2019).

Zzyym v. Pompeo, 18–1453 (2020, May 12).

Zzyym v. Pompeo, 341 F. Supp. 3d 1248 (2018).

Zzyym v. Pompeo (Tenth Circuit, 2015).

Chapter 7

Next Steps

Chapter Content

Federal policies granting lesbian, gay, bisexual, transgender, and queer (LGBTQ) rights and protections began to emerge in the past 15 years. In 2003, the U.S. Supreme Court decriminalized same-sex behavior, granting lesbians and gays the same rights to personal intimacy as opposite-sex couples (*Lawrence v. Texas*, 2003). This was a major and historic step in moving LGBTQ people from the category of criminal to citizen. Prior to 2003, same-sex couples could be arrested, jailed, and fined for engaging in personal intimacy, which often led to being harassed or fired by their employer, making it difficult to obtain work and creating financial hardship. Next, in 2011, Congress passed the Don't Ask Don't Tell Repeal Act of 2010 (Pub. L. 111–321). As a result, lesbians and gays have been openly serving in the U.S. military. Two years later, in 2013 the U.S. Supreme Court struck down Section 3 of the Defense of Marriage Act and redefined marriage to include same-sex couples (*U.S. v. Windsor*, 2013). For same-sex married couples who lived in states that legalized same-sex marriage, the ruling also extended more than 1,100 federal spousal benefits including health insurance, military benefits, social security, and estate and property tax rights. These new government benefits in the form of economic tax breaks and reduced health care costs significantly increase the wealth and prosperity of same-sex married couples. These are benefits and rights opposite-sex couples have always enjoyed but now extend to same-sex married couples. In 2015, the U.S. Supreme Court ruled marriage was a fundamental right and made same-sex marriage legal across the country (*Obergefell v. Hodges*, 2015). It was a landmark ruling, creating marriage equality and granting federal spousal economic benefits to same-sex married couples nationwide. It also provides the social recognition of marriage and spouses in American society. Prior to the ruling, gay couples hid their marriage or partner in fear of being outed and ostracized by society. Today, they are treated similarly to opposite-sex married couples (same tax benefits). In 2016, the U.S. Supreme Court ruled 9–0 in *V.L. v. E.L.* (2016) that an adoption by a same-sex couple in one state had to be recognized by all other 49 states. For example, this means when a same-sex married couple who resides in Kansas drives across the state border to Missouri, the state government of Missouri has to recognize the adoption from its sister state of Kansas, a legal right opposite-sex married couples have always enjoyed in every state across the nation. In 2020, the U.S. Supreme Court delivered a landmark ruling that 'sex' under Title VII of the Civil Rights Act of 1964 includes sexual orientation and gender identity (*Bostock v. Clayton County*, 2020), expanding employment protections to LGBTQ people. The court ruled it is a violation of federal law to discriminate against homosexual and transgender people in employment. The momentous ruling, made by a conservative majority court and penned by conservative Justice Gorsuch, is a sea change in LGBTQ employment protections and highlights the court's political independence. LGBTQ people no longer have to live in fear of being fired based on being gay or transgender. They can now get married on Sunday and announce their marriage at work on Monday with no adverse actions. Being gay or transgender is no longer 'fireable' offenses. The *Bostock v. Clayton County* (2020) ruling is broad-reaching, impacting 4 million LGBTQ people, and potentially impacting more than 100 federal laws which provide statutory protections based on sex. The ruling will likely extend antidiscrimination LGBTQ protections in credit, education, health care, housing, and a myriad of federal programs that prohibit discrimination based on sex. The *Bostock v. Clayton County* (2020) ruling was viewed as a push back on President Trump's attempt to reverse President Obama's legacy of LGBTQ protections in the Affordable Care Act, Fair Housing Act, and executive order on employment.

Five landmark U.S. Supreme Court decisions, four of which were delivered by the Roberts' court, have collectively created a set of new legal rights and property (government benefits) for LGBTQ people and extend the umbrella of civil rights to include sexual orientation and gender identity as protected traits. This is seismic and groundbreaking. For the past 50 years, sex under the Civil Rights Act of 1964 has meant women and men (biological sex), and now sex includes homosexuals and transgenders as protected traits. And the Stonewall Inn in New York, which birthed the LGBTQ movement, now stands as one of our country's national parks, reminding visitors of the long, hard-fought journey in securing LGBTQ rights and human rights in America. The court's impact on LGBTQ rights in public administration is broad-reaching. Policy implementation (Pressman & Wildavksy, 1984) and compliance of the court's decisions will impact all three levels of government and has nationwide implications. It will be important to ensure judicial policies are implemented efficiently, effectively, economically, and equitably. In terms of social equity, it will be important to measure procedural due process, distributional equity, process equity, and outcome disparities (National Academy of Public Administration, n.d.). In terms of the field of public administration, it is an ever-evolving field (Peters & Pierre, 2017; Perry & Christianson), with a strong history of administrative reforms (Durant, 2020). Policies, practices, training, and textbooks will need to be updated to reflect the court's decisions on LGBTQ legal protections in adoption, employment, health care, marriage, and a range of other policies. The rulings directly impact administrative law, human resources, and public personnel.

Next Steps

Enormous advancements have been made on LGBTQ Protections and political representation. However, more work needs to be done in securing LGBTQ parenting rights in foster care and adoption, transgender violence protection, government identity cards and vital statistic certificates, and political representation.

Adoption and Foster Care

Regarding foster care and adoption, there are several pending court cases on whether religious organizations contracting with the federal and state government to provide foster care and adoption can discriminate against LGBTQ people based on religious exemptions granted by the U.S. Department of Health and Human Services. One case involves a contractor refusing to license foster parents unless they are Evangelical Protestant Christians, excluding people who are Catholic or Jewish (*Rogers v. U.S. DHHS*, 2019) regardless of whether couples are same sex or opposite sex. These cases need to be monitored to ensure the best interest of children is placed at the forefront of the decision making. There are approximately 500,000 children languishing in the U.S. child welfare system, and they need a permanent home before they age out of the system. There is a shortage of foster parents and adoptive parents. No adoption equates to no families to guide and direct these children as young adults. The outcomes are tragic. Without an adoptive family, our foster children are more likely to quit school, be unemployed, abuse drugs, and become homeless. Our foster children have basic needs (food, shelter, clothing, education, and family). The criteria utilized to select foster parents and adoptive parents should be a loving home that can meet basic needs, regardless of religious affiliation. The number one priority should be securing permanent homes for children.

U.S. Census

The U.S. Census should add sexual orientation and gender identity as options in the demographic variable sex when collecting census data. The recent *Bostock v. Clayton County* (2020) ruling defined *sex* to include sexual orientation and gender identity in Title VII of the Civil Rights Act of 1964. It will be critical to collect data on LGBTQ employment to ensure policy compliance with the Equal Employment Opportunity Commission (*Bostock v. Clayton County*, 2020) ruling. The U.S. Census tracks employment data and income. More broadly, the U.S. Census is utilized to determine political representation and funding allocation for over $650 billion for roads, highway, hospitals, schools, and policing. LGBTQ people have unique education, health care, housing, and public accommodation needs. To ensure distributional equity, LGBTQ people need to be counted in the census, and it starts by recognizing them based on sexual orientation and gender identity.

Government ID

We need to update our government identity document (ID) policies. It is critical for federal, state, and local governments to have accurate information on its citizens (*Zzymm v. Pompeo*, 2020). The best strategy to ensure accuracy is to collect accurate information (update the forms) and make data collection uniform (a federal policy). This means that policies need to be updated to reflect medical and scientific evidence on human sexuality (intersex). The binary sex model no longer captures accurate information on the entire population. Gender X needs to be an option on government forms for sex, including the passport, state-issued drivers licenses, and birth certificates. The United Nations and other countries accept and issue ID with the X marker. As it stands now, the U.S. lags behind its European peers.

Transgender Protection Policies

Additional policies are needed to protect transgender people from discrimination and violence. The *New York Times* has labeled the brutal killing of transgender people an epidemic (Rojas & Swales,

2019). According to the U.S. Federal Bureau of Investigation, each year approximately 25 transgender people are murdered based on gender identity. In 2009, Congress passed historic legislation, the Matthew Shepard Jr. and James Byrd Hate Crimes Prevention Act, which classifies murders based on sexual orientation and gender identity as hate crimes and carries a more severe penalty. This policy is important in capturing hate crime statistics but does not address the root causes of hate and discrimination. For example, on June 12, 2016, one of the largest mass shootings in U.S. history took place in Orlando, Florida. Known as the Orlando Nightclub Massacre, the killer, Omar Mateen, was an American who identified himself as an Islamic soldier. Mateen opened fire at a gay nightclub called the Pulse, killing 49 people and wounding 53. That specific night was "Latin night," and as such, the majority of people killed and wounded in the club were Hispanic LGBTQ people. Mateen was killed by police in the shootout. As such, Mateen's real motives will never be known, but the massacre is the largest and deadliest attack against the LGBTQ community in U.S. history. More recently, in April 2020, two transgender women from New York City were found dead in a burned car during a visit to Puerto Rico (Levenson & Garcia, April 30, 2020). These examples illustrate the need for new federal legislation to prevent individual attacks and mass violence against LGBTQ people. Research shows that when heterosexual people get to know someone of a different sexual orientation or gender identity, they become less biased, less discriminatory, and more accepting and supportive. As a result, more public service announcements, education, and training are needed in the form of media campaigns, including television advertisements, print, billboards, and social media, to decrease violence, discrimination, and bias against LBGTQ people. Regarding specific transgender rights, a federal public accommodations policy is needed for bathrooms, gyms, locker rooms, and dressing rooms to ensure their safety. When transgender people (adults and youth) use bathrooms based on gender identity instead of birth sex, it often results in bullying, harassment, and violence.

Military Service

To ensure equal treatment and full citizenship, the transgender military ban should be lifted. This means we need federal legislation or court intervention to provide a long-term sustainable. The rights of gays and transgenders to serve in the U.S. military should be based on allegiance to country and willingness to serve.

Religious Freedom Versus Equal Protection

Historically, legal rights for LGBTQ people have been framed as a cultural and political war. Blue liberal states support LGBTQ legal protections and red conservative states support religious freedom, reflecting the political divide in the country (Kettl, 2020; Swan, 2014). It sets religious freedom against equal protection, which has deep roots in American history. The fight for religious freedom began at the country's inception and was debated at length by our Founding Fathers (Myerson, 2012); it is a debate that has been ongoing for over 200 years and will most likely continue. Rights on LGBTQ, abortion, guns, and religion, are primal policy issues and define us at our core. The "Baby, Guns, and Jesus," debate model asks us to determine our core beliefs. Underneath the political debate is our culture, which is composed of core values and beliefs (Khademian, 2004; Schein & Schein, 2017). There are two core questions: First, what do you believe about sexual orientation and gender identity? If you believe people are born gay, homosexual at birth, then you tend to believe that gays should have equal rights and equal treatment like their straight, heterosexual peers. If you believe people being gay is a choice (learned or environmental), then you are less likely to support equal rights and equal treatment. The same logic can be applied to transgender people. When Americans were asked this core question the majority believe gay people are born gay. A poll by the Pew Research Center shows that over half of Americans polled believe that homosexuality is innate, it is something people are born with and can't change. It is also widely understood by the American Psychological Association, the American Psychiatric Association, and the medical community at large that homosexuality is innate; people are born gay or lesbian As such, Americans support LGBTQ protections and legal rights in marriage equality, adoption, employment, and housing. The second question is, What do you believe about America? Should America protect all its citizens? Should we protect the "tired and poor" as stated on the Statue of Liberty? Protecting vulnerable and unpopular political groups may not be an easy task, but it is a task we are legally and politically called to do if we believe in "liberty and justice for all."

References

Asmelash, L. (2020, June 10). West Virginia just elected its first openly transgender official. *CNN*. www.cnn.com/2020/06/10/us/rosemary-ketchum-west-virginia-transgender-trnd/index.html

Bostock v. Clayton County, Georgia, 590 U.S. _ (2020).

Defense of Marriage Act of 1996. (Pub. L. 104–199).

Don't Ask Don't Tell Repeal Act of 2010 (Pub. L. 111–321).

Durant, R. F. (2020). *Building the compensatory state: An intellectual history and theory of American administrative reform*. Routledge.

Kettl, D. (2020). *The divided states of America: Why federalism doesn't work*. Princeton University Press.

Khademian, A. M. (2004). *Working with culture: The way the job gets done in public programs*. CQ Press.

Lawless, J. (2012). *Becoming a candidate: Political ambition and the decision to run for office*. Cambridge University Press.

Lawrence v. Texas, 539 U.S. 558 (2003).

Levinson, M., & Garcia, S. E. (2020, April 30). Two arrested in killings of transgender women in Puerto Rico. *New York Times*. www.nytimes.com/2020/04/30/us/puerto-rico-transgender-murder-arrests.html

Myerson, Michael I. (2012). *Endowed by our creator: The birth of religious freedom in America*. Yale University Press.

National Academy of Public Administration. (n.d.). *Social equity*. www.napawash.org/aa_social_equity/index.html

Obergefell v. Hodges, 576 U.S. 644 (2015).

Peters, G. B., & Pierre, J. (2017). *The next public administration: Debates and dilemmas*. Sage.

Pressman, J. L., & Wildavsky, A. (1984). *Implementation: How great expectations in Washington are dashed in Oakland* (3rd ed.). University of California Press.

Rogers v. U.S. Department of Health and Human Services, DSC 6:19-cv-01567 (2019).

Rojas, R., & Swales, V. (2019). 18 Transgender killings this year raise fears of an 'epidemic.' *New York Times*. www.nytimes.com/2019/09/27/us/transgenderwomen-deaths.html?auth=login-email&login=email

Schein, E., & Schein, P. (2017). *Organizational culture and leadership*. John Wiley & Sons.

Swan, W. (2014). Framing the same-sex marriage decisions: The context and the possibilities. *Journal of Health & Human Services Administration, 37*(2), 184–206.

U.S. v. Windsor, 570 U.S. 744 (2013).

Zzyym v. Pompeo, 18–1453 (2020, May 12).

Glossary

Asexual: not attracted to either males or females
Binary: either female or male
Bisexual: attracted to both males and females
Cisgender: an individual's biological sex matches their gender identity
Gay: males who are attracted to males
Gender Identity: an individual's perception of their gender; does not have to match their biological sex (male or female reproductive organs)
Gender Fluidity: sexuality is viewed on a spectrum, nonbinary
Intersectionality: layered identities based on variables such as race, gender identity, and gender expression
Intersex: no established sex
LGBT: lesbian, gay bisexual, transgender
LGBTQ: lesbian, gay, bisexual, transgender, queer
LGBTQIA: lesbian, gay, bisexual, transgender, queer, intersex, asexual
Lesbian: females who are attracted to females
Nonbinary: neither male or female; sexuality on a continuum
Questioning: an individual who is uncertain about their sexuality or gender identity
Trans: short for transgender
Transgender: gender identity does not match or conform to their birth sex
Transgender and gender-nonconforming (TGNC): gender identity does not match or conform to their birth sex

Appendix

List of Federal Statutes Protecting Sex Discrimination

Source: *Bostock v. Clayton County*, 2020, pp. 66–81. Listed in chronological order.

Congressional Budget and Fiscal Operations; Federal Mandates (2 U.S.C. Section 658a(2)
Congressional Accountability; Extension of Rights and Protections (2 U.S.C. Section 1311(a)(1)
Unfunded Mandates Reform (2 U.S.C. Section 1503(2)
Presidential Offices; Employment Discrimination (3 U.S.C. Section 411(a)(1)
Merit System Principles (5 U.S.C. Section 2301(b)(2)
Prohibited Personnel Practices (5 U.S.C. Section 2302(b)(1)
Labor-Management Relations; Definitions (5 U.S.C. Section 7103(a)(4)(A)
Labor-Management Relations; Unfair Labor Practices (5 U.S.C. Section 7116(b)(4)
Antidiscrimination Policy; Minority Recruitment Program (5 U.S.C. Section 7201(b)
Antidiscrimination; Other Prohibitions (5 U.S.C. Section 7204(b)
Supplemental Nutrition Assistance Program (7 U.S.C. Section 2020 (c)(1)
Immigration; Numerical Limitations on Individual Foreign States (8 U.S.C. Section 1152(a) (1)(A)
Visa Waiver Program for Certain Visitors (8 U.S.C. Section 1187(c)(6)
Authorization for Programs for Domestic Resettlement of and Assistance to Refugees (8 U.S.C. Section 1522(a)(5)
Uniform Code of Military Justice; Article 132 Retaliation (10 U.S.C. Section 932(b)(4)
Protected Communications; Prohibition of Retaliatory Personnel Actions (10 U.S.C. Section 1034(j)(3)
Directors of Federal Reserve Banks; Number of Members; Classes (12 U.S.C. Section 302)
Prohibition Against Discrimination on Account of Sex in Extension of Mortgage Association (12 U.S.C. Section 1735–5(a)
Antidiscrimination; Other Prohibitions (5 U.S.C. Section 7204(b)
Federal Deposit Insurance Corporation; Insurance Funds (12 U.S.C. Section 1821(d)(13)(iv)

Federal Deposit Insurance Corporation; Corporation Moneys (12 U.S.C. Section 1823(d)(3)(D)(iv)
Farm Credit System Insurance Corporation; Corporation as Conservator or Receiver; Certain Other Powers (12 U.S.C. Section 2277a-10c(b)(13)€(iv)
National Consumer Cooperative Bank; Eligibility of Cooperatives (12 U.S.C. Section 3015(a)(4)
Foreign Bank Participation in Domestic Markets (12 U.S.C. Section 3106(1)(B) and (2)(B)
Wallstreet Reform and Consumer Protection; Powers and Duties of the Corporation (12 U.S.C. Section 5390(a)(9)(E)(v)
Aid to Small Business (15 U.S.C. Section 631(h)
Small Business Administration (15 U.S.C. Section 633(b)(1)
Alaska Natural Gas Transportation; Civil Rights (15 U.S.C. Section 719)
Federal Energy Administration; Sex Discrimination; Enforcement; Other Legal Remedies (15 U.S.C. Section 775)
Equal Credit Opportunity Act (15 U.S.C. Section 1691(a)(1)
Equal Credit Opportunity Act (15 U.S.C. Section 1691d(a)
Full Employment and Balanced Growth; Nondiscrimination (15 U.S.C. Section 3151(a)
Deprivation of Relief Benefits (18 U.S.C. Section 246)
Special Hearing to Determine Whether a Sentence of Death is Justified (18 U.S.C. Section 3593(f)
Higher Education Resources and Student Assistance; Antidiscrimination) (20 U.S.C. Section 1011(a)
Disclosures of Foreign Gifts (20 U.S.C. Section 1011f(h)(5)(D)
Historically Black College and University Capital financing; Limitations on Federal Insurance bonds Issued by Designated Bonding Authority
Federal Family Education Loan Program (20 U.S.C. Section 1071(a)(2)
Federal Payments to Reduce Student Interest Costs (20 U.S.C. Section 1078(c)(2)(F)
Federal Family Education Loan Program; Special Allowances (20 U.S.C. Section 1087–1e
Student Loan Marketing Association (20 U.S.C. Section 1087–2(e)
Discrimination in Secondary Markets Prohibited (20 U.S.C. Section 1087–4)
Discretion of student financial Aid Administrators (20 U.S.C. Section 1087tt(c)
Education Programs; Use of Funds Withheld (20 U.S.C. Section 1231e(b)(2)
Title IV of the Education Amendments of 1972 (20 U.S.C. Section 1681)
Equal Educational Opportunities; Congressional Declaration of Policy (20 U.S.C. Section 1701(a)(1)
Equal Educational Opportunities; Congressional Findings (20 U.S.C. Section 1702(a)(1)
Denial of Equal Educational Opportunity Prohibited (20 U.S.C. Section 1705)
District Lines (20 U.S.C. Section 1715)
Equal Educational Opportunities; Definitions (20 U.S.C. Section 1720)
Remedies with Respect to School District Lines (20 U.S.C. Section 1756)
Career and Technical Education; Federal Laws Guaranteeing Civil Rights (20 U.S.C. Section 2396)
Department of Education; Congressional Findings (20 U.S.C. Section 3401(2)
Magnet Schools Assistance; Applications and Requirements (20 U.S.C. Section 7231d(b)(2) (C)
Strengthening and Improvement of Elementary and Secondary Schools; Civil Rights (20 U.S.C. Section 7914)
Foreign Relations and Intercourse; Equal Employment Opportunities (22 U.S.C. Section 262p-4n)
Human Rights and Security Assistance (22 U.S.C. Section 2304(a)(1)
Furnishing of Defense Articles or Related Training or Other Defense Service on Grant Basis (22 U.S.C. Section 2314(g)
Discrimination Against United States Personnel (22 U.S.C, Section 2426)
Peace Corps Volunteers (22 U.S.C. Section 2504(a)
Foreign Contracts or Arrangements; Discrimination (22 U.S.C. Section 2661a)

Discrimination Prohibited if Based on Race, Religion, National Orign, or Sex (22 U.S.C. Section 2755)
Foreign Service; Congressional Findings and Objectives (22 U.S.C. Section 3901(b)(2)
Foreign Service; Personnel Actions (22 U.S.C. Section 3905(b)(1)
Foreign Service; Definitions (22 U.S.C. Section 4102(11)(A)
Foreign Service; Unfair Labor Practices (22 U.S.C. Section 4115(b)(4)
International Religious Freedom; Findings; Policy (22 U.S.C. Section 6401(a)(3)
Office of Volunteers for Prosperity (22 U.S.C. Section 8303(c) (2)
Federal Aid Highways; Nondiscrimination (23 U.S.C. Section 140(a)
Highways; Prohibition of Discrimination on the Basis of Sex (23 U.S.C. Section 324)
Housing Assistance for Native Hawaiians (25 U.S.C. Section 4223(d)(2)
Tax Court; Employees (26 U.S.C. Section7471(a)(6)(A)
Duties of the United States Sentencing Commission (28 U.S.C. Section 994(d)
Trial by Jury; Discrimination (28 U.S.C. Section 1862)
Trial by Jury; Challenging Compliance with Selection Procedures (28 U.S.C. Section 1867(e)
Equal Pay Act of 1963 (29 U.S.C. Section 206(d)(1)
Family and Medical Leave; Effect on Other Laws (29 U.S.C. Section 2651(a)
Workforce Development Opportunities; Nondiscrimination (29 U.S.C 3248)
Research Funds to Institutes (30 U.S.C. Section 1222(c)
Government Accountability Office; Personnel Management System (31 U.S.C. Section 732(f)
Federal Payments; Prohibited Discrimination (31 U.S.C. Section 6711)
Federal Payments; Definitions, Application, and Administration (31 U.S.C. Section 6720(a)(8)
Prohibition of Federal Control Over State and Local Criminal Justice Agencies; Prohibition of Discrimination (34 U.S.C. Section10228(c)
Juvenile Justice and Delinquency Prevention; State Plans (34 U.S.C. Section 11133(a)(16)
Community Schools Youth Services and supervision Grant Program (34 U.S.C. Section 12161(g)
Violent Crime Control and law Enforcement; Civil Rights for Women (34 U.S.C. Section 12361)
Crime Victims Funds; Administration Provisions (34 U.S.C. Section 20110€
Emergency Federal Law Enforcement Assistance (34 U.S.C. Section 50104(a)
Air Force Sergeants Association; Membership (36 U.S. C. Section 20204(b)
Air Force Sergeants Association; Governing Body (36 U.S. C. Section 20205(c)
American GI Forum of the United States; Membership (36 U.S.C. Section 21003(a)(4)
American GI Forum of the United States; Membership (36 U.S.C. Section 21004(b)
American GI Forum of the United States; Membership (36 U.S.C. Section 21005(c)
The American Legion (36 U.S.C. Section21704A)
Amvets; Membership (36 U.S.C. Section 22703(c)
Amvets; Governing Body (36 U.S.C. Secton22704(d)
82nd Airborne Division Association, Incorporated; Membership (36 U.S.C. Section 60104(b)
82n Airborne Division Association, Incorporated; Governing Body (36 U.S.C. Section 60105(c)
Fleet Reserve Association; Membership (36 U.S.C. Section 70104(b)
Fleet Reserve Association; Governing Body (36 U.SC. Section 70105(c)
Military Order of the World Wars; Membership (36 U.S.C. Section 140704(b)
Military Order of the World Wars; Governing Body (36 U.S.C. Section 140705(c)
Non Commissioned Officers Association of the United States of America, Incorporated; Membership (36 U.S.C. Section 154704(b)
Non Commissioned Officers Association of the United States of America, Incorporated; Membership (36 U.S.C. Section 154705(c)
Retired Enlisted Association, Incorporated; Membership (36 U.S.C. Section 190304(b)

Retired Enlisted Association, Incorporated; Membership (36 U.S.C. Section 190305(c)
United States Olympic Committee; Eligibility Requirements (36 U.S.C. Section220522(a)(8) and (9)
Vietnam Veterans of America, Inc.; Membership (36 U.S.C. Section230504(b)
Vietnam Veterans of America, Inc,; Governing Body (36 U.S.C. Section 230505(c)
Federal Property and Administrative Services; Prohibition on Sex Discrimination (40 U.S.C. Section 122a)
Appalachian Regional Development; nondiscrimination (40 U.S.C. Section 14702)
Military Benefits (42 U.S.C. Section 213 (f)
Projects for Assistance in Transition from Homelessness (42 U.S.C. Section 290cc-33(a)
Children with Serious Emotional Disturbances; Requirements With Respect to Carrying Out Purpose of Grants (42 U.S.C. Section 290ff-1€(2)(C)
Public Health Service; Prohibition Against Discrimination on Basis of Sex (42 U.S.C. Section 295m)
Public Health Service; Prohibition Against Discrimination by Schools on Basis of Sex (42 U.S.C. Section 296g)
Preventative Health and Health Services Block Grants; Nondiscrimination Provisions (42 U.S.C. Section 300w-7(a)(2)
Block Grants Regarding Mental Health and Substance Abuse; Nondiscrimination (42 U.S.C. Section 300x-57(a)(2)
Block Grants to States for Temporary Assistance for Needy families (42 U.S.C. Section 603(a)(5)(I)(iii)
Maternal and Child Health Services Block Grant; nondiscrimination Provisions (42 U.S.C. Section 708(a)(2)
Duties of Civil Rights Commission (42 U.S.C. Section 1975a(a)
Civil Rights; Public Education; Definitions (42 U.S.C. Section 2000c(b)
Civil Rights; Public Education; Civil Actions by the attorney General (42 U.S.C. Section 2000c-6(a0(2)
Equal Employment Opportunities; Unlawful Employment Practices (42 U.S.C. Section 2000e-2)
Equal Employment Opportunities; Other Unlawful Employment Practices (42 U.S.C. Section 2000e-16(a)
Employment by Federal Government (42 U.S.C. Section 2000e-16(a)
Government Employees Rights Act of 1981 (42 U.S.C. Section 2000e-16a(b)
Discriminatory Practices Prohibited (42 U.S.C. Section 2000e-16b(a)(1)
Intervention by Attorney General; Denial of Equal Protection on Account of Race, Color, Religion, Sex or National Origin (42 U.SC. Section 2000h-2)
Discrimination on the basis of Sex Prohibited in Federally Assisted Programs (42 U.S.C. Section 3123)
Fair Housing Act; Discrimination in Residential Real Estate-Related Transactions (42 U.S.C. Section 3605)
Fair Housing Act; Discrimination in the Provision of Brokerage Services (42 U.S.C. Section 3606)
Fair Housing Act; Violations; Penalties (42 U.S.C. Section 3631)
Intergovernmental Personnel Program; Congressional Findings and declaration of Policy (42 U.S.C. Section 4701)
Domestic Volunteer Services; Nondiscrimination Provisions (42 U.S.C. Section 5057(a)(1)
Nondiscrimination in Disaster Assistance (42 U.S.C. Section 5151(a)
Community Development; Non-discrimination in Program and Activities (42 U.S.C. Section 5309(a)

Development of Energy Sources; Sex Discrimination Prohibited (42 U.S.C. Section 5891)
Public Works Employment; Sex Discrimination; Prohibition; Enforcement) (42 U.S.C. Section 6709)
Public Works Employment; Nondiscrimination (42 U.S.C. Section 6727(a)(1)
Weatherization Assistance for Low-Income Persons (42 U.S.C. Section 6870(a)
Low-Income Home Energy Assistance; Nondiscrimination Provisions (42 U.S.C. Section 8625(a)
Community Economic Development; Nondiscrimination Provisions (42 U.S.C. Section 9821)
Head Start Programs; Nondiscrimination Provisions (42 U.S.C. Section 9849)
Community Services Block Grant Programs; Limitations on Use of Fund (42 U.S.C. Section 9918(c)(1)
Family Violence Prevention and Services; Formula Grants to States (42 U.S.C. Section 10406© (2)(B)(i)
Enterprise Zone Development; Waiver of Modification of Housing and Community Development Rules in Enterprise Zones (42 U.S.C. Section 11504(b)
National and Community Service State Grant Program; Nondiscrimination (42 U.S.C. Section 12635(a)(1)
Investment in Affordable Housing; Nondiscrimination (42 U.S.C. Section 12832)
Loans to States and Political Subdivisions; Discrimination Prohibited (43 U.S.C. Section 1747(10)
Outer Continental Shelf Resource Management; Unlawful Employment Practices; Regulations (43 U.S.C. Section 1863)
Federal communications Commission (47 U.S.C. Section 151)
Public Broadcasting; Equal Opportunity Employment (47 U.S.C. Section 398(b)(1)
Cable Communications; Equal Employment Opportunity (47 U.S.C. Section 554(b) and (c)
Cable Communications; Limitation of Franchising Authority Liability (47 U.S.C. Section 555a (c)
Virgin Islands; Voting Franchise; Discrimination Prohibited (48 U.S.C. Section 1542(a)
Discrimination Prohibited in Rights to Access to, and Benefits From, Conveyed Lands (48 U.S.C. Section 1708
Duties of the Secretary of Transportation; Prohibited Discrimination (49 U.S.C. Section 306(h)
Public Transportation; Nondiscrimination (49 U.S.C. Section 5332(b)
Air Commerce and Safety; Prohibitions on Discrimination (49 U.S.C. Section 40127)
Airport Improvement; Nondiscrimination (49 U.S.C. Section 47123(a)
Selective Service System (50 U.S.C. Section 3809(b)(3)
Anti-Boycott Act of 2018 (50 U.S.C. Section 4842(a)(1)(B)

Index

Note: Page numbers in *italic* indicate a figure and page numbers in **bold** indicate a table on the corresponding page.

Abandoned Infants Assistance Act 49–50
accreditation 7
Achieving Social Equity (Guy and McCandless) 8
Adarand Constructors v. Pena 11, 76
Administrative Law for Public Managers (Rosenbloom) 8
Administrative Procedure Act (APA) 60
adoption 48, 135; *see also* domestic adoption; international adoption; state bans
Adoption and Safe Families Act 49, 50
Adoption Awareness Act 49
adoption legal cases **62**
Adoption Opportunities Act 50
Adoption Promotion Act 50
affirmative action 8
African American women 15
Age Discrimination Act 14, 73
Age Discrimination Employment Act 14, 71, 73
Alaska State Supreme Court 26
Altitude Express v. Zarda 79
American Civil Liberties Union 51, 55
American Disabilities Act (ADA) 118–119
American Psychiatric Association 22
American Psychological Association (APA) 14
American Society for Public Administration (ASPA) 6–7
Americans with Disabilities Act 71, 73
Anti-Polygamy Act 24
Arthur, J. 21
assisted reproduction technology (ART) 46, 47, 57–59

Baker, R. J. 25
Baker v. General Motors Corp 53
Baker v. Nelson 26, 35
Bergrud, E. 6
Best Article Award 6
Bilchik, S. 51
biological children 47
Bipartisan Budget Act 50
Bi-Partisan Legal Advisory Group (BLAG) 31

birthright citizenship 59–60
Blessett, B. 5, 7
Blixt v. Tillerson 60
Bostock, G. 79
Bostock v. Clayton County 60, 61, 67, 68–70, 73–74, 78–79, 83, 86
Bowers v. Hardwick 28, 29, 39
Boynton v. Virginia 11
Breaking the Silence (Swan) 8
Brown v. Board of Education Topeka I 11
Brown v. Board of Education Topeka II 11
Brunet, J. R. 5
Bryant, A. 47, 51
Bureaucracy and Representative Government (Niskanen) 8
Byrd, J. 13

Cammermeyer, M. 95, 98–99
Carroll, J. 119
Catholic Charities of the Diocese of Springfield v. Madigan 53
Catholic Social Services 53
child abuse 48–49
Child Abuse and Treatment Act 50
Child Abuse Prevention and Enforcement Act 49
Child Abuse Prevention and Treatment Act 49, 51
Child Abuse Prevention and Treatment Amendments 49
Child and Family Services Improvement and Innovation Act 50
Child Citizen Act 50
Child Placing Agencies (CPA) 55
citizenship 50; aspects of 95; birthright 59–60; documentation for 123; intercountry adoption 57; passport 124
City of Cleburne v. Cleburne Living Center, Inc. 11
Civil Rights Act of 1964 12–13, 14, 70–72, 111, 112–113
Civil Rights and Women's Equity in Employment Act 14, 73
Civil Rights Restoration Act of 1987 117–118

Civil Service Reform Act of 1978 71, 73
class action lawsuit 37–38
Cleveland Board of Education v. LaFleur 11
Cohen, A. 61
Colorado Anti-Discrimination Act 1
Colorado Civil Rights Commission 1
Colorado Court of Appeals 1
Colvin, R. 6
Commission on Equal Employment Opportunity 13
Commission on Peer Review and Accreditation 7
Conference of Minority Public Administrators (COMPA) 6
Congress 4, 13–14
Constitutional Competence for Public Managers (Rosenbloom) 8
constitutional interpretation 11
Court Appointed Special Advocates (CASA) 79
Craig v. Boren 11
Crenshaw, K. W. 15
Cultural Competence for Public Managers (Borrego and Johnson) 8
Cultural Competency for Public Administrators (Norman-Major and Gooden) 8

D'Agostino, M. 6
Davis v. Beason 38
Dawson v. Bumble & Bumble 79
DeBoer v. Snyder 35
Defense of Marriage Act (DOMA) of 1996 11, 26, 27–28, 33, 39, 101
defiance 36
demarcation 21
Department of Human Services (DHS) 53, 104
DHS *see* U.S. Department of Homeland Security (DHS)
Dictionary Act 27
discrimination against women 101–102
distributional equity, social equity 5
DoD *see* U.S. Department of Defense (DoD)
Doe v. Trump 104
DOJ *see* U.S. Department of Justice (DOJ)
domestic adoption 48
Don't Ask, Don't Tell Policy (DADT) 99, 103
Don't Ask Don't Tell Repeal Act 95, 100–101
Dumont v. Gordon 54–55
Dvash-Banks v. Pompeo 60

Economic Growth and Tax Relief Reconciliation Act 50
Edmunds-Tucker Act 24, 38
Educational Amendments 14, 20, 113–115, 117–118, **120**, 122
EEOC *see* U.S. Equal Employment Opportunity Commission (EEOC)
Eighth Amendment 121
Elias, N. 6
eligible spouse 32

Ely, M. 37
Ely v. Saul 37
Employment Non-Discrimination Act (ENDA) 69–70, 72
employment opportunity 13
equal access 113
Equal Employment Opportunity Act 14, 70, 73
equality 3
Equality Act 72
Equal Pay Act 14, 72
equity, defined 3; *see also* social equity
Esplin, B. 55
Evans v. Georgia Regional Hospital 79
Executive Orders 75

Fair Access Foster Care Act 50
Fair Housing Act 14
Fair Labors Standard Act 72
Families Violence Prevention and Services Act 50
family creation 47–48
Family First Prevention Services Act 50
Family Medical Leave Act (FMLA) 32–33, 73
federal antidiscrimination employment laws 72–73
federal antipolygamy laws 24
federal benefits 32
Federal Bureau of Investigation 10
federal case law 78–80
Federal Equal Employment Opportunity (Rosenbloom) 8, 71
federal ID 125
federal laws 12–13
federal legislation 70–71
federal policy, public accommodations **120**
federal REAL ID 123–124
Federman, P. S. 6
Fifth Amendment 10, 12, 23, 30–31, **39**, 45, 105
First Amendment 1, 24, 38
Food Stamp Act of 1964 11
formal policy 97–99
foster care 45–63, **62**; adoption legal cases and 61; ART 57; child abuse and neglect 48–49; *Dumont v. Gordon* 54–55; family creation 47–48; federal adoption 49–51; foster care laws 49–51; *Fulton v. City of Philadelphia* 53–54; international adoption 56–57; international surrogacy and birthright citizenship 59–60; *Kiviti v. Pompeo* 60; *Marouf v. Azar* 55–56; marriage equality and children 46; *Mize v. Pompeo* 60; overview 45–46; *Pavan v. Smith* 58–59; public support 46–47; *Roe v. Patton* 57–58; state adoption bans 51–52; *Strickland v. Day* 59; successful surrogacy 61; *V.L. v. E.L.* 52–53
Foster Care Independence Act 49
Fostering Connections to Success Act 50
Fourteenth Amendment 3, 10, 11, 12, 21, 23, 28–29, 33–35, **39**, 45–46, 122
Frederickson, H. G. 8

Free Speech/Free Exercise Clauses 1
Frontiero v. Richardson 11, 102
Fulton v. City of Philadelphia 53–54, 61

gay: couples 1–2, 21, 47; marriage 21–22, *22*; parenting 51; *see also* LGBT rights
Gay, Lesbian, Bisexual, and Transgender Civil Rights (Swan) 8
Gay, Lesbian, Bisexual, Transgender Public Policy Issues (Swan) 8
gender identity 14–15, 67–68, 82
gender nonbinary people 14
Genetic Information Nondiscrimination Act 71, 73
Gerton, T. 4
Ginsburg, J. 2, 29, 31, 33, 35, 39, **39**, 58, 106
Glaser, M. A. 9
Glasser v. U.S. 11
Gloria Hobson Nordin Social Equity 6
Gloucester County School Board v. G.G. 121–122
Gooden, S. T. 3–4, 9
government identity documents (ID) 112, 122–125, **127**, 135; *see also* state identity records
Gregg, J. 60
Guy, M. E. 3

Handbook of Gay, The (Swan) 8
Harris, G. L. A. 15, 101, 102
hate crimes 100
Hawaii Supreme Court 26
health care 84–86
Heart of Atlanta Motel Inc. v. United States 11, 54
Hein v. Freedom from Religion Foundation 56
Help America Vote Act 126
HHS *see* U.S. Department of Health and Human Services (HHS)
High Tech Gays et al. v. Defense Industrial Security Clearance Office 100
Hobbes, T. 3
Hobson, G. 6
Hollingsworth v. Perry 30, 33–34
homosexuality 21–22, 97–98, 99, 100
homosexuals 77, 96–97; assimilation of 99; banned 96; DOD ban on 99; high-level security clearances 96, 100–101; military ban of 99; policy on 96–97
Hope for Children Act 50
housing 86–87
HUD *see* U.S. Department of Housing and Urban Development (HUD)
Human Immunodeficiency Virus (HIV) 98

identification documents (ID) 112
Immigration and Nationality Act (INA) 49, 59–60
implications 83–84
Intercountry Adoption Act 49
Interethnic Adoption Provisions of the Small Business Job Protection Act 49
international adoption 48, 56–57

international surrogacy and birthright citizenship 59–60
intersectionality 15

Janus Society 25
Johnson, N. J. 4
Johnson III, R. G. 6, 9
Justice for All: Promoting Social Equity in Public Administration (Johnson and Svara) 4, 8

Karnoski v. Trump 104
Keeping Children and Families Safe Act 50
Kennedy, J. 1, 29
Kiviti, K. 60
Kiviti v. Pompeo 60
Korean War 96
Krislov, S. 8

Larson, J. 5, 7
Lawrence v. Texas 11, 28–30, 98
Ledbetter v. Goodyear Tire & Rubber Co., Inc 73
Lemmon, D. 61
lesbian, gay, bisexual, transgender, and queer (LGBTQ) 2
Levine, H. 6
LGBT Advocacy Alliance 6
LGBTQ employment discrimination 69
LGBTQ employment protections 67–89, *74*; classifications 75–76, **76**; EDNA 72; Executive Orders 75; federal antidiscrimination employment laws 72–73; federal case law 78–80; federal legislation 70–71; LGBTQ employment discrimination 69; overview 67–68; public opinion 69–70; scrutiny levels 75–76, **76**; state bans 73–74; UN human rights 68–69; U.S. Supreme Court cases 77–78; U.S. Supreme Court ruling on Title VII 80–88
LGBT rights 2, 95–106; DADT Repeal Act 100–101; discrimination against women 101–102; formal policy 97–99; hate crimes 100; lesbians, gays, and bisexuals 96–97; overview 95–96; policy on homosexuals 96–97; policy reversal 103–104; public opinion on transgender military members 106; same-sex marriages (SSM) 101; security clearances 99–100; *Stone v. Trump* 104–106; transgender people 102–103; U.S. Military Service 95–106
Lily Ledbetter Fair Pay Act 73
Linking Social Equity and Performance Management (Larson) 5
local government–issued ID 127
Locke, J. 3
Los Angeles Department of Water Power v. Manhart 81
Loving v. Virginia 11, 76
Lujan v. Defenders of Wildlife 34

Management Matters 4
Managing Diversity in Public Service Workforces (Riccucci) 8
manifesto, social equity 9–10

Manual for Courts-Martial 96
Marouf, F. 55
Marouf v. Azar 55–56
marriage: boundaries of 25; constitutional right 23–24; defined 27, 31, 101; domestic relation 25; federal antipolygamy laws 24; gay 21–22, *22*; overview of 23–26; state bans on gay marriage 25–27; state regulation 25
marriage equality 21–40; children and 46; class action lawsuit 37–38; defiance 36; DOMA of 1996 27–28; family medical leave 32–33; federal benefits 32; first wave of state bans 26; impact of ruling 36–37; international comparison of marriage 22–23; *Obergefell v. Hodges* 34–36; overview 21–22; overview of marriage 23–26; rainbow rulings 34; same-sex marriage polls 38; second wave of state bans 26; social security benefits 32; third wave of state bans 26–27; U.S. Supreme Court cases **39**; U.S. Supreme Court rulings 28–32; veteran spousal benefits 33
Massachusetts State Supreme Court 26
Master of Public Administration (MPA) 7
Master of Public Policy 7
Masterpiece Cakeshop, Ltd. 2
Masterpiece Cakeshop, Ltd. v. Colorado Civil Rights Commission 1–2
Matlovich, L. 95, 97, 98
Matthew Shepard Jr. and James Byrd Hate Crimes Prevention Act of 2009 13, 14
Maynard-Moody, S. 9
McCandless, S. 3, 7
McConnell, J. M. 25
McDonald, B. 37
Melk, H. 25
Meyer, S. 6
military service 136
Minnowbrook Conference 3, 9
Missouri Commission on Human Rights 67
Missouri Human Rights Act 67
Mize, D. 60
Mize v. Pompeo 60
Morrill Act 24
Mostel, C. 6
Moving From Theory to Practice (Blessett) 5
Multi-Ethnic Placement Act 49
Musheno, M. 9
Myers, S. L. 3–4

Nance, B. 87–88
National Academy of Public Administration (NAPA) 4–5
National Association of State Secretaries 126
National Center for Transgender Equality 69
National Equity Atlas 5–6
National Labor Relations Act 72

National LGBT Bar Association 56
National Voter Registration Act 126
Naylor, L. A. 5
neglect 48–49
Network of Schools of Public Policy, Affairs, and Administration (NASPAA) 7
Newland, C. 6
New Public Administration 3
Ngyuyen, T. 6
Nordin, J. 6

Obergefell, J. 21
Obergefell v. Hodges 11, 34–36, 37, 39, 46, 51, 58, 60, 76, 86
O'Connor, J. 29
Office of Administrative Courts 1
Office of Refugee Resettlement (ORR) 55–56
Oklahoma Habitual Sterilization Act 38
Oncale v. Sundowner Offshore Services, Inc. 77, 81
outcome disparities, social equity 5
Overby, P. 47

Patient Protection and Affordable Care Act 84
Pavan v. Smith 58–59
People (magazine) 61
Personnel Management in Government (Naff) 8
Pew Research Center 21
Philips v. Martin Marietta 81
Plessy v. Ferguson 11
policy: on homosexuals 96–97; reversal 103–104
Politics of Representative Bureaucracy (Peters) 8
Powell v. Alabama 11
Pregnancy Discrimination Act 14, 71, 73
Preventing Sex Trafficking and Strengthening Families Act 50
Price Waterhouse v. Hopkins 77, 78, 80
Princeton Survey Research Associates 69
procedural fairness, social equity 5
process equity, social equity 5
Promise of Representative Bureaucracy, The (Selden) 8
Promoting and Valuing Diversity in Municipal Government Workforces (Riccucci) 8
Promoting Safe and Stable Families Amendments 50
public accommodations: bathroom bills 119–121; federal policy **120**; government identity documents (ID) 122–125; legislative history 112–119; overview 111–112; state identity records 126–127; U.S. Supreme Court rulings 121–122; U.S. transgender population 112
public administration 7
Public Administration and Law (Rosenbloom) 8
Publication Administration Review (Glaser) 9
public opinion: on LGBT employment protections 69–70; on transgender military members 106
Public Personnel Management: Current Concerns, Future Challenges (Riccucci) 8

Public Personnel Management: Contexts and Strategies (Llorens) 8
Public Service Award 6

rainbow rulings 34
REAL ID Act 123–124
Refugee Act 56
religious exemptions to Title IX 115–117
religious freedom *vs.* equal protection 136–137
Representative Bureaucracy and the American Political System (Krislov and Rosenbloom) 8
Representative Bureaucracy: Classic Readings and Continuing Controversies (Dolan and Rosenbloom) 8
R.G and G.R. Harris Funeral Homes v. EEOC 79–80
right to liberty 29
right to privacy 29
Robinson v. California 121
Roe, A. 57
Roe, K. 57–58
Roe v. Patton 57–58
Rogers, E. 45
Romer v. Evans 11, 77
Rosenbloom, D. H. 8
Routledge Handbook of LGBTQIA Administration Policy, The (Swan) 8
rule of law 10–11
ruling impact 36–37
Rushin, S. 119
Russell, E. W. 3
Rutgers University 7
Rutledge, P. 4

Sabharwal, M. 6
same-sex marriage (SSM) 22; bans on 25–27, 33, 34–35; couples 36; issue of 27–28; legalized 2, 21, 22–23, 31, 34–35, 37, 46, 60, 133; polarizing issue 21; polls 38; recognition of 101; religious objections to 49; rights 30; violate 1; white Protestant Evangelicals 21
Section 504 of the Rehabilitation Act 117
Section on Women in Public Administration (SWPA) 6
security clearances 99–100
Sellars, M. D. 6
Serving in Silence (Barwood Films) 99
sex-based harassment 69
sexual intercourse 28
sexual orientation 52, 67–68, 82
Sexual Orientation and U.S. Military Personnel Policy 99
Shafritz, J. M. 3
Shelley v. Kraemer 11
Shepard, M. 13
Simonton v. Runyon 79
Sixth Amendment 11
Smithkline Beecham Corporation v. Abbott Laboratories 76
Smith v. Allright 11

social equity 111; defined 3–4, 5; distributional equity 5; federal laws 12–13; gender identity 14–15; institutionalizing 4–7; intersectionality 15; issues 6; manifesto 9–10; measurement criteria for 5–6; NAPA 4–5; outcome disparities 5; overview 1–2; principles 9–10; procedural fairness 5; process equity 5; public administration and 1–16; research 7–9; rule of law 10–11; standards 7; theory 2; U.S. Supreme Court decisions 11–12
Social Equity and Leadership Conference 4
Social Equity and Public Administration (Frederickson) 8
Social Equity in a Time of Change (Johnson) 8
Social Security Act 48, 49, 50
social security benefits 32
Social Security Supplemental Income (SSI) 32
Sotomayor, J. 2, 31, 33, 35, 39, **39**, 58, 80, 106
Spyer, T. 30
state bans: adoption 51–52; gay marriage 25–27; LGBTQ employment discrimination 73; LGBTQ employment protections 73–74
state identity records 126–127, **127**
State University of New York 7
Steffan, J. 98
Stockman v. Trump 104
Stone v. Trump 104–106
Strengthen social equity 6
Strickland v. Day 59
successful surrogacy 61
surrogacy 61
Svara, J. H. 4, 5
Swan, W. 8

Teaching College Students Communication Strategies for Effective Social Justice Advocacy (Johnson) 8
Texas Penal Code 28
Theory of Justice, A (Rawls) 3
Thorne, T. 98
TIME (magazine) 97
Title IX of the Educational Amendments 14, 113–115
To Look like America (Naff) 8
transgender 14, 102; LGBT rights 102–103; population 112; prohibition of 103; rights of 103
Transgender Myth: Through the Gender Looking Glass, The (Overby) 47
transgender protection policies 135–136
Transgender Service in the U.S. Military 105
Transportation Security Administration (TSA) 119

Unaccompanied Alien Child Program 56
Unaccompanied Refugee Minor Program 56
UN human rights 68–69
Uniform Adoption Act 49
Uniform Code of Military Conduct (UCMC) 96
Uniform Code of Military Justice (UCMJ) 96, 100
United Nations (UN) General Assembly 68
United States v. Windsor 11

Universal Declaration of Human Rights 68
University of Baltimore 7
University of Cincinnati 7
University of Massachusetts Amherst 7
U.S. Armed Forces 95–96
U.S. Census 135
U.S. Census Bureau 5
U.S. child welfare system 48
U.S. Conference of Catholic Bishops (USCCB) 55–56
U.S. Department of Agriculture v. Moreno 11
U.S. Department of Defense (DoD) 95, 97, 99, 102, 104
U.S. Department of Education 113, 115
U.S. Department of Health and Human Services (HHS) 45, 48, 55–56
U.S. Department of Homeland Security (DHS) 119
U.S. Department of Housing and Urban Development (HUD) 86
U.S. Department of Justice (DOJ) 113
U.S. Election Commission 127
U.S. Equal Employment Opportunity Commission (EEOC) 67–68, 69, 79
U.S. Federal Bureau of Investigation 112
U.S. foster care 48
U.S. General Accounting Office 98
U.S. House of Representatives 5
U.S. Military service *see* LGBT rights
U.S. Office of Personnel Management 71
U.S. Passport 124
U.S. Secretary of Defense Dick Cheney 98
U.S. Social Security Act 32
U.S. Social Security Administration 37
U.S. Supreme Court ruling on Title VII 80–88; health care 84–86; housing 86–87; implications 83–84
U.S. transgender population 112
U.S. v. Windsor 25, 30–32, 34, 46, 68, 76, 86, 101

Vermont State Supreme Court 11, 26
veteran spousal benefits 33
Victims of Child Abuse Act Reauthorization Act 51
Vietnam Era Veterans' Adjustment Act 73
Vietnam War 3, 96
Virginia Commonwealth University 7
Virginia Performs 5–6
Visionary Award 6
V.L. v. E.L. 52–53
Vocational Rehabilitation Act 71, 73
voter registration cards 126–127
Voting Rights Act 14

Waldo, D. 3
Walsh, M. 87–88
Walsh v. Friendship Village of South County 87–88
Watkins, P. 98
Welch, B. 45
white Protestant Evangelicals 21
Wildhaber, K. 67
William Wilberforce Trafficking Victims Protection Reauthorization Act 56
Winchell, Barry L. 100
Windsor, E. 30–32
Women's Armed Forces Integration Act 102
Women Veterans: Lifting the Veil of Invisibility (Harris) 101
Wooldridge, B. 4, 6
World War II 96

Young Men's Christian Association (YMCA) 114
Young Women's Christian Association (YWCA) 114

Zarda, D. 79
Zzyym v. Pompeo 124–125